ALSO BY **Cheryl and Bill Jamison**

The Big Book of Outdoor Cooking and Entertaining

Good Times, Good Grilling

American Home Cooking

Chicken on the Grill

A Real American Breakfast

WILLIAM MORROW

AN IMPRINT OF
HARPERCOLLINS PUBLISHERS

· THE ULTIMATE CULINARY ADVENTURE ·

CHERYL AND BILL JAMISON

The names of some individuals, and identifying features including physical descriptions and occupations of other individuals, have been modified in order to preserve their anonymity. In some cases, composite characters have been created or timelines have been compressed, in order to further preserve privacy and to maintain narrative flow. The goal in all cases was to protect people's privacy without damaging the integrity of the story.

FIRST EDITION

DESIGNED BY JANET M. EVANS

Library of Congress Cataloging-in-Publication Data
Jamison, Cheryl Alters.
    Around the world in 80 dinnners : the ultimate culinary adventure / Cheryl and Bill Jamison. — 1st ed.
        p.   cm.
    ISBN 978-0-06-087895-5
    1. Cookery, International.   2. Jamison, Cheryl Alters—Travel.   3. Jamison, Bill—Travel.   I. Jamison, Bill.   II. Title.   III. Title: Around the world in eighty dinners.
    TX725.A1J2855 2008
    641.59—dc22   2007022010

---

08   09   10   11   12   WBC/RRD   10   9   8   7   6   5   4   3   2   1

For the Neale family:
our daughter, Heather; son-in-law, J. B.;
grandchildren, Riley, Bronwyn, and Chloe;
and the youngsters' Flat Stanleys

CONTENTS

Acknowledgments

If we've had any success at all in relating our tale, much of the credit goes to three talented and inspirational ladies. Our former editor Harriet Bell suggested we take a pause from writing cookbooks and try our hands at a new genre, in which she gave us important early guidance. Doe Coover, our hard-toiling agent, made us see and understand some of our initial mistakes and how to correct them. Carolyn Marino, who took over as the editor, went through our first draft with a sharp pencil and piercing insight, cutting extraneous material and showing us what needed tightening. None of them, of course, shares any of the blame for blunders that remain.

We also want to thank Sam Daniel; Rebecca, the reservation agent; and other employees at American Airlines who assisted us so ably in putting together our flight plans for an around-the-world trip. In a modern take on medieval alchemy, they turned frequent-flier miles on paper into fifty thousand actual miles with wings.

AROUND
THE
WORLD
IN
80 DINNERS

OFF TO EAT THE WORLD

NOTHING SPOILS A DAY MUCH MORE THAN SAM DANIEL CALLING TO SAY THAT you have too many legs.

"Mr. Jamison?" he asks cheerfully when Bill picks up the phone, signaling in one short breath that he's a stranger we probably don't want to hear from.

"Yes," Bill answers warily, holding the phone askance.

In a soothing, sonorous voice—imagine Bill Clinton on Valium—Sam introduces himself and says, "I'm with American Airlines, assigned to the office that coordinates AAdvantage award travel involving our partner carriers in the ONEworld alliance. Our committee of all the airline representatives met yesterday and reviewed the around-the-world Business Class itinerary you booked recently. We found that it contains more than sixteen legs, or flight segments, the maximum permitted."

Bill is fully alert now and determined to remain tactful, contrary to his natural instincts. "Sam, I've read all the published rules for this kind of award travel many times, and they don't include any limitation on the number of legs."

"Yes, sir. It's a new policy."

"Do you have it in writing somewhere so I can review it?"

"No, not yet, but the committee feels strongly about it."

Bill thinks back quickly to the long conversation he had two days earlier with Rebecca, the perky international agent who obligingly booked our three-month trip without a single protesting peep about the number of flights. "Why didn't Rebecca catch this? She's clearly sharp and professional."

"She doesn't know about it yet. We haven't had an opportunity to inform the reservation agents."

"Sam," Bill says in a slight slippage from the most diplomatic approach, "you sound like a decent and intelligent guy. You don't by any chance think I'm a total fool, do you, the kind of guy who might, for instance, pay the delivery charge on a truckload of bullshit?"

It's either that or else a crackpot committee has put him in an untenable jam, changing the award rules after a booking, which of course he would not admit. Sam assures Bill that he doesn't consider him a fool and promises, "I'll help you make adjustments as painlessly as possible." Needing time to consider the agony of amputating legs, Bill lies about an imminent appointment in town and schedules another call with Sam later in the day.

For us, this is the adventure of a lifetime, not the kind of thing you want to see hacked to pieces in advance. For decades now, ever since each of us spent a year studying and traveling in Europe during college, we've dreamed—separately at first and then together—of circling the globe with enough time to genuinely enjoy places that intrigue us. To make the spree affordable, it's essential for us to use frequent-flier miles to cover most of the air expenses, but Sam threatens to clip our wings for taking undue advantage of American's AAdvantage program.

Bill immediately confers with Cheryl about response tactics. The most obvious option is combative confrontation, refusing to yield ground to a fickle bully, whoever the culprit is. Bill in particular likes this approach viscerally but doubts it will work. Drawing from his many years of poker experience, he says, "Aggression succeeds when you've got the best hand or can effectively bluff an opponent. We have decent cards in this case, because of the late, clumsy shift in policy, but they control the awards. They're holding pocket aces, known ironically in poker slang as 'American Airlines' because of the A.A. initials. About all we can hope for is a split pot."

Cheryl asks if he could get help from friends in London at British Airways, one of the major ONEworld alliance partners. Two decades ago, when the airline was in transition from public to private ownership, Bill served as a management consultant at the highest levels of the corporation's marketing, information management, and strategic planning departments. "Everyone I could call for advice has left now, but I know something about the power politics of the business. If we overreach, they'll squash us like pesky bugs."

After talking through the situation for more than an hour, we decide to try accommodation, at least at first, to give Sam a chance to fulfill his promise of painless surgery. When Sam calls back shortly, Bill affects a nonchalant air, asking him for suggestions on salvaging our travel plans. "We can cut three legs in the United States if you simply pay for direct, nonstop flights—much better, don't you agree, Mr. Jamison?—between your home airport in Albuquerque and your overseas departure city of Los Angeles."

"That's reasonable, Sam," Bill says, not mentioning that we've been considering the idea anyway.

"Then for some of the additional frequent-flier miles still in your accounts, we can switch your three flights inside Australia on Qantas to a separate reward package, removing them from this itinerary." Bill balks briefly at this, mostly as a bluff, until Sam offers to rebate some of the miles later.

These changes bring us down to seventeen legs, one of which is the gap, or "open jaw" in airline lingo, between our arrival and departure cities in Australia, covered now by the separate set of tickets. In other conversations over the next two business days, Sam encourages Bill to propose another cut. Bill has one in mind as a last resort—paying for our relatively inexpensive flights between London and Nice—but he politely protests that a simple break in the itinerary between destinations should not be counted as a flight segment. Sam asks, almost in exasperation, "Why aren't you getting angry with me? Everyone does."

Bill changes the subject to avoid the question but thinks to himself, "Aha, now he's beginning to feel defensive." Apparently Sam convinces the committee to allow Bill's point about the open jaw because he graciously stows the scalpel without mentioning the matter again.

By this time we regard Sam as a genuine ally, a savvy manager trying to balance assistance to customers of his airline against demands laid down by other airline partners providing us most of our free Business Class seats. He never implies in any way that he's caught in the middle of this situation, but it seems increasingly likely to us. In looking back on the problem after the trip, we suspect the impetus for the after-the-fact rule change came from a foreign partner, perhaps Qantas, which unlike the other ONEworld carriers, consistently treated us like hobo free-loaders, often authorizing only Coach Class tickets and refusing to upgrade them, as Sam said they would, when Business seats sat empty.

In the end, despite the minor glitches, everyone wins. The committee flexes its muscles, Sam negotiates skillfully, and we keep our itinerary wholly intact, emerging in fact with more than seemed likely to us before our initial conversation with Rebecca. For 220,000 frequent-flier miles each, four ONEworld members—American, British Airways, Cathay Pacific, and Qantas—give us $20,000 worth of Business Class award travel taking us around the globe to ten countries over thirteen weeks. It takes almost half as many miles for a similar ticket to just one European city and back, so we feel like we're absconding with the little pot of gold at the end of the frequent-flier rainbow.

As much as people complain about the difficulties of collecting awards from frequent-flier programs, neither of us has encountered many problems in more than twenty different experiences on various airlines. This time we anticipated more trouble than usual because of all the destinations involved, the need to construct routes between them on several ONEworld carriers, and the tangle of rules that govern the travel. Bill spent many hours on the Alliance Web site figuring out which partners flew where, when, and, most important, how often, knowing that the chances of scoring a ticket increase in direct proportion to the frequency of flights. He built a preferred itinerary on this basis and then developed backup alternatives to ensure our flexibility, often one of the keys required to unlock the treasure chest.

The other critical key is making reservations as soon as possible after they become available, generally about eleven months before the last flight. Airlines allocate a limited number of seats for reward travel—the main constraint in obtaining free flights rather than frequently blamed blackout dates—and the early birds claim the spoils. Bill called the international AAdvantage desk several times to get an exact availability date for us from different agents. Opinions varied on whether it was 330 or 331 days from the end of the trip, but the agent who got his attention advised starting a little earlier than either of those dates because you have two weeks to complete the booking process. Bill selects January 12, 2005, for a launch date, a week ahead of 330 days from a mid-December return, and phones that morning.

On the initial call, he tries to get Qantas seats from Los Angeles to anywhere in Australia, the most logical first stop geographically. No seating availability at all for the whole month of September. Then Bill claims a need to rethink plans, hangs up, and verifies this information with another agent. Rebuffed again, on his third call he goes to backup plan number one, flying Cathay Pacific to Bali (originally our second stop) and hopping from there to Australia next. This time the agent is the genial Rebecca, who tells him there is wide-open availability on Cathay Pacific almost every day of the month. Bill books our departure for September 18 and proceeds through the rest of the reservations, accepting several changes as necessary in ideal flight days and routes but otherwise raking in a bonanza more fully and easily than expected—at least before Sam springs his surprise forty-eight hours later.

On the evening after concluding the final arrangements with Sam, Cheryl tests a few recipes from our cookbook in progress, *The Big Book of Outdoor Cooking and Entertaining,* submitted to the publisher shortly before our departure and released in the spring of 2006, after our return. When we sit down for dinner to enjoy the dishes—including a spectacular grilled shrimp with romesco sauce—with a bottle of Côte du Rhône wine, the conversation naturally drifts to our big trip ahead. Cheryl says, "Sam played a major role in making this happen, didn't he?"

Bill raises his wineglass and proposes a toast. "To Sam, our favorite amputator."

Cheryl clicks her glass to his and adds, "A leg man any woman can love."

> >

Our planning for the journey began four years earlier, in the winter of 2001. Both of us had accumulated about fifty thousand frequent-flier miles on two airlines, American and Delta. It wasn't enough yet for a trip abroad—we don't do domestic with our valuable miles—but it seemed an apt time to set a goal and start focusing the collection of additional mileage on one of the two carriers. Early conversations centered on single countries and regions, mainly India, South America, and Southeast Asia. One night a little lightbulb blinked on above Cheryl's head, just as if she were Cathy from the comics: "Let's check out around-the-world possibilities. Maybe we can go to all these places and others, too."

The next morning Bill leaped into the research, first on the Internet and then on the phone with AAdvantage and SkyMiles representatives. American and Delta both offered around-the-world rewards in conjunction with foreign airline partners, but at the time at least the American program appeared broader in scope, less limited in restrictions, and clearer on the parameters. So he began playing on the ONEworld Web site, constructing fantasy itineraries to test the feasibility of stringing together a bunch of wonderful destinations. By the end of the week he told Cheryl, "A brilliant idea. This baby is gonna fly."

"I've been thinking," Cheryl said, "about the timing. Would it be possible to save up enough miles and arrange our future work schedule so we could make the trip in late 2005 to celebrate our twentieth wedding anniversary?"

Bill smiled and patted himself on the back. "I sure was smart to marry such a genius."

Neither of us could be certain at that point whether the timing would pan out, but we immediately settled on it as our target. From early in our marriage we've commemorated major milestones in our lives with special vacations, focused increasingly over the years on great eating opportunities. The idea goes back to our wedding, when we wrestled with a choice between diamond rings for Cheryl or a honeymoon in Kauai, Kyoto, Hong Kong, and Bangkok. The bank account wouldn't cover both, and Cheryl ultimately decided on the Pacific escape, selecting for her finger a more unusual and less expensive band featuring her favorite stone, blue topaz. It turned out to be a fantastic decision for us, a memory to share forever and an experience to repeat in different ways over and over.

Our tenth anniversary took us only as far as Las Vegas, but we met up there with three long-term friends who paid more to travel to our wedding than we did for the event itself. The five of us paraded up and down the Strip on a neon-lighted New Year's Eve and grazed our way through the most compelling menus in town at the time, early in the reign of the all-star absentee chef in Vegas, when Mark Miller and Wolfgang Puck shared the throne and Emeril Lagasse, still learning to talk good on TV, was merely a parvenu prince opening his first restaurant in town. Emeril's suffered from start-up jitters on our visit (in such obvious ways that the maître d' comped the dinner), but the kitchen teams at Miller's and Puck's places put together fine spreads.

When Cheryl's fiftieth birthday approached, she planned a party at La Combe en Périgord, a lovely manor in southwestern France that serves as the base for annual weeklong culinary adventures we lead in the Dordogne. Arriving early, we picked up a rental car in Barcelona and carefully collected a couple of cases of wine for the occasion from small, independent vintners along the French Mediterranean between Collioure in the south and Bandol on the lip of the Riviera. Many of the bottles came from Jean-Benoît Cavalier at Château de Lascaux in Vacquières, who greeted us fresh from his fields in a faded polo shirt and half-zipped work pants, and proudly shared tastes of all of his handcrafted creations while meticulously explaining the differences in the soils where he grew each of the grape varietals. At La Combe, Cheryl's mother and a number of good friends joined us for a two-day feast covering more courses than you need for a Ph.D. in gastronomy.

For Bill's sixtieth birthday, he staged an elaborate dine-around at our favorite restaurants and joints in pre-Katrina New Orleans, beginning with warm-up meals at the Acme Oyster House, Central Grocery, and Mother's, then building up the tempo at Galatoire's, Uglesich's, and Brigtsen's before a rousing climax the final evening at Commander's Palace. Totally satiated, we went from there to Orlando to take our young grandkids on a five-day romp through Disney World, and afterward ended up at baseball spring training in Vero Beach, Florida, where our Dodgers hone the season's strategy for losing as many critical games as possible without being demoted to a bowling league.

So we're not total rubes in putting together celebratory trips. Still, planning an around-the-world jaunt presented immense challenges, which excited us from the beginning. For starters, we had to save up money as well as frequent-flier miles, though we also had to spend the former to accumulate the latter on credit-card purchases. From the inception of the idea to our departure, every expense possible—groceries, utility bills, the deposit on a new Volvo C70 convertible, even small stuff such as Cheryl's daily postworkout iced tea—went on a Citibank AAdvantage card, always paid off right away to avoid any burdensome debt. Each of us had cards connected with our AAdvantage accounts, with second cards for the spouse, and we switched back and forth between them, accepting upgrades that offered extra miles and tracking progress with every monthly bill. It took us most of the time available to reach the goal, plopping down the plastic for the last charge with only months to spare.

The most daunting but fun challenge was picking our destinations, another process begun immediately and not completed until near the end. The number of places related, of course, to the time available. Two months seemed too rushed and four months pushed the limits for being out of work. Quick research on the Internet suggested fall as the best travel season overall for weather, but we wanted to avoid any stragglers from the summer tourism stampede and hoped to be back for the December holidays. From sometime in September to mid-December gave us roughly three months to roam, allowing us an average of nine days for unhurried visits to each of ten countries.

One of the early stops, we decided right off, would be dedicated to a second honeymoon. In these days of any-gimmick-goes tourism, every town from Calgary to Calcutta hypes itself as a honeymooners' paradise. If you fancy getting married locally as well, or require a large hot tub for your reception, the chamber of commerce has a special bureau to provide you a directory of vendors. The last time we took the word of a tourism tout, about fifteen years ago in the Caribbean, the ferry left St. Kitts for Nevis thirty minutes early, with our checked luggage but without us, requiring us to hire a speedboat to catch up with our bags, which were sitting stranded on the dock in Charlestown. Our tack since then: Don't ask and don't listen.

Bali emerged as our choice for the encore tryst on the basis of little more than romantic hankering. It's in the Pacific region for one thing, where we honeymooned before, and the island's exotic allure has long attracted both of us. The clincher came when Kathy Loo, a friend who's been to more places than the Rolling Stones on tour, told us, "I know a blissful small hotel in Ubud you would love." Bill looked it up on the Internet and, sure enough, the resort inn offered a honeymoon package and suite, and all the sweeter, at an affordable price.

After an invigorating date in Bali, we were bound to be hungry. So the question became, for the rest of our itinerary, where do we want to eat? Even keeping a tight focus on places with strong local food traditions, rather than worldly pretensions, our appetites went overboard on the prospects, suggesting enough possibilities to keep us running like a perpetual-motion machine for a decade. The problem became elimination, deciding which good options to leave on the table for a future meal. That eventually included virtually all of Europe, where enjoying food is akin to folk art. Since we visit regularly and wanted new experiences for this trip, it was cut to a single stop in Nice, scheduled partially because we needed a layover someplace in the neighborhood to get between

South Africa and Brazil on ONEworld airlines, and also because our favorite hotel anywhere is a couple of hours away via the autoroute in Les Baux-de-Provence.

Brazil ranked as a priority from the beginning, or at least Salvador, the capital of the northeastern state of Bahia. The historic city boasts a vibrant Creole culture and cuisine, a fascination of ours for many years, as well as a lively music scene and beautiful beaches. Of all the tempting destinations in South America, it's long been at the top of our wish list. Flights to Salvador go through Rio de Janeiro, so it became a bonus stop.

South Africa fell into place quickly, too. The country's got game, literally and figuratively, plus the alluring Winelands, one of the world's emerging hot spots for creative cooking and winemaking. Cape Town—lovely by all reports— seemed to warrant some time and so did a safari, eventually planned in the Eastern Cape near Port Elizabeth rather than the more popular and expensive area around Kruger National Park. If the safari had been an overriding interest, our chief focus, we would have gone to Kruger, but traveling to the park from the distant Cape Town–Winelands region took too much time and money for our purposes.

Thailand excited us on our honeymoon more than our other destinations combined, and it produces lustfully flavored food, so it easily rated a return. Our last visit was too short and limited in scope, making it important in this case to stay longer and move around. ONEworld airlines go only to Bangkok, putting it on our map for sure, and we also decided to see Chiang Mai and Phuket, the former for its remarkable highlands culture and the latter because of its spectacular rise in the late twentieth century into international tourism renown.

A friend of Bill's from college lives most of the year in Chaozhou, China, where he and his wife own and run a ceramics factory that exports its products to the United States. They have urged us to visit for years and this could be our only opportunity before they retire. It became definite when Bill found an article saying the residents love food so much the children used to memorize and sing a ten-thousand-word ballad just about the local snacks, skipping completely over all the goose and crab main dishes. Hong Kong provides the best gateway to Chaozhou, so we add it to our stops.

Everywhere else involved compromises and trade-offs. At first we wanted to linger for a month or more in the South Pacific, New Zealand, and Australia. That proved impractical for a number of reasons, primarily because the ONEworld airlines generally serve the South Pacific through cooperative arrangements with other carriers, putting the flights off-limits for frequent-flier rewards. The only appealing island chain we could reach without a lot of hassles was New Caledonia, a Qantas port of call relatively close to Australia. It finally made the cut as a destination due to its French background and relatively unspoiled setting. New Zealand fell out of the competition around the same time, as we preferred to focus on Australia, specifically the wine regions near Adelaide and the capital of "Mod Oz" cuisine, Sydney.

In India, the whole enormous country enticed us. Cheryl made a strong pitch for Agra, the site of the Taj Mahal—"How can we miss, on a twentieth-anniversary trip, the world's most famous monument to love?"—and Bill pushed Khajuraho, where Hindu art reached its apex in the erotic sculpture of the numerous temples—"Talk about love, this place is like a three-dimensional version of the Kama Sutra." Both of us wanted to visit Rajasthan, especially the legendary cities of Jaipur, Jodhpur, and Udaipur, and hoped as well to time our arrival for the annual camel fair in Pushkar. Given the unpredictable and sluggish state of internal transportation in India, however, we realized it would take weeks to see these places, and we simply didn't have the time on this trip. Ultimately, food ruled. Our flights would go in and out of Mumbai (formerly Bombay), so a short stop there became a given, and then we chose to head south to Kerala, known for a spicy, distinctive style of cooking much different from the northern Indian fare usually associated with the country.

Near the end of the planning, we added Singapore to the itinerary and scratched the Seychelles. Both Singapore and Kuala Lumpur caused us to dither from the beginning. Modern cities in an international mode, they had little personal appeal to us beyond the eating possibilities. Singapore got the nod eventually because of its extraordinary wealth of street food. The Seychelles, a high priority at first, posed too many problems coming and going. Airline connections from Mumbai, the closest city on our trip, are wretched, much worse than from Paris, where we find ourselves often enough to travel to the islands at another time.

Ready finally by the fall of 2004 with ample AAdvantage miles and a preferred list of stops, we waited impatiently for the January 12 booking date, wondering what was going to fall through the cracks, convinced something would with so many destinations and flights. When everything goes great with Rebecca, and Sam's changes turn out to be minor, relief and elation overwhelm us. For a whole day.

> >

Now out of the dreaming and scheming stage, we've got to move on immediately to the hundreds of details that need attention before our mid-September departure. As soon as our frets about the booking process fade from our minds, a more urgent question arises: What can go wrong on the trip? The answer comes from a little demon who hovers above our pillows each night, saying in a giddy Robin Williams voice, "You dummies! Everyone in the world who didn't already hate Americans certainly does at this point after the Iraq fiasco. They also think all Americans are rich, so thieves will target you. If you escape vitriolic ridicule and robbery, you'll probably catch an exotic tropical disease never seen before in the United States. At the very least, an airline will lose your luggage in an Asian country where the largest clothes on the market wouldn't fit a normal American child, much less overindulgent eaters like you."

An omen of the potential pitfalls arises ominously even before our departure. Only a few nations on our itinerary require visas in advance of arrival, a formality we expect to be simple and straightforward. It isn't in the case of Brazil, our last stop, because the consulate in Houston won't begin work on a visa until ninety days before your plane ticket (copy necessary) indicates you will land. Our British Airways flight gets into Rio de Janeiro on the seventy-eighth day of our journey, giving us a dozen days in our window of opportunity immediately before our departure from the United States—during which time our passports have to vacation with the Brazilian bureaucrats in Texas.

The consulate insists on at least five working days for its toil, and five more get lost to the weekend between working days, the Labor Day holiday, the anniversary celebrating Brazilian independence from Portugal, and the day between these two holidays, since no one wants to work then. Bill calls frequently to monitor progress and we start to fear that one of us will need to fly to Houston to retrieve our passports in person, with or without the visas. Finally, FedEx delivers all the official documents to our door just forty-eight hours ahead of our first flight. If we've got a maze like this to stumble through before leaving home, what obstacles lurk ahead in the wide, wide world out yonder?

It's imperative first of all, according to our nighttime demon, to look un-American, something war enthusiasts have called us at times but nothing we've ever felt or tried deliberately to appear. Our hometown travel store in Santa Fe—the founding owners of which referred to themselves as "the bag ladies"—helps right away by selling us luggage tags featuring an image of the Canadian flag; obviously from the copious supply of these on hand, other travelers have similar concerns. More important, we need to avoid clothes that announce our nationality: athletic shoes (particularly when worn with white socks), Top-Siders and most loafers (particularly when worn with no socks), sweat suits, shirts with button-down collars, khaki pants or shorts, baseball caps, and casual pullovers decorated with little polo players, alligators, or any other branded emblem, miniature advertising billboards few other people in the world pay to display.

The one allowed exception, definitely American in tone, is what Bill calls his "bulletproof blazer," a TravelSmith sport coat that's completely indestructible, wrinkle-free, and machine or hand washable. It's as shiny as an oversized flagpole at an auto dealership, and almost as suspect in character, but he needs the jacket on flights and in airports because it contains an array of secret, zippered pockets to securely hold our wad of airline tickets, passports, cash, and credit cards. The downside of the portable safe is the risk of losing everything at once if Bill leaves the coat behind somewhere, certainly a possibility in untoward circumstances.

Nothing can prevent stupid mistakes, but we seek protection from actual pilfering on the streets by leaving all valuables at home, wearing cheap watches and costume jewelry, and taking big manila envelopes to seal up things placed in hotel safe-deposit boxes, which will always include our passports, plane tickets, one of our ATM cards, extra credit cards, and ten one-hundred-dollar U.S. bills. For identification when we're out, in the unlikely event it's ever required, we'll carry a photocopy of the main page of both passports on a single sheet of paper. The wallet Bill carries in his back pocket serves only as a decoy for pickpockets, holding just a little local money and some fake credit cards. With the real goods stashed unobtrusively in a zippered front pocket, the simple ruse saved us from disaster once in Barcelona, when a thief in an almost empty bathroom "accidentally" splattered Bill with urine and pretended to help him clean it off while cleaning out his back pocket instead.

Next, it's essential to get as much protection as possible from strange diseases. Our doctor for many years until his recent retirement, Don Romig, an internist with a distinguished reputation in infectious diseases, devoted a half day of his office schedule each week to emporiatrics, a rather obscure term for travel medicine. In our old, trusty *Random House College Dictionary*, the only similar word is "Emporia," denoting a city in Kansas, so we've always figured Don invented the specialty and named it for the precautions you would want to take in visiting Emporia or any other similarly exotic destination.

The doctor who bought his practice, Mary Ellen Lawrence, reviews our medical records and notes that we don't need the shots for hepatitis B, taken for previous trips, but wants us to get boosters for tetanus, diphtheria, and polio. Then she pulls out a world atlas of maladies, showing precisely where every dangerous microbe hangs out. "Let's check yellow fever," she says, comparing the maps and our list of destinations. "You'll be okay with that"—a relief to Cheryl since yellow doesn't really suit blondes—"but malaria will be a concern."

At a dental cleaning a week earlier, our hygienist asked Bill, "Want to hear a cautionary tale about malaria?" She knew he did since she had him sprawled out speechless on his back with his mouth propped wide open. "A pal of mine relied on some of our popular Santa Fe–style 'natural medicine' for protection in Africa against malaria, which she caught and barely survived. She was an awful mess for a long time."

When the hygienist finally released his jaw and he could talk again, Bill quickly reassured her. "Some of our best friends are drugs."

Dr. Lawrence gives us a prescription for malaria pills and also a onetime dose of something to combat typhoid fever. Continuing to write, she says, "Now let's get a generous supply of an antibiotic to control diarrhea."

"While you're doing that," Cheryl interjects, "it would be useful to have another antibiotic in case of a tooth infection."

Bill adds, "And two kinds of sleeping pills for flights of different lengths, one that leaves the body after a few hours and another that will keep us down longer." By the end of the appointment our stack of prescriptions weighs as much as the *Physicians' Desk Reference*.

Insurance covers none of the cost, of course, which adds up to hundreds of dollars. Blue Cross Blue Shield will pay tons more if we pass on the medicine and get malaria, typhoid fever, or polio, but won't ante up even a dime for prevention. Sure makes us proud of our health-care system.

On to the luggage our demon says an airline will lose. It seems important to rely on carry-on bags as much as possible, but the restrictions on these are tighter in Asia, Africa, and South America than at home, often prohibiting any more than one suitcase weighing a maximum of seven kilograms, the equivalent of 15.4 pounds. Our existing regulation-size carry-on bags are so heavy by international standards that packing a single change of skivvies could put us over the allowed kilos.

Among the scores of suitcases on the American market labeled "lightweight," a few actually are. Each of us gets a new Eagle Creek six-pound rolling bag plus a smaller, matching tote suitable for either carry-on or checking, depending on the flight. In addition, we take a sturdy cloth briefcase from our collection to check always with hefty, replaceable items such as books. Stashed away inside these five bags, we'll carry a couple of extremely light, fold-up totes to haul absolutely irresistible purchases, mainly those things Cheryl makes a real stink about.

Obviously, the limited luggage restricts our wardrobes, and because of that, all the clothes need to be washable by hand when necessary. Fortunately, the weather should be consistently warm everywhere except France—a time for layering—since the other destinations lie south of the equator, where it will be spring.

Other than his blazer cum safe, Bill won't bring much more than three wrinkle-resistant gray slacks with expandable waistbands and zippered pockets, a half dozen casual shirts with banded bottoms that hang loosely outside pants, two pair of shorts (one navy blue, the other charcoal), a swim suit, sandals, and a rain poncho. Care goes into the selection of walking shoes. They must be comfortable, of course, but also dressy enough for a fancy restaurant, easy to slip on and off at Asian homes and places of worship, and European in styling to reinforce our faux Canadian pedigree.

Cheryl takes much longer than Bill in selecting her clothes, which, naturally, cost a lot more than his, even though she gives little attention to trendy fashion statements. The priority is a flexible ensemble, equally suitable in myriad combinations for dining out in Sydney, bounding across a savannah on a South African safari, riding an elephant in Thailand, and strolling the seaside promenade in Nice. She needs to be as modestly dressed in India as the heat allows and as immodestly attired as she dares on the hot sands of Ipanema Beach.

The search begins in the late winter, when stores and mail-order catalogs start promoting warm-weather wear. She settles ultimately on six tops and four bottoms, all predominately black and made mostly of lightweight, crinkly fabrics. The tops, purchased in several cases at Chico's, include a camisole that can be worn under anything, a patterned V-neck T-shirt, a tank, a long-sleeved knit, a hooded gauze tunic, and an old travel favorite, a sleeveless, loose-fitting cotton-rayon blouse with bright tropical accents set against a black background. The latter develops a small hole during the trip, which Cheryl patches with duct tape on the inside without detracting from its external appearance.

Her favorite Capri pants don't fare as well, falling apart into shreds halfway through the journey. The misfortune leaves her with one other pair of Capris in a cotton-spandex blend, stretchy "travel-knit" slacks, and a skort that makes her look like a refugee from the LPGA tour but offers the comfort of shorts with the more respectable appearance of a skirt.

To dress up the outfits, Cheryl will adorn her shoulders with a silky, diaphanous scarf that folds up to the size of a small fist. Her new rain jacket, in reversible shades of blue, looks just as stylish and also scrunches up compactly. For protection against the sun, she gets a wide-brimmed crushable Tilley hat with lots of mesh to keep her head cool. She's susceptible to insect bites, so some of her shirts and socks come from Buzz Off, a manufacturer that impregnates its clothes with permethrin. The tags say the garments are 99.48 percent fabric and .52 percent insect repellent, and carry a warning: "It is a violation of Federal Law to use this product in a manner inconsistent with its labeling." This worries us a bit for Singapore, where the strict disciplinarians who run the country might mete out lashes to her feet if she's caught employing the socks as an emergency doggie bag.

For walking shoes, Cheryl packs a pair of Wolky sandals—black, of course—that look fine for evening wear in dark restaurants after the day's dust is brushed off. As a backup, she originally chooses a pair of Pumas, the chic closed-toe athletic shoes of the moment. Then she spots and stops a speed-walking woman on a Santa Fe street to ask about her shoes, which seem to be exceptionally comfortable and are less typically American in appearance. They are Cole Haans with Nike Air-Soles, a bargain she swears to Bill at three times the cost of the Pumas, now tossed aside.

The selection of swimsuits turns out less generous in options. Determined to avoid shopping in the "mature swimsuits" section of local stores, Cheryl heads instead to online and catalog merchants, who all report as early as March that her size is already sold out—or more likely in her mind, not really made—except in special spandex models. She orders a few of these "miracle" suits, advertised for their ability to shear off "at least ten pounds!" Once she manages to wedge herself into the industrial-strength spandex, she realizes immediately that the ten pounds is simply squeezed outside the fabric, making the extra adipose tissue bulge more prominently. In the end, she sticks with an old two-piece tankini suit, and vows to take up swimwear design in her next life.

In addition to clothes, our bags must hold an assortment of other stuff, much of it purchased especially for the trip. Our old cell phone works only in the United States and doesn't handle e-mail. Out it goes for a new T-Mobile PDA model with international calling and Internet capabilities, dubbed by Cheryl "Mobi Deux" (or just Mobi for short) after a French phone we bought once for use in Europe. Our digital camera, just a few years old, is already pixel-challenged and must be replaced; and to take notes on the fly, we need a downsized microcassette recorder small enough to carry in a pocket or purse.

The rest of the packing list includes a dozen mysteries, eating guides to Singapore and Sydney (both ordered online from the respective cities), many maps, vitamins for both of us, a customized first-aid and over-the-counter drug kit, the travel charger for Mobi and the appropriate electrical adapter plugs, lots of blank microcassette tapes, umbrellas, a small sewing kit, laundry supplies, and as vital as anything, duct tape for on-the-go repairs of all kinds. To treat food and drink spills on clothes, a frequent problem for us, we've got several Tide to Go stain remover sticks.

Instead of lugging along a load of guidebooks and language manuals, we review them before the trip, photocopy some important pages, and decide what other information should be summarized succinctly in destination notes on each of our stops. It still amounts to a substantial amount of paper, but it gets left in hotels on our departure from countries and slowly dwindles to nothing, providing growing room for purchases. The notes cover basics about the cuisine, recommended restaurants, tipping expectations, ideas on sightseeing and other activities, and pronunciation instructions for key words such as "hello," "please," and "thank you" (despite knowing many words in French and Spanish, we can only handle verbs with any fluency in English). To haul around the notes on-site, as well as maps and water bottles, we bring a light, mesh unisex tote.

While dealing with packing decisions, we find amusement in researching and reserving hotels, a favorite parlor game of ours. For more than a decade at one point in our past, before we started teaching and writing about cooking for a living, we coauthored three accommodation guides in Houghton Mifflin's *Best Places to Stay* series on Hawaii, Mexico, and the Caribbean. The job required us each year to see and review hundreds of hotels in all cost ranges and styles, providing us an intensive education in the hospitality business. From this practicum, we developed a strategy for selecting hotels and particular rooms for ourselves, an approach that's hardly infallible but sometimes works spectacularly well.

Many people think that highly regarded top-end establishments offer the finest accommodations in a town. They frequently do if you can afford one of the better suites. Their regular rooms, from our observations, tend to be dully conventional. Instead, we usually opt for the best and priciest quarters at smaller, less prestigious local inns and hotels, which generally cost considerably less and often provide more space, better views, a truer sense of place, and greater romantic appeal. On this trip three expensive hotels attract us for short splurges along the way, each for a different reason, but mostly we reserve the prime rooms at more affordable places well located for our culinary sleuthing and grazing. The choices usually serve our needs—particularly the penthouse suite in Hong Kong at the YMCA—but also let us down occasionally, like in Sydney, where the guesthouse's historic charm crowds out much hope of comfort.

The first step in the selection process for us is checking guidebook, magazine, and Internet recommendations. These sources always seem suspect to us because they frequently favor the new and trendy, sometimes act as disguised forms of advertising, and often reflect the views of unseasoned travelers or reviewers with entirely different agendas than ours. Still, they provide a useful starting point, particularly in identifying hotels praised by multiple people with varied perspectives. After narrowing the field of options, we investigate the prospects as fully as possible, going to their Web sites, doing Internet searches, locating them on maps.

How to book becomes the next consideration. In our *Best Places to Stay* days, hotel executives talked constantly about clueless customers booking through third-party agents such as reservation services and wholesalers, usually in an effort to get minor discounts. Maybe the guests saved a few dollars, but they also got the worst room available and impersonal service. The managers told us they rewarded patrons who dealt with their hotel directly, sometimes with better rates as well as preferred accommodations. So that's what we do most of the time, relying on fax and e-mail contact in foreign countries.

The actual booking process turns out a little differently with each hotel on our trip. In the case of the three splurges, for example, we negotiate with the Oriental in Bangkok via fax; with the Amanpuri in Phuket through the Web site, which presents a fifty percent discount; and with the Taj Mahal in Mumbai through an Internet reservation service selling our ideal room package at a much better price than the hotel will provide. In Bali, all our communication is with the general manager herself, who gives us a great break. In Salvador, Brazil, our contact is an obsessive pen pusher who requires more paperwork from us than a bankruptcy court would demand.

Our itinerary also requires us to reserve rental cars in several spots and extra flights to destinations not served by ONEworld airlines. Enter Ingrid of Globe World Travel, our trusty travel agent for twenty years even though she lives a long way from us, in Salem, Oregon. We've never met her personally, and we don't even know her last name, but a friend told us about her once as a resource and she and Bill became phone buddies who speak regularly in an arcane travel language only occasionally resembling English. In her biggest coup on our behalf, Ingrid convinced him a few years ago to purchase a Renault Mégane on a guaranteed buy-back plan rather than renting a car in Europe, saving us bundles of money and giving us the pleasure of driving a vehicle with a distinctive and ample rear end advertised on French TV as suggestively sexy. She books us more conventional cars this time in Adelaide, Cape Town, and Nice, and all the flights except the ones in Brazil and South Africa, which Bill gets more cheaply himself on the Internet on discount airlines that sell internationally only through their Web sites.

As Bill deals with the reservations, Cheryl turns her attention to house-sitting arrangements, another major piece of nitty-gritty. A close colleague of Cheryl's from years ago, when they both worked for the City of Dallas Arts Program, Diana Clark loves to visit Santa Fe and often stays at our place during long trips we take. This time she can come for the early and late stages of our absence. To handle the rest of the three months, Cheryl talks with a friend and neighbor, Diane Dotts, who happily agrees to stop by daily to check on everything. Both of them will pick up our mail and newspapers, throw away all the Christmas catalogs, and shred the glut of credit card offers from CapitalOne and other nuisance banks. Each will also pay a couple of bills, but Cheryl sets up almost all our regular expenses on automatic disbursement plans.

In the anxious final days of waiting for the return of our passports from the Brazilian consulate, we occupy ourselves with last-minute chores. Cheryl calls our credit-card companies to tell them exactly where we'll be and when so their skittish security personnel won't think aliens abducted our plastic for a burn-the-earth spending spree. Even when we've taken this precaution in the past, issuing banks have disrupted several vacations by calling our home phone and leaving urgent messages to contact them about possibly fraudulent charges in precisely the place we told them we would be.

Bill takes care of most of the housecleaning, as he usually does. Our place seldom gets more spick-and-span than right before we leave town in anticipation of Diana's imminent arrival. You never know where a guest will stumble across a mess, so Bill puts on his obsessive face—always near at hand—and scours every surface, including those hidden under furniture and rugs.

Diana comes in the afternoon before our departure day, when we're finally beginning to relax about the details, and the three of us catch up over dinner. She raises a question that other friends ask as well. "How will you manage to get along all that time, with the constant closeness and the strains of travel?"

Bill says, "Because I'm so good-natured."

Ignoring him, Cheryl answers more seriously: "It's pretty easy for us actually. For all of our marriage, as you know, we've worked and played together, often on long trips." She pauses and updates figures in her head. "If you count revised editions as well as the originals, the two of us have collaborated fully on twenty-nine books, not something you want to attempt unless you're pretty simpatico."

Bill nods while thinking to himself, We'll see.

The next morning, Mobi announces, as only a PDA can, "Around the World Trip—All Day Event." Diana takes us to the Albuquerque airport after lunch and in the evening Cathay Pacific boards us in Los Angeles for the flight to Hong Kong, our connecting point for Bali. When the attendants in the Business Class cabin offer us a full multicourse dinner as we approach cruising altitude, Cheryl notices a lighter alternative on the menu, a bowl of noodles in broth, with sliced roast pork and greens, available at any hour. The dish instantly makes our top-ten list of airline meals, particularly after adding the Asian chile sauce always on board. Two mornings later, when the plane has crossed the international dateline during our overnight snooze, breakfast also excels, especially Bill's rice porridge congee with clams and abalone.

Despite restful sleep, we land in Hong Kong in a jet-lagged daze, barely alert enough to find Cathay Pacific's large, luxurious Business Class lounge. After claiming two adjoining sofas in the nearly empty space—one apiece—Bill digs out his toiletries bag and heads to the men's room. He washes his face, shaves, brushes his tangled hair, and leisurely thumbs through an airline magazine in a bathroom stall before returning to his seat.

"Good grief! Where's your blazer?" Cheryl shrieks.

Befuddled, Bill looks at his bare arms and glances around our sitting area, certain it must be draped somewhere in the vicinity. Then he realizes he hung it on a hook in the stall and dashes back to retrieve it. Thieves, hooey. Save us from ourselves.

Late the same afternoon, almost thirty-six hours in real elapsed time after leaving home, our connecting Cathay Pacific flight arrives in Bali. It's elating to emerge from the confines of a plane into the tropical sunshine, but our hotel driver—provided as part of our honeymoon package—deflates the mood by reminding us that the town of Ubud, our final destination, is still another ninety minutes away by car. When he drops us off at the inn, we're little more than putty, eager to collapse into bed after an early and quick dinner. As we're nestling into the sheets, Cheryl suddenly remembers our favorite American Airlines employee, the guy who helped us to get here. After bidding Bill sweet dreams, she says with a big grin, "And good night to you, too, my leg man Sam."

MAYBE IT'S BAD LUCK TO TAKE A TRAVELING COMPANION on a second honeymoon. It certainly causes us grief in Bali, though it's not really Flat Stanley's fault—the only thing we agree on. "It's all your fault," Bill says adamantly to Cheryl.

"No, it isn't. If you need to blame someone, it's got to be that damn rogue monkey."

Flat Stanley, a paper-doll replica of a children's storybook character, refuses to take sides, an advantage of his difficulty in forming and expressing opinions. In Jeff Brown's popular tale, Stanley yearns to travel but his parents can't afford it. When he's sleeping one night, a bulletin board falls on him and flattens him, leaving him capable of flying off anywhere he wants in an envelope for the mere cost of the postage. As part of a first-grade project in their school, our grandchildren send Stanley on trips with us in preparation for putting together show-and-tell presentations. For Riley, Cheryl took Stanley with her to New York, where he attended a special, hush-hush committee meeting of food professionals, and now, for Bronwyn, we're escorting him around the world.

Stanley even carries his own bag on the trip—or more accurately, it carries him. His hotel room is our unisex purse, where he rests securely with our camera, cell phone, and tape recorder. The lightweight, compact bag slips easily across our bodies to foil drive-by purse snatchers, all too common these days on streets everywhere, and comes with steel-reinforced straps to prevent a thief from snipping it off of us. Stanley leaves the safety of his room only for photo ops to document his adventure.

Cheryl decides it's one of those occasions shortly after we reach Bali. On a stroll through the Sacred Monkey Forest in Ubud, we're admiring the ancient Hindu temples and the cute long-tailed macaques scampering constantly underfoot. The monkeys, who play heroic roles in Balinese religious epics, beg tourists to feed them, and many people oblige. Cheryl spots a group of successful supplicants gulping down bananas, stands Stanley in front of them a sensible distance away, and focuses the camera. Before she has time to snap the shutter, another macaque leaps from behind her and kidnaps Stanley, ripping him limb from limb and eating as many of the body parts as he can stuff in his tiny mouth. "Holy crap," Bill screams. In our careful planning about potential dangers on this trip, sacred cannibals never made any of the threat lists.

Cheryl races after the scoundrel, full of the ferocity of a lioness defending her cub but less commanding—all observers would agree—in the requisite speed and dexterity. In the ensuing scuffle, she rescues only one each of Stanley's arms and legs. Staring horrified at the sundered limbs, she breaks into tears while Bill says, a little too harshly, "How could you be so careless?"

"And how can you be so uncaring?"

After calming down a bit, we panic together about what to do. "Should we explain the truth to Bronwyn," Cheryl asks, "that Stanley experienced a life-defining spiritual conversion and went to live in a religious sanctuary?"

Bill considers the possibility but says, "No, we can't admit he's gone and leave her without a Stanley show."

"Then how, pray tell, do we put our Humpty Dumpty back together again?"

"Let's look for a copy of the storybook with the same cutout doll that Bronwyn used. Maybe we can find it here or next week in Australia." Local bookstores, it turns out, carry plenty of Western fairy tales—a young Balinese girl sits in the aisle of one shop avidly reading Cinderella—but no Stanley stories. Panic deepens.

After his third beer that evening, Bill gets another idea. "Everyone in Bali is reincarnated after death. Why not Stanley?"

Unlike most of the predominantly Muslim nation of Indonesia, the island of Bali is historically Hindu and devout in its practice of the faith. According to carefully prescribed rites, the family of the deceased, with the help of almost everyone in the village, cremates the body in a lively public ceremony. This is the only way to free the soul to return to earth in another form. Neither of us knows much more than that, but we're planning to attend a cremation in a few days. "That's a perfect opportunity for us," Bill says, "to see how it's done. Then we can reenact the whole thing for Stanley and bring him back to life in a new form."

"And since he was so young," Cheryl proposes without consulting any spiritual authorities other than her own bottle of brew, "he should look much the same—enough to fool Bronwyn if we dare—even though the body must be different. We can redraw him on another kind of paper, freeing us from the need of a book, and add color with crayons from Bali. The rescued arm and leg give us the right dimensions for everything." As an art major in college, as well as a suspected accomplice in the homicide, Cheryl takes on the responsibility of giving birth to Stanley the Second. She actually delivers triplets, so we've got the Third and Fourth on hand for future insurance purposes.

Elaborate ceremonies accompany every stage of a person's life in Bali, we soon learn, but the last of these, cremation, is the biggest and most important, requiring considerable preparation. Members of the community bring food to the family of the deceased, who in turn feed people participating in the rite and entertain them with gamelan music performed by a drum, xylophone, and gong orchestra. The family asks a Hindu priest to identify an auspicious day for the event, which he does by consulting the *tika*, a complex 210-day-per-year calendar that governs rituals. They build a funeral tower and lay out the body in a special house to be blessed with holy water, bathed, and wrapped in cloth.

Guests must prepare for the day as well. The tourism office, in booking the transportation for our six-hour excursion to the nearby village holding the cremation, tells us to bring our own water and food, which for us consists of cashews, dried fruit, and Double Stuf Oreos. Most critical, the agent says, we must wear sarongs and sashes, widely available in the Ubud central market for around four dollars per outfit. At 10:00 in the morning of the appointed day, we leave the tourism office with a small group of other visitors in a minibus long past its expiration date, air-conditioned only by the sliding door on the side that won't shut.

When our entourage arrives at the house where the body rests, a gamelan group plays for the hundreds of local people milling about awaiting the procession that carries the deceased to the cremation grounds. In addition to sarongs, the men wear scarf head wraps, a range of casual to dressy shirts, and running shoes usually. The women look more stylish, attired often in silks. Several family members bring out the casket, swathed in fabric, and with the help of others, lift it into the brightly colored, pagoda-shaped funeral tower made of bamboo, paper, cloth, mirrors, and flowers. At least fifteen feet tall, it rises like a pyramid in eight tiers, indicating the high social status of the deceased lady. A photograph of her hangs on the tower, along with the image of a turtle protected by two fierce dragons. Her eldest son climbs up beside the casket and ropes himself into place, holding a scepter topped with a paradise bird that will escort her into the afterlife. Rows and rows of men from her birth village get ready to hoist poles under the tower and carry it for almost a mile to the cremation site.

A troupe of women leads the procession, balancing baskets on their heads full of offerings favored by the deceased, including coconut, rice, and eggs. The gamelan band brings up the rear, playing as they go. This is anything but a stately funeral march. The people in charge try to prevent the living soul from returning to the dead body, confusing it as much as possible by rushing along, shaking the tower, running it around in circles, and constantly dousing it with water from a fire truck that stays in the thick of the procession the whole way. The hose drenches everyone as we hustle to keep pace with the hectic parade.

At the cremation grounds, men remove the body from the casket and place it in a golden-horned black bull sarcophagus, another sign of elite position. The bull sits on a pyre fired by propane and logs, and the women bearing offerings put them alongside. The body burns for several hours until nothing remains except ash, which the family takes to the ocean or to a river to wash away. Most of the attendees, including us, hang around until near the end, chatting, eating, and occasionally looking up to check the progress of the flames.

Now it's Flat Stanley's turn. After breakfast the next morning, we prepare for a procession and cremation on our hotel room balcony, facing the mountains, the most sacred direction in Bali. Obviously, we can't do everything the same—the fire truck poses the most insurmountable problem—but we try to come close. Bill improvises a casket for the salvaged body parts from a paper napkin on our terrace dining table. It's equally easy to assemble an appropriate funeral offering, borrowing a small incense basket from the hotel grounds and filling it with freshly dropped flower petals and a Double Stuf Oreo, almost certainly one of Stanley's favorite foods.

Donning our sarongs again and tying the sashes around them, we head outside to the veranda. With the offering basket balanced on her head, Cheryl leads the march across the balcony toward an ashtray pyre at the far end. Bill plays the role of the funeral tower, lofting the mortal remains in his upraised arms, and spins and bobs behind Cheryl to confound Stanley's soul. When he reaches the ashtray, he places the remains inside and ignites the fire, reducing the relics to ash, which we toss over the terrace railing into the river far below.

Stanley the Second makes his debut just before noon, enjoying a photo op by a lotus pond.

> >

If Stanley had been consulted in advance, he couldn't have picked a more serene and spectacular spot for his cremation and reincarnation. The expansive balcony of our honeymoon suite at the Ulun Ubud Resort and Spa peers over a deep river gorge at an untamed jungle climbing the sheer wall of the opposite slope up to a flat summit of terraced rice paddies. At the far end of the veranda, the bathroom shares the open-air setting and views. When either of us is taking a bath or shower, we're literally hanging off the cliff in the midst of a tropical fantasy, with frogs and geckos to keep us company and vines and giant bamboo forming a curtain around us.

The large, long room inside is pleasantly simple in most respects, with minimal furnishings, but the king bed faces the balcony and enjoys the same perspective through a wall of windows and glass doors, allowing the sun to rise vividly in the morning right in front of our eyes.

The only downside for us is the trek into and out of the suite, the bottommost of twenty or so thatched stone guest cottages that sprawl like a Balinese village on a hill beneath the hotel's lobby. A winding outdoors pebble-and-concrete pathway, composed of 125 giant-size steps, connects all the facilities, starting at the top in the lovely reception area—full of striking woodwork, towering tropical plants, and local statuary—and descending precipitously to a terrace restaurant, a spa, the lodging, and near the end, just above our bungalow, a swimming pool watched over by the granite figures of a man and a woman, he pissing fountain water into the pool, and she squirting the same from one of her nipples.

Bill compares the trail to the one down the Grand Canyon, which he hiked right after his fortieth birthday to prove some kind of manly point that has long since seemed irrelevant. "It feels almost as steep and taxing, but it's a damned sight shorter at least." Hardly a comforting thought to a flagging Cheryl, who keeps threatening to spend the night in the lobby.

In addition to the suite, our $130-a-day honeymoon package includes two complimentary dinners at the hotel, as well as free breakfasts, an art tour, and a massage. For our first, arrival-night dinner, Ulun Ubud's general manager, a shyly confident young woman named Wulan, asks, "Would it be okay with you if we present some of our specialties, instead of you selecting from the menu?"

"Please do," Cheryl says, and the food just starts coming. The appetizer is a soothing potato soup with a coconut milk base, served in coconut shells with a garnish of whole, decoratively cut scallions. The main course consists of two plates, one of grilled beef topped with a cheese sauce and the other vegetarian, mainly fried items such as batter-dipped cauliflower and miniature spring rolls. "Hindus serving beef?" Cheryl asks, and then answers herself. "Yeah, I'm sure some of them do eat it."

"Even if they have a little to learn about cooking it," Bill says. The spring rolls feature a hint of curry in the creamy vegetable filling, and turn out to be the best version we find in Bali. A wonderful dessert—fresh tropical fruit cubes suspended in a yogurt and coconut milk mixture—wraps up the meal.

When the waiter clears our dishes, bowing as he leaves, he asks, "You meet the chief?" Most of the warm, generally reticent staff speaks some English, but only Wulan is proficient. Given the context, we assume he wants to introduce us to the chef, and that's who shows up at the table. Bill mumbles something he hopes vaguely resembles "thank you" in Indonesian, and switches rapidly back to English to compliment the spring rolls and the dessert in particular. The chef silently extends his hand to shake and beams with humble gratitude.

Another bowing young man brings our breakfast to the room in the morning, an option we take each day in preference to a round-trip schlep to the hilltop dining room. The menu includes simple Western fare such as eggs and toast, but both of us always order the *nasi goreng* (Indonesian fried rice) or *mie goreng* (a similar dish of fried noodles). For extra flavor after a few days, we learn to ask for an over-easy egg on top and we pick up a local hot sauce in town to add some zip. Fresh fruit comes on the side, usually a plate of mixed tropical choices from the island. Sitting at a small table on our terrace, in swiveling rattan and cane chairs, we savor the view with the food.

"I'm not sure what to make of all the bowing," Bill says one morning early in our stay. "It appears like a guileless gesture of respect, but it also bothers my populist soul."

"Lighten up," Cheryl responds. "Deference is part of the culture. The staff seems to me as gentle and gracious as saints in waiting."

"Yeah, the karma quotient around here must be off the charts."

We leave the room after breakfast and the first thing we see, about twenty feet directly ahead, is a Hindu shrine, where the employees leave offerings every day. More of these pop up in other areas of the property, which the local owner converted in the 1980s from agricultural use to one of Ubud's earliest hotels. The shrines, the architecture, the focus in the accommodations on the natural bounty outside, the art and local music in the lobby, all signal a firm intent to remain fully Balinese, rather than to provide a Balinese slant on international style, the route taken by many of the newer hotels in town. This is clearly where we want to be.

"Ulun Ubud" means "on top of Ubud," an accurate tag. The heart of the town is about two miles downhill along the main street, astraddle the same river that meanders far below our balcony. The hotel provides free van transportation to and fro, which we usually take twice a day, going out in the morning until midafternoon and then again in the evening. On the initial jaunt, we typically wander the streets (only about five square blocks), browse some shops and galleries, have lunch, and check e-mail at an Internet café, since our cell phone/PDA, Mobi, fails to get reception in Ubud. Cracks and potholes make the sidewalks a minor hazard, and many buildings appear rustic at best, but local artistry pops brightly through the blemishes, in a terra cotta basin with floating pink and coral hibiscus blossoms, in stone warriors draped with floral headdresses, in fuchsia daisies tucked behind the ears of statues of Ganesha, the elephant-headed Hindu god. At night, when our driver is usually the gregarious Agum, we head off for dinner and often also attend a ceremonial dance and music performance.

Ubud reigns unchallenged as the cultural center of Bali, but it remains relatively quiet and largely aloof from the tourism boom of the last few decades. Most people who visit the island stay in one of the dozen beach areas, passing through Ubud, if at all, only on a bus tour of the countryside. Even the ones who stop overnight in the town generally do it briefly at the end of a beach vacation. Adopting the opposite approach, we spend our whole ten days here except for one six-hour excursion to a few of the beaches, which don't seem to us to be especially enticing. Lacking in local character, they could be anywhere in the world. The sands in Nusa Dua sparkle brilliantly, certainly more so than those in and around Kuta, but the resort development teems with convention facilities, golf courses, and hotel chains such as Hilton, Hyatt, and Club Med. You might as well be in Cancún.

In Ubud, plenty of shops and restaurants, and an increasing number of inns, cater to the tourist trade, but overall the residents maintain a good balance between commerce and tradition. Whatever they do for income, they tend to adhere to time-honored local customs, values, and beliefs, in ways easily noticeable around town. Every business, from souvenir stands to liquor stores, sets out a fresh religious offering on the front sidewalk when they open daily. Usually small, square woven baskets, they contain rice, flowers, crackers, burning incense, and sometimes more. All students learn Bali's ceremonial dances at school and are expected to participate in them on a regular basis as adults, one means of earning individual, karmic merit and the main reason for the many nightly performances in and near Ubud. Multiple generations of a family live together as often as possible in the same compound, which always contains a small private temple for worship. Everyone in a village, even if they have genuine conflicts, tries to attend major community functions such as cremations and religious festivals at the numerous public temples. All over Bali, including areas overtaken by tourism, these practices remain ideals, but around Ubud they prevail as realities.

One night when Agum ferries us back from dinner to the hotel, he explains the difficulties he's having in rearranging his work schedule to participate in a semiannual event in his nearby hometown. "This is the biggest feast day of the year, when all families prepare food to share and decorate the temple together. I will feel disgraced if I can't participate, but so far I haven't found anyone to trade days off."

The spiritual underpinnings of this way of life leap out vividly in the dances and art we see. Most of the inspiration for the creative work comes from two epic Hindu poems, the *Ramayana* and the *Mahabharata*, which portray the everlasting struggle between good and evil to illustrate the virtues the faithful need to advance toward holiness. In the kinetic Kecak dance—especially enjoyable on the terrace of the temple in the hamlet of Junjungan, where members of all 150 resident families participate in the performance—the hero and heroine, Rama and Sita, face incredible tribulations in maintaining their commitment to each other and vanquishing the wicked giant Ravana. In a climactic battle, an army of monkeys provides the decisive edge for the forces of good, unlike in the case of poor Flat Stanley.

The Sunda Upasunda dance relates the attempt of two giants to usurp the power of the gods and conquer their paradise of Swarga Loka. To thwart the takeover, the king of the gods sends a beautiful goddess and her heavenly nymphs to seduce and deter the schemers. Leaving this show in a driving rainstorm, we add some drama of our own to the plot: Cheryl trips on a slippery step and falls. Ahead of her and unaware, Bill keeps going until one of the nymphs taps him on the shoulder, eliciting a moment of surprised anticipation. His pipe dream crashes quickly, of course, as she points back to indicate the problem. Luckily, Bill, feeling the pain of the confounded giants, is more hurt than Cheryl, who's still sitting in a puddle when he rushes to help her up. She asks, "How did you figure out what happened?"

"A heavenly nymph chased after me," he says, getting Cheryl laughing so hard she loses her grip and splashes down again.

Later in the same storm, when we stop to pick up some cash, drama turns into disaster as Bill leaves his ATM card in the machine in a rush to get out of the rain. Not carrying old-fashioned traveler's checks or any American dollars except for emergency purposes, we're relying on our two ATM cards as a lifeline to our money supply for the whole trip. The next morning, gathering stuff for a return to Ubud, Bill realizes the magic plastic is missing. "Shit, where's my bank card?"

"Did you get it back last night?"

"Oh my God." Bill hustles into town ahead of Cheryl to the scene of the debacle, finds nothing, and e-mails our Santa Fe bank to cancel the card and issue a new one. The bank, in its typically clumsy fashion, never responds to the message, and on our departure from Bali a few days later, Bill uses a credit card to call from an airport pay phone about midnight our time after the bank opens back home, incurring a bill for almost U.S.$100. "Yes, we got your e-mail," the clerk says, surprised that someone thousands of miles away wouldn't just trust that, "and we'll send a new card and PIN to your home address in a week or two."

As soon as you wake up and go to work, Bill thinks but doesn't say. Our house sitter e-mails us the new PIN and forwards the card by FedEx to the friends we're staying with in China several weeks later, but in the meantime Cheryl's ATM card offers our only access to cash.

If you lose it, she tells Bill, "You can swim home to get more money."

The art tour provided in our honeymoon package focuses on the importance of painting and wood carving in the culture, taking us to galleries and co-op studios in villages such as Batuan and Mas. The hotel sends us out with I Nyoman Rusma as our driver and guide, a good choice since he's an artist himself. When he stops in Celule, a town known for metal craftsmanship, Cheryl almost buys some silver jewelry but decides instead to get a matching necklace and bracelet she's been eyeing in Ubud.

Driving between these places, we talk with Nyoman about food. "Do you have any favorite restaurants?" Cheryl asks.

"No, not really. Like most Balinese people, I eat mainly at home. My mother and wife fix food in the morning for our whole family, and everyone helps themselves during the day when they feel hungry."

"Are there particular dishes you really like?"

"I like all Balinese food, but, I guess, *sate* and duck are my favorites."

"We've been trying to order *bebek betutu*," Bill says, referring to a smoked duck specialty marinated for hours or days in a spice-and-herb paste. "It's on a lot of restaurant menus, but never actually available that day according to the waiters. Is it good?"

Completely surprising us, Nyoman says, "Come see for yourself at my house. My wife makes a great version."

"Are you sure she won't mind?" asks the only wife in the car.

"Not in the least. Would Sunday evening work for you?"

"Absolutely."

> >

Unlike on all the other stops on our trip, food didn't figure prominently in our decision to come to Bali. The island seemed ideal for a twentieth-anniversary celebration and second honeymoon because of other factors, notably the culture, way of life, and exotic setting. Local food always attracts us, anywhere we visit, but our minimal experience with Indonesian cuisine in other places tempers our expectations.

On our second day in Ubud, in search of a spot to have lunch, we stop to check out the menu at Bumbu Bali, one of the few restaurants downtown that specializes in Balinese food. Cheryl notices a sign by the front door advertising daily cooking classes. "Maybe that's what we need to expand our horizons."

Bill peers through the window and sees a lesson in progress in the otherwise empty dining room. "Tell you what, let's eat here and eavesdrop on the session. If it sounds worthwhile, we can sign up for the next class." The young instructor appears knowledgeable and enthusiastic, and the limited space for students ensures full participation, so we register for the following morning.

The teacher, Kutut, who also cooks at the restaurant, gives us some background at the beginning. Except for ceremonial occasions, he says, food and cooking are regarded in Bali more as routine necessities than as something special. "In a family compound, the kitchen—along with the bathroom—is considered an impure area, to be located in one of the least auspicious spots, away from the holiest part of the land facing the mountains. At home, the Balinese usually eat quickly and alone, holding a plate in their left hand and scooping food into their mouth with their right hand. Outside the home, they snack at street-side food stalls, often on heavily sweetened fare." Much of the description sounds uncomfortably familiar, like maybe we didn't really leave the United States after all.

A market visit dispels that notion. Kutut takes us and today's other two students into the depths of the central market complex to a subterranean food area we haven't discovered yet on our own. He leads us single file through precarious, ceiling-high displays of ingredients—one false step away from burying us—and points out common staples such as chiles, garlic, shallots, shrimp paste, coconut and palm oils, and several kinds of rice. "Rice," he says, "constitutes the heart of any Balinese meal. Everything served with it functions like a side dish."

Back at the school, Kutut demonstrates another core element of the cooking, *base gede,* a basic spice paste used on poultry, fish, vegetables, and soybean products. His version incorporates shallots, garlic, chiles, galangal, lesser galangal, turmeric, coriander seeds, candlenuts, shrimp paste, salt, pepper, and other seasonings of less importance. When he pauses to pass around tastes, Cheryl asks him about a big, domed earthen oven behind his prep table. "Is that used for the famous local roast pig?"

He laughs heartily. "No, it's a pizza oven we fire up in the high season to tempt tourists who won't eat anything else."

Two of the most characteristic local dishes we help to prepare, *opor ayam* (a chicken curry) and *sate lilit* (kebabs of ground meat, poultry, or fish), start with the base gede, and all the others involve similar flavoring in abbreviated forms. The spice paste tastes especially good to us in a pork sate lilit, where Kutut mixes it into bowls of the minced meat before coaxing Bill and another student to come forward and squeeze small handfuls of the pork onto lemongrass stalks to grill. Unlike in the conventional Indonesian sate, the base gede provides the zest rather than a spicy peanut dipping sauce. If you want a sauce as well, Kutut notes, you would opt for a *sambal*, chiles with various other ingredients such as oil, garlic, shallots, tomatoes, lime, and salt.

All the class dishes taste better than the menu versions of the same things at Bumbu Bali and most other Ubud restaurants, mainly because the seasonings are freshly prepared. Many of the popular establishments in town put more emphasis on atmosphere and décor than on exemplary food. This is the case at Cafe Lotus, which enjoys a fabulous location overlooking a quarter-acre lotus pond and temple; at the expat favorite Batan Waru; and at the sleekly contemporary Ary's Warung, where only the fresh greens on the side of the plate salvage the mediocrity of two different Asian-style fish choices.

When we ask at the hotel about where to try *bebek bengil*, crispy fried duck, the staff, so warmly sage in most respects, encourages us to go to the Dirty Duck, set in lovely candlelit jungle surroundings. The beloved local dish, basically a simplified riff on the Peking duck theme, has great potential, but all we get are crispy fried bones. In the end, our waitress delights us much more than the food. After being reserved and retiring most of the meal, when she brings us the receipt for our American credit-card charge, she stiffens her back to reach a fully erect five feet and says, "I think your president did a very bad job in dealing with Hurricane Katrina," still current news at the time. Like scores of other people we meet everywhere on the trip, she's more up-to-date on world events than most Americans, and she clearly separates the actions of a national government from the people of the country, able to denounce the one while respecting the other. It's a relief to us to avoid guilt by association and also an embarrassment that many of our compatriots don't make the same simple distinction.

A few pretty places deliver better on the local cooking. The restaurant of the grand Four Seasons Hotel, several miles outside town, provides us, along with lunch salads, an outstanding off-the-menu sampling of their sambals. The waitress brings a platter of five different types to nibble with crispy breads: tiny rounds of fiercely hot yellow-green chiles and shallots fried briefly in oil; a subtle blend of shrimp paste with green chile; a more typical tomato and red chile combo; a buttery ground candlenut and red chile sauce; and a lemongrass variation—our favorite—with lots of the tender inner stalks of the herb in oil with a generous quantity of shallots and kaffir lime leaves.

The dining room at the ultra-luxe Amandari hotel offers two tasting menus in the evening, one Western and the other Indonesian. The predominantly Japanese guests pick the former, which leaves us as the only patrons who order the latter. Most of the banquet comes on one huge platter lined with banana leaves. The array of dishes includes a succulent lamb sate with piquant peanut sauce, pork loin fried with savory little vegetables, gorgeous prawns farm-raised in Bali, mahimahi poached in galangal and lemongrass broth, tofu with potatoes, spinach and carrot salad, wonderful cucumbers with vinegar and ginger, and an assertive sambal of tomatoes and chile. Our dessert is spectacular, a superb rendition of the local favorite known as *bubur injin,* a pudding made with black and sticky rice, palm sugar, and coconut milk. The meal probably approaches the summits of Indonesian gastronomy, but still the style falls short of some other Asian cuisines in the complexity of flavors and textures.

Our most remarkable food experiences are in far humbler settings than the Amandari and Four Seasons. One evening when we're leaving our regular Internet café to attend a dance performance, a young man calls out "Mr. William," the name on Bill's passport and hotel registration. He turns out to be one of Ulun Ubud's young employees, who had mentioned to us earlier that he worked at night at his family's street-food stand. Sitting with his sister on the sidewalk, fanning the flames of a simple ground-level charcoal grill, he asks us shyly but proudly, "You like to try my sate lilit?"

The prospect makes us a little nervous in a completely unregulated environment where tap water isn't safe for drinking, but we can't refuse without being rude. After a couple of bites, Bill says truthfully, "This is the best sate I've tasted in Ubud," and Cheryl seconds the sentiment. The cook's silent sister, who probably speaks no English, then takes two portly, leaf-wrapped packets off the grill and hands them to us, motioning for us to open them. As we do, she picks up a small jar of homemade sambal and spoons a little on the sweet-potato filling inside. It's also delicious, which we try to convey with lip smacking and other facial expressions. Bill pulls out his wallet to pay for the treats, but they won't accept any money, the brother merely saying, "Gift, gift."

Another day we relish lunch near the center of Ubud at Ibu Oka, where the total tab for both of us together with drinks reaches only $3.80. The open-air eatery sells just one item, *babi guling*, or roast pig, cooked until the turmeric-basted skin is crackling crisp. As you approach the entrance from the town's main street, you have to dodge the butt of the young hog hanging over the sidewalk at the end of the carving table, stand in line for the chow, pay your dues, and sit either on floor cushions at low tables in a covered pavilion or outside on wobbly stools at a higher table draped with a Coca-Cola oilcloth. Taking a stool each, we start sampling the contents of our paper plates.

"Wow," Cheryl says. "This reminds me of the pork at a good Southern barbecue joint, with bits of the dark outer meat mixed with slices of the juicy inside meat." Bill agrees, but then laughs about the likelihood of an American pitmaster serving the same side dishes, a small piece of well-seasoned blood sausage, a scoop of rice, and some *lawar* (a finely chopped salad with grated coconut), made in this case with green beans. A shared sugar bowl of an incendiary sambal sits at the center of the table, daring diners to indulge. With or without the sauce, this is pigging-out at its best.

Another feast awaits us Sunday night at Nyoman's home. Neither of us has any idea what to expect, so we review cultural protocols, reminding ourselves to avoid pointing feet at anyone when we're sitting (an offensive gesture), to refrain from patting a child on the head (the holiest part of the body), and to eat only with the right hand (the left is reserved as necessary for sanitary functions). At the appointed hour, whether we're prepared or not, Nyoman picks us up at the hotel for the short drive to his family compound. Like others we've seen from the street, an elegantly carved doorway leads inside, where modest residential buildings border the property around a small private temple in the center. Chickens scratch around the open spaces.

Nyoman escorts us to the front terrace of one of the houses and seats us on low couches around a small table covered with a batik cloth. Nodding toward the inside, he tells us, "This is where I live with my wife and our three-year-old son, Wayam."

"Is that Wayam?" Bill asks, indicating a photo above the front door of a child in a basketball uniform.

"Yes, and the paintings on the wall are some of my recent works." Pointing across the courtyard, he says, "My parents live there. We all share a kitchen and bathroom in the far corner. Behind you, next to the temple, the low stone platform is our death bed, where we're laid out temporarily when we die."

At this point Nyoman's father drops by briefly to smile a warm greeting and shake hands with Bill. Nyoman says, "No one else in my family speaks any English, but all of them are grateful for you coming to our home."

He steps inside and brings out two large bottles of local Bintang beer and three glasses, along with bowls of peanuts and crispy crackers that resemble fried wonton wrappers dusted with dried chile. After we drink, nibble, and talk awhile, his wife appears from the kitchen with a tray of fish sate lilit. She acts demurely welcoming and amiable, but Nyoman doesn't introduce her by name and she never joins us. The vigorously spiced sate tastes terrific.

She returns again a little later with the bebek betutu. Residents always refer to it as smoked duck because it's cooked slowly over a wood fire, but like our hostess, most cooks wrap it in banana leaves so that it actually steams. She seasons the skin nicely in this version, and prepares the bird whole, leaving his head drooping around his neck. She stuffs the cavity, à la turkey dressing, with a lawar that's predominantly jackfruit with shredded coconut. Dessert is her rendition of *bubur injin*. She boils down the rice pudding into a sticky candy mixture and then spreads it inside corn husks, which to us resemble miniature tamales. The young Wayam ventures out timidly at this point and eats the sweets by the fistful.

It's a wonderful evening, delighting us again with the people of Bali. It's usually seemed to us in our travels that almost everyone is friendly, even in places where others talk about rudeness (such as Paris) or caprice (say, Mexico), but we've never encountered before this kind of self-effacing generosity of spirit. It's what we'll remember the most about our visit, the truly tender people. Their extraordinary level of human care and kindness provides a perfect, love-affirming blessing for honeymoon number two.

THE NITTY-GRITTY

ULUN UBUD RESORT AND SPA
www.ulunubud.com
Jln. Raya Sanggingan, Ubud
62-361-975-024   fax 62-361-975-524
A beautiful retreat with bargain rates.

I NYOMAN RUSMA
Ubud
fax 62-361-975-073
An astute driver, guide, and painter.

BUMBU BALI
Jln. Monkey Forest, Ubud
62-361-976-698
Lunch, dinner, and cooking classes.

FOUR SEASONS RESORT
www.fourseasons.com/sayan
Sayan, Ubud
62-361-977-577
The restaurant is open for breakfast, lunch, and dinner.

AMANDARI
www.amanresorts.com
Kedewatan, Ubud
62-361-975-333
The restaurant is open for breakfast, lunch, and dinner.

IBU OKA
Jln. Suweta
Across from the Tourist Office and Palace, central Ubud (no reservations)
Serves lunch only until the roasted pig is gone.

Fish Sate Lilit

MAKES ABOUT 2 DOZEN SATE

Lemongrass stalks, enough to make 2 dozen 6- to 8-inch skewers, plus 1 longer stalk to use as a basting brush

- 3 medium shallots
- 2 to 4 fiery small fresh red or green chiles, such as Thai chiles, seeds removed, or 1 fresh red or green serrano chile
- 6 plump macadamia nuts
- 3 fresh ginger "coins," sliced ¼ inch thick
- 2 teaspoons sesame seeds
- 1 tablespoon palm sugar, turbinado sugar, or dark brown sugar
- 2 teaspoons freshly ground black pepper
- 1½ teaspoons Southeast Asian shrimp paste or fish sauce
- 1 teaspoon ground coriander
- ½ teaspoon ground white pepper
- ½ teaspoon ground cumin
- ¼ teaspoon ground nutmeg
- ¼ teaspoon salt
- 1 kaffir lime leaf, finely chopped or crumbled
- ¾ pound mild-flavored but somewhat firm white fish fillets, such as snapper
- ¼ pound peeled shrimp
- 1 tablespoon coconut oil or vegetable oil
- 1 tablespoon fresh lime juice
- ¼ to ½ cup coconut milk

A few additional tablespoons of coconut oil or vegetable oil

Cut about a half-dozen ¼-inch deep notches into the top 3 inches of each lemongrass skewer to help the fish mixture absorb the herb's flavor. Make a basting brush from the longer lemongrass stalk, first cutting off about ½ inch of the hard fibrous knob end of the stalk. Discard the knobby end. Give the sliced end of the stalk a few whacks with the side of a chef's knife or meat mallet, just enough that the fibers fray at least a half inch. Reserve.

Chop together in a food processor the shallots, chiles, nuts, ginger, sesame seeds, sugar, black pepper, shrimp paste, coriander, white pepper, cumin, nutmeg, salt, and lime leaf until finely minced. Scrape out into a medium bowl.

Without washing the food processor, plop the fish and shrimp into it. If either the fish or shrimp has been frozen and thawed, blot well on paper towels to remove lingering moisture before putting in the processor. Using quick pulses, mince the mixture evenly, but do not let it turn into a paste. Scrape into the bowl of spice paste. Stir together thoroughly, then mix in the coconut oil and lime juice. Add enough coconut milk to make a very moist but not soupy mixture. Switch to your fingers and knead the sate mixture for about 30 seconds. (The mixture can be made to this point up to a day ahead, then covered and refrigerated.)

Fire up a grill to medium-high heat.

Wrap the fish mixture around the lemongrass skewers shortly before you plan to grill the sate. (It may split and fall off if formed more than a hour before grilling.) Wet your hands with cold water, then form a ball with a rounded tablespoon of the fish mixture. Holding a skewer with the notched portion upright, balance the ball on top of the skewer, then start pulling the mixture down the skewer, using your thumb and the two fingers closest to it. Turn the skewer slowly as you pull the mixture down, winding it around the top 3 to 4 inches of the skewer and tapering it as you reach the lower handle portion of the skewer. It should look in shape a bit like a miniature corn dog. Place on an oiled plastic-wrap- or Silpat-covered baking sheet. Repeat with the remaining fish mixture and skewers, wetting your fingers again before forming each one, to avoid sticking. Cover and refrigerate for about 15 minutes.

Transfer each of the sates to a well-oiled cooking grate with their lemongrass handles away from, or off of, the heat. Grill for 4 to 5 minutes, turning the sate on all sides. Using the lemongrass brush, baste each skewer lightly with oil on all sides, and grill for about two minutes more, until cooked through with some nicely browned edges. Serve immediately.

THE ALARM CLOCK JARS US AWAKE RUDELY EARLY ON
our first full day in Australia. It's a Saturday, the only day of the week when the
Barossa Valley farmers market opens its stalls for trade in the small town of Angaston, near the center of the famed wine region. An expat American couple active in
the market, Thalassa Skinner and Tony Bogar, tell Bill, "As long as you don't encounter any problems on the highway, you can get here from your Adelaide hotel
in just over an hour." Bill laughs, because there's an obvious problem before we
even leave our room: Australians are lefties, ignoring the consensus among most
of the world's population that cars belong on the right side of the road.

The quaint custom, inherited from the idiosyncratic British, requires us to
allow more than ample time for the trip. Bill takes the wheel because he has experience driving on the left, even when perfectly sober. He only dimly remembers the last occasion, however, and in every instance in the past the cars felt
American because the driver's seat was on the left. Not so in our rental car here,
where the wheel is on the locally proper and (for most people) safer right side.
He takes off slowly, looking for a quiet street to practice shifting the manual
transmission with his left hand. When that proves possible, Bill hits the highway,
where the difficulties begin. He keeps reflexively flicking the lever on the left of
the steering column to indicate lane changes, as you would in an American
car, but instead turns on the windshield wipers, as though he's battling a private

rainstorm on this sunny spring day. Despite the frenzied flapping of blades at the worst possible moments, he avoids mishaps and we arrive safely and on time. Cheryl emerges from her imaginary hiding place on the floor of the backseat, where she mentally placed herself for the past hour, and we go into the large wine-storage shed that houses the market.

An Illinois girl from agrarian stock and the former chair of the volunteers' fund-raising board for the Santa Fe Farmers Market, Cheryl loves farmers, at least the ones who raise crops in sustainable ways to sell at local markets. Before we left home, she e-mailed so many people for information about the Barossa Valley market that eventually word of her interest reached Thalassa and Tony. They offered to show us around, and Cheryl eagerly accepted.

Thalassa finds us instantly, as soon as we open our mouths at the information booth. "You must be the Americans we're expecting. We don't get many accents like that around here."

"You pegged us," Cheryl acknowledges.

"Well, let me give you some background on the market, then we'll round up Tony and look around. This is modeled in many ways on the kind of farmers' markets that have become so popular in the United States in recent years. Local growers raise everything they sell, from the top-notch produce to the chickens that lay the eggs and the livestock that gives milk for the dairy products. Everyone in the Barossa Valley lives in easy driving distance of each other and the market, so many vendors and buyers show up each week, year-round. We all know one another in the valley, so it's like a community gathering spot."

"How did you and Tony get involved?" Bill asks.

"We moved here from California several years ago, about the time that people began talking about a local market. We already knew many Barossa residents because my father grew up in South Australia before emigrating to the States. So they asked us about California markets, and we quickly got drawn into the planning. Here's Tony now. He can start showing you around, and I'll catch up in a minute when I finish some business at the booth."

As soon as she introduces us to Tony, he spots and stops a friend heading outside with a cigarette and lighter in his hand. "Peter, I won't keep you from your smoke, but I want you to meet these Americans."

"More of your kind, eh? Are we being invaded?"

"The wisecracker," Tony says to us, "is Peter Lehmann, the one we all fondly call 'the Baron of Barossa.'"

Thrilled to run into the legendary winemaker, Bill says, "We're coming to your winery this afternoon. Will you be there?"

"Nope, going fishing. But I'll ask Margaret, my wife, if she can give you a few nips of the good stuff."

"Wow," Bill tells Tony when Lehmann leaves, "that's like bumping into Robert Mondavi at the Oakville Grocery and being invited to a private tasting at the estate. Barossa really is a small and laid-back world, isn't it?"

"Yep, it's nothing at all like Napa."

Thalassa joins us again and the couple gives us a guided tour of the forty stalls, introducing us to most of the vendors and telling us about their goods, which include spring fruits and vegetables, pastries and breads baked as much as possible with local products, and lots of Germanic pickles of green tomatoes, onions, cucumbers, figs, grapes, horseradish, and more. Tony says, "German farmers settled much of the Barossa, and their food and wine traditions still flourish. They planted the original vineyards just to make wine for themselves. Nothing changed substantially until recent decades, when wine became a big business here and elsewhere. Even today, many of the Barossa farms and vineyards remain small-scale operations."

"Oh, look," Thalassa interrupts, "there's Maggie Beer. Would you like to meet her?"

"Of course we would," Cheryl says. "She's the Alice Waters of Australia," referring to the founder of Berkeley's Chez Panisse, who helped stimulate American interests in fresh, local produce. "We're going to Maggie's restaurant for lunch." Thalassa handles the introductions while Cheryl gropes into her purse for the camera and Flat Stanley, handing him to Bill while shoving both toward Maggie for a photo of the three of them together. It's now barely 9:00 A.M. and already, it feels, we've met half of the valley and had a week's worth of adventure.

"Speaking of lunch," Tony asks us, "have you eaten breakfast?"

"No," Bill answers. "We thought there might be some food around here."

"Allow me, then, to make one final introduction, to the best breakfast sandwich in the world. Follow me." He leads us to a stand in the corner of a second room where volunteers sell coffee, other drinks, and snacks as a fund-raising activity for the market. He tells us what to get and we follow his orders, right down to the cups of hot chocolate concocted with rich Jersey milk from a neighborhood dairy "to take the chill off of the morning air." For the sandwich, the cooks start with a roll from a local bakery, then layer in it bacon produced in the valley, a fried egg fresh from the hen, pickled onions, and a tangy chutney from one of the vendors. Even though we've written a cookbook on breakfast with a whole chapter of great sandwiches, this gem tops them all, in part because of the ingredients' sterling freshness.

After thanking Thalassa and Tony profusely for their help and offering them room and board if they're ever in Santa Fe, we head off to explore some of the back roads of the Barossa. Bill gets lost immediately in the parking lot, going to the wrong front door of the car, pretending he's there just to let Cheryl in, and finally getting behind the wheel again on the other side. He takes us through gently rolling hills awhile and then down into the valley, where fields of intensely yellow rapeseed and splashes of other wildflowers pop out of the lovely, manicured landscape. A canopy of eucalyptus branches overhangs some of the byways and sheep graze in the meadows. Scattered stone houses in shades ranging from cream to light gray flaunt beds of fiery poppies and rosemary bushes budding blue. Except for a few too-cute B&Bs, little looks overly precious or tarted up for tourists, an affliction of many prominent wine areas.

Along the way, we stop at Yalumba, Australia's oldest family-owned winery. Dru Thomas greets us at the long bar of the cellar door (Aussie-speak for "tasting room") and pours samples of a range of wines, starting with a 2004 Chardonnay fermented with wild yeast from the vineyards and concluding with a just maturing 2000 Coonawarra Cabernet Sauvignon. Many of the choices surprise us with their superb balance between fruit and acid. Bill tells Dru, "Most Australian reds we've purchased at home tend to be sweet, sometimes dreadfully so, but there's no hint of that in these bottles."

"You blokes have helped to make that the reigning international style, you know. Some Australian wineries add sugar for export sales." If so, that's a shame for everyone.

Our drive eventually leads to Maggie Beer's Farm Shop. It's still a little before noon, the time of our reservation, so we wander over to another wine tasting in progress, not realizing at first that the pourer is Maggie's husband, Colin, handing out samples of his Beer Bros. Wines. The couple began raising pheasants on their farm in the 1970s and opened the award-winning Pheasant Farm Restaurant, which they ran for fifteen years before tiring of the toil. They then focused on making pantry products, such as verjuice, an acidic liquid based on unfermented grapes that Maggie champions in cooking. Today, the Beers sell their goods, and serve food as well, at the Farm Shop.

The dining room conveys a casual, country mood, but there's nothing casual about the kitchen's attitude toward food preparation. All diners start with a serving of Maggie's signature pheasant pâté—magnificently buttery and fleshy—with caramelized onions and brioche flecked with orange zest. Cheryl follows with Berkshire Gold pork and fennel sausages with French du Puy lentils, verjuice-glazed apples, and wilted spinach, a masterpiece of meat and produce. Bill opts for an equally tasty game pie with roasted carrots and fennel and a cabernet sauce, saying as he savors the last bite, "I don't know why more places in the States can't offer this kind of affordable but refined food in such a relaxed setting."

A short drive brings us to the winery founded by and named for Peter Lehmann. From the fifth generation of a German immigrant family, he began his winemaking career at Yalumba at the age of seventeen and progressed to the top vintner's job at Saltram thirteen years later. Crisis struck the Barossa in 1978, when the supply of grapes greatly exceeded the needs of wineries. Lehmann's bosses ordered him to break standing agreements with vineyard owners, but he refused, knowing the farmers might face financial ruin from their unsold surplus. Instead, he formed a new company, named Masterson after the Damon Runyon character Sky Masterson, a gambler, and adopted the Queen of Clubs as the logo. Through the firm, he bought the grapes himself and started making his own wine, soon rechristened under his name. He gambled on an uptick in the fortunes of the Barossa and raked in a big pot, for himself and the whole valley.

At the cellar-door bar, we tell the lady in charge about our chance encounter with Peter this morning and his suggestion of the possibility of a tasting with Margaret. "Oh, yes," she says. "Let me get her." Margaret comes out and proposes that we join her in the private tasting room, where we can all sit down. The baroness, who has been widely quoted as stating that the Barossa was the original Garden of Eden, gives us her perspective on the valley. She says, "The terrain encompasses an incredible range of microclimates and soil types, conditions that promote a rich diversity in types of grapes that grow well. Our winery alone works with 190 growers and 900 patches of grapes, allowing the company to produce a variety of premium wines." Margaret mentions that Peter jokes about how boring it would be to wake up each day and only be able to make Château Lafitte.

To illustrate the bounty, she grabs a few bottles to sample. First, she pours the 2004 Eden Valley Riesling, nimbly mineral in character. "Consider this as a base," she says, opening another bottle, "and then try the 2001 vintage of the Reserve Riesling, a four-time winner of an award for the world's best dry Riesling."

Both of us sip in awe, with Cheryl finally breaking the silence. "It's easily the best Riesling I've ever tasted. Just magnificent."

"I know," Margaret confidently concurs. "Take the rest of it back to your hotel for later."

Next Margaret uncorks two vintages of Shiraz, the 2001 Eight Songs and the 1999 Stonewell, the former soft, rich, and ready to drink, the latter still young and brooding but well balanced and long in the finish. "The Stonewell has serious guts," Bill says. "In a few years, it's going to rival the finest of French Syrahs."

Thanking Margaret as we leave for being such a charming and generous hostess, Bill asks, "Would you consider coming home with us to be our fairy godmother?"

"Sorry," she declines. "I've got to cook Peter's fish for dinner."

What a day, we agree on the drive back to Adelaide. "Certainly the best of our trip so far," Cheryl declares.

"I love the strong sense of community there and the easygoing way of life," Bill says. "It's a place I could live." Just at that moment, he starts to change lanes and flicks on the windshield wipers once again. "As soon as they switch over to the right side of the road."

> >

Neither of us really grasped the vastness of Australia before we began planning our visit. In a week to ten days, we assumed naively, it should be possible to see Sydney, our main priority, and get a good glimpse of several other places, including maybe the Adelaide area, Melbourne, Tasmania, the Great Barrier Reef, and the Outback. Fat chance. The country is so huge it constitutes a continent, one of those miscellaneous facts from fourth-grade geography that our brains inconveniently misplaced.

In the end, Bill pushed to limit ourselves to Sydney and one other destination, so we didn't waste half our time in planes and airports. For him, the natural choices for the second spot on a food adventure seemed to be Melbourne, a worldly city many Aussies prefer to Sydney, or Adelaide and its nearby wine regions, or possibly Tasmania, an island growing quickly in international culinary renown. Cheryl settled the matter firmly. "I'm going where we've got the best chance of finding kangaroos and koalas in the wild. That's been a dream of mine since childhood. If one of your three places offers the opportunity, sign me up. If not, keep looking."

Her best hope, it turns out, is Adelaide, which serves as the gateway to nearby Kangaroo Island, a ninety-mile-long oasis in the ocean set aside in large part as a nature reserve for Down Under species. Eager to enjoy the South Australian wines, Bill cheerfully accepted the provincial city as a stop and booked both of us to Kangaroo Island on a nonrefundable day-trip package with airfares included. Unhappily for him, when the appointed day arrives, he wakes up with a horrible cold, the result, he suspects, of the overnight ordeal of getting here from Bali two nights earlier on a sleepless red-eye flight involving an extended 4:00 A.M. stopover in Darwin. Bill decides that Cheryl should go alone on her wildlife quest. "I don't want to risk eardrum damage on a plane"—a close friend of ours went deaf in one ear from that—"and I should probably rest and conserve my strength."

Bill stays true to his word, leaving bed only to hand-wash his laundry and to seek out a pharmacy and fast-food lunch near our small downtown business hotel, the Rockford. Cheryl has a much more exciting time with Ron and Phil of Adventure Charters, who take her and six other people in an all-terrain Laingley to explore the middle third of Kangaroo Island. The outing fulfills all her lifelong aspirations, as she indicates to Bill repeatedly over the next few days in stories filled with exclamation points.

The tour guides, who refer to the rest of the country as "the northern island," focus in the morning on the marvels of the eucalyptus forests, which flaunt eight hundred varieties of the stately native tree and such splendid birds as glossy black cockatoos and the scarlet parakeets called rosellas. When Cheryl brags about spotting three koalas in the branches, Bill teases her about the feat. "Aren't there thirty thousand koalas on the island—so many, the authorities are sterilizing them and may start culling the herd?"

"Yes, that's true, but seeing three is good because they are solitary animals that avoid people! So phooey on you."

Kangaroos, as you might expect, abound on the island named for them. As they drive around, the group comes across some hopping through open fields and even more grazing in the bush, leaning back on their tails between bites. "Once," Cheryl tells Bill, "when we rounded a corner, there was a big 'roo standing upright beside the road, just like he was hitchhiking!"

"Probably trying to get away from the swarming koalas."

For lunch, Ron and Phil prepare a cookout picnic for their charges, frying fillets of freshly caught whiting over a propane fire to serve with crusty potato wedges, a green salad, and a selection of local cheeses and wine. Cheryl uses the break to get acquainted with the only other Americans on the excursion, a couple who happen to live part-time in our hometown. She makes plans to get together with them during the December holidays, right after our return from the trip.

In the afternoon the tour continues to Seal Bay, populated by sea lions rather than fur seals. To remain unobtrusive, everyone crawls across a stretch of beach to watch the animals lolling on the sand and playing in the water. "Guess what they eat," Cheryl says to Bill.

"Tuna-fish sandwiches?"

"No, smart-ass. They gobble whole crustaceans, shell and all. After munching on a lobster or similar creature, they chew rocks to break up the shell they swallowed and then regurgitate the stones!"

"Now that would have been a sight worth seeing."

Bill thinks the same, and Cheryl agrees, about the Adelaide Hills and McLaren Vale wine regions, both in different directions from Adelaide than the Barossa Valley and even closer to the city. In the heart of the Hills, the large Petaluma winery owns the historic Bridgewater Mill, where the company produces some of its wines, provides tastings of all its labels at a cellar door, and operates the most famous lunch-only restaurant in Australia. The enticing combination of treats lures us to the old mill and ultimately detains us for most of an afternoon.

In the cellar door, we meet a couple of enthusiastic employees, Kate Wall and

Mike Mudge, who take turns pouring us samples of various wines, including superb examples of a sparkler (named Croser after founder and winemaker Brian Croser), a Riesling, and a Shiraz. After lunch, when the tasting room slows down substantially, the two give us a tour of the building, showing us the huge nineteenth-century waterwheel and the up-to-date processing facilities for the champagne-style sparklers.

As amiable and eager to please as Kate and Mike are, the man who makes our day is Chef Le Tu Thai. A Vietnam boat refugee, born of Chinese parents, he came to Australia in traumatic circumstances at the age of sixteen, beginning his career in the culinary field by taking a job as a dishwasher in a French restaurant. With pluck, luck, and lots of talent, he rose from tender of the suds to the top of his profession, gradually honing one of the most respected repertoires in the country for contemporary Australian cooking, often called "Mod Oz" cuisine.

Le's constantly changing menu offers superlative ingredients from the area in classic preparations frequently brightened with Asian accents. Appetizer choices might include quail sausage wrapped in prosciutto with white bean tortellini, soy-beans, and black cabbage, or maybe seared yellowfin tuna with tempura oysters, soba noodles, and baby leeks. Today, Cheryl begins with a beautifully balanced dish featuring a gorgonzola and caramelized onion tart with apple, celery, and pickled-walnut dressing. Bill orders one of the regular starter specialties, daz-zling grilled Kangaroo Island marrons (giant crayfish) with crustacean mous-seline, shellfish essence, truffle cream, and a salted duck egg, which he follows with a hearty, rare steak dressed with meaty oxtail samosas and robust Moroccan chile jam. For her main course, Cheryl opts for roasted Kangaroo Island chicken with scampi and Armagnac sauce, perfectly prepared and wonderfully flavored.

It's a magnificent introduction to the sophisticated tastes of Mod Oz food, even to Bill with his deepening cold, but at the time we fail to grasp anything much about the essence and significance of the style. Until we gain more experi-ence with the cooking in Sydney, the lunch is merely an outstanding meal, easily the most elegantly delightful yet on the trip. Within a few days, it becomes part of a revelation.

The drive to McLaren Vale yields surprises more immediately. Bill maneu-vers deftly through Adelaide's morning rush-hour traffic, gaining confidence in his left-of-the-road skills, and gets onto an expressway heading south. After a few miles, Cheryl notices something peculiar about the highway we're barreling down: an abundance of traffic signs face the opposite direction than Bill is headed. "Could we be going the wrong way?" she asks.

"If so, we've got lots of company. There could be a helluva pileup ahead."

Later, after our arrival in McLaren Vale, locals tell us the highway department ran out of money to purchase land, so it only built half of the projected road. Traffic flows south in the morning, then access shuts down for two hours, and after that, it runs north for the rest of the day. At least the strange arrangement solves Bill's problem about driving on the appropriate side of the street.

A smaller area than Barossa, composed of one village and the surrounding hills, McLaren Vale enjoys a similar kind of bucolic allure. At the head of Main Road, the only street in the valley with any red lights or commercial activity, Bill pulls into a wine information center to get a map. It's not open yet, but Mary Hamilton, chair of the McLaren Vale Wine Marketing Committee, shows up to drop off some paperwork. Cheryl asks her about special places to visit, and Mary invites us to join her for a cup of coffee downtown. "I handle sales for my parents' business, Hugh Hamilton Wines," she tells us, "and that takes me regularly to the United States, where we export much of our production." She shows us one of their labels, pointing out the black sheep logo and the slogan "Every family has one." "That's my father, our black sheep," Mary says with pride. "You should meet him for sure."

Following directions she provides, we drive up to the winery's cellar door, perched on a hilltop offering panoramic views over the Vale. Hugh and Mary's mother, Pam, are both in the tasting room, chatting and laughing with guests. Several open bottles sit on the bar: Loose Cannon Viognier, Scallywag Un- wooded Chardonnay, Mongrel Sangiovese Blend, Jekyll & Hyde Shiraz- Viognier, Ratbag Merlot. When Hugh comes over to pour us our first choice among the wines, Bill says, "Looks like you keep some pretty shady company."

"I do indeed. The wines are named after different good friends."

"Ratbag?"

"In Aussie slang, that's an affable rascal. May need to change that label. It scares off American buyers for some reason."

Pam offers us some olives from the estate, which she has laced with rose- mary, garlic, and a hint of chile, and also pieces of bread with the Hamiltons' olive oil and dukkah, a Mideastern mixture of nuts, seeds, and spices that's popular locally because of a profusion of almond trees. The snacks go pertly with the wines, particularly the unoaked Chardonnay ("Just ran out of barrels one day and discovered the pure grape flavor for the first time") and the Merlot, which boasts vigorous structure, backbone, and tannin.

As we drink and nibble, Hugh tells us about the winery. "I'm the fifth generation of a family that planted vineyards here in 1837, less than a year after the first European settlers came to South Australia. When I grew up in the 1950s, my parents distilled much of their grape juice because so few people in Australia cared at all for dry wine. I've seen the whole progression in interest since then, a seismic shift in my lifetime."

Nearby at Coriole, the Lloyd family got into the wine business more recently, in 1967, but their estate dates back to 1860 and some of their Shiraz vines first budded in 1919. The cellar door, in an old stone barn building, sits astride a hill along with a cottage garden, a plot of Flanders poppies, and an amphitheater for Shakespeare in the Vines performances. The lady at the bar offers us glasses of Chenin Blanc, Sangiovese, and Shiraz wines, all well crafted, along with samples of olives and cheeses for sale in the tasting room. The Lloyds raise the olives on their property and also own Woodside Cheese Wrights, a respected maker of artisanal goat cheeses. In lieu of a lunch stop, we buy stocks of both products for a picnic.

If Bill had been feeling well, we would have eaten instead at d'Arrys Verandah Restaurant, located in the old family homestead at McLaren Vale's best-known winery, d'Arenberg. Perusing the posted menu near the entrance, Cheryl speculates about the choices. "Maybe I would get the warm cuttlefish salad with sugar snap peas, pine nuts, pea tendrils, and chard, or possibly the red-elk pie with glazed pot-roasted onions." Waiters whiz by us with some of the dishes, a sight sufficient to drive a sick man to drink.

The staff is pouring sips of most of the wines except the Extremely Rare Daddy Long Legs Tawny Port, priced in the same league as BMWs. The most impressive of the selections, predictably, are d'Arenberg's three iconic reds, the Dead Arm Shiraz, the Coppermine Road Cabernet Sauvignon, and the Ironstone Pressings Grenache, Shiraz, Mourvèdre. The 2003 vintage of each is tannic and tight but showing brawny potential. On our way out, Cheryl spots a display of chocolates, d'Arry's truffles filled with fortified Shiraz, and decides promptly on a purchase. "I'm going to need a couple of these for a roadie dessert."

By the time of our afternoon return to Adelaide, the expressway has gone into reverse, sending us back on the same lanes of asphalt that brought us south hours earlier. Our original plan for dinner calls for trying one (or maybe even two) of the city's plain, value-priced Chinese restaurants that residents rave about for urbane fare—on nearby Gouger Street alone, Ying Chow wins plaudits for northern Chinese fare, the Mandarin House for its handmade noodles, and Ming's Palace for Peking duck. Bill feels worn down, however, so we sup instead at our hotel dining room, not expecting much from the food.

Each of us orders South Australian oysters to start, since it's their high season. Some come on the half shell and others are baked briefly in the locally popular Kilpatrick style, topped with bits of crispy bacon and a light brush of Worcestershire sauce. The oysters are plump and tasty—and briny enough to stand up to the Kilpatrick kick. Our main course, fresh whiting fillets fried in a tempura batter, shines as well. "Even better than the whiting I had on Kangaroo Island," Cheryl says.

"This may be more amazing than your three koalas. Here in a small, provincial city in rural Australia, a business-hotel kitchen wows us!"

> >

The next day, with Bill tanked up to his hair roots in decongestants, we fly on to Sydney and check into the Russell Hotel. Despite being too much like a B&B in interminable quaintness and inadequate storage space, the inn claims a prime location in The Rocks historic district just across a small park from Circular Quay, the transportation hub for the city, and provides grand views from a rooftop garden encompassing the harbor, Harbour Bridge, and the Opera House. Even acerbic Bill finally says, "The advantages probably outweigh the dangers of choking on the Victorian charm."

Our friend Liz Gray picks us up out front when she gets off work. The three of us met in France a year earlier, when she attended a culinary-adventure week that we lead annually in the Dordogne at a wonderful country retreat called La Combe en Périgord. Our planning for this trip by then already called for a definite stop in Sydney, and Liz volunteered to advise us on our visit and make restaurant reservations for us. This evening she's taking us to a couple of her favorite places in town and showing us, at our request, a Sydney institution known as Harry's Cafe de Wheels.

Harry's opened at the end of World War II, originally as a street-food cart pushed into place every day to serve sailors working on the nearby wharfs. After it gained some fame among celebrities visiting Sydney and eventually acquired historic status, the café gave up its wheels and became a permanent fixture. It stays busy now eighteen hours a day, selling meat pies—such as the beefy "Tiger," the nickname of the founder, complete with mushy peas, mashed potatoes, and gravy— and chili hot dogs, the biggest of which contains the namesake ingredient along with garlic, onions, mushy peas, and cheese. It looks fun, but we pass on the chow.

Liz escorts us down the same block to the more posh surroundings of the lobby bar in the W Hotel, part of a sleek new residential development. After we've taken seats in cushy chairs around a low table and ordered wine, Liz leans over to Cheryl and whispers, "I've heard Russell Crowe and Tom Cruise maintain flats upstairs in the private wings."

"No kidding," Cheryl says, almost knocking over her glass trying to look in every direction at once.

The sightseeing turns out to be more successful on the drive to dinner. "I'll take you on a detour across the Harbour Bridge," Liz tells us, and accidentally makes the round-trip twice, giving us magnificent nighttime views of the city around us and the boats below, both aglow. "A lot of tourists," our guide mentions, "join organized groups to climb the built-in ladders to the very top of the structure."

"Good thing we're not joiners," Bill says.

Liz eventually parks on the waterfront near the end of the bridge and leads us into The Wharf, a restaurant operated by the Sydney Theatre Company, with spectacular harbor views from the end of the same pier that houses the stage. Among the three of us, we try almost half the items on the Mod Oz menu, including zucchini and ricotta "dumplings" (clouds of cheese dusted with flour and wrapped in thin zucchini strips), red bell pepper soup accompanied by a scrumptious Chinese steamed pork bun, salt-and-pepper-crusted calamari, and warm, luscious scallops folded in a thin omelet and topped with bok choy in a mirin vinaigrette.

"This is all fabulous," Cheryl says to Liz. "Tell us about Mod Oz cooking."

"The term is just a catchy nickname for today's leading-edge Australian cooking, which often blends European and Asian flavors, sometimes in pretty extraordinary ways. When I was growing up, Australians ate a lot of British-style meat pies, like those served at Harry's, and they are still comfort food for many people. But in the 1970s the country abandoned a century-old whites-only immigration policy, established back in British colonial days, and this led to an influx of Asian settlers. Since then, we've become a truly multicultural society, and the cooking reflects that, particularly in good restaurants like this one. Our top chefs are always trying to outdo each other in creative new dishes."

"I didn't doubt your judgment about this place," Bill says, "but I did see that the popular *Good Food Guide* gives it fifteen points out of a possible twenty for quality. Dozens of other restaurants score higher. Are they really better?"

"Maybe so. Everyone respects the *Good Food Guide*—our main newspaper has put it out for many years—but I like The Wharf personally, partially because it raises money for the Sydney Theatre Company. I made your reservations for Tetsuya's and est., two of the most highly regarded places. See what you think."

"I only wish we were able to get to more of the honor roll restaurants," Bill says. "We've read great things about Neil Perry, Peter Gilmore, Luke Mangan, and other chefs, but we don't have time to sample their food."

"To try all the serious restaurants, you would have to spend your entire three months here. Even a devoted Sydneysider like me wouldn't suggest that."

The next morning, we each buy a three-day Sydney Pass, providing us with a choice of several harbor cruises and unlimited travel on city ferries, trains, and a couple of on-and-off tourist buses that make circuits of the major sights. One of the buses gets us to the Darlinghurst neighborhood for a glorious breakfast at bills, the eponymous establishment of Bill Granger. The small corner-storefront café features three treasured and much copied morning dishes: corn fritters, scrambled eggs, and ricotta hotcakes with banana and honeycomb butter. All sound as simple as a pot of tea, but that's what stumps the imitators. Ordering a plate of each, we find them robust but subtly complex, perfectly cooked, and brimming with sterling ingredients.

Another bus on the same sightseeing line takes us to the other side of downtown, the site of the Sydney Fish Market. A large, full-bore operation, it encompasses a working fishing port, wholesale suppliers, retail sales, and food and beverage outlets—even a seafood cooking school. With more than one hundred familiar and exotic species available daily, it brags about offering the greatest variety in the world except for Japanese markets. Eating with our eyes at the retail counters, which together extend the length of a football field, we devour a broad range of just-shucked oysters, scallops on the half shell with their crimson roe attached, "bay bugs" that resemble lobster tails, cobalt blue swimmer crabs, cooked red spanner crabs, glistening green-lipped mussels, hefty Tasmanian black dover mussels, and loads of fresh fish of every shape, size, and color. Cheryl says, "This is as good as snorkeling, with the same kind of Technicolor flash."

The market makes us want to take to the water and that's what we do for most of the afternoon, lounging comfortably on a ferry deck during a two-and-a-half-hour cruise of the harbor. The boat leaves from busy Circular Quay, in the area where the first English settlers landed in 1788 after an eight-month journey by ship. They passed from the ocean into the harbor through the narrows known as the Sydney Heads, one of our destinations. Our captain hugs the southern shore on the way toward the open Pacific, passing closely to the Opera House, the Royal Botanical Gardens, lots of waterfront homes (some bungalow-style, others grandly opulent), pretty bays, and several beaches (one nudist, most more dressy). Near the Heads, we cut into Middle Harbour under the raised center section of Spit Bridge, giving us access to the maze of waterways in North Sydney. It's a lovely, serene area, distant in spirit if not time from the bustle of the city.

This is our night for Tetsuya's, the most acclaimed restaurant in Australia, well known in food circles around the globe. Liz made the reservation for us seven months in advance to assure a table. A receptionist leads us through an impressive collection of contemporary art to an elegantly restrained dining room overlooking the spare, contemplative Japanese garden just outside a wall of windows. A waitress brings water and informs us that chef-owner Tetsuya Wakuda does without a printed menu, wanting his staff to describe choices personally. After listening as attentively as possible to the long recitation, both of us order the evening's tasting menu with paired wines.

The first course offers yellowfin tuna tartar over sushi rice, avocado cream, and tiny firm fish roe. You could easily find a cousin of this in Los Angeles, but not on this level of refinement. Alongside it, the server places a diminutive cup of sweet corn soup with a wee scoop of basil ice cream floating on top. Next comes a New Zealand scampi swimming in a chicken-liver parfait and a grilled scallop on the half shell with its roe, snuggling with lemon and mildly briny wakame seaweed that adds a touch of gelatin to the scallop juices. A Clare Valley Riesling couples well with both of these plates, and like all the wines except the sweet one at the end, it's bottled in Australia especially for the restaurant.

Then the chef sends out his signature ocean trout confit with ocean trout roe, which the *Good Food Guide* calls "the most photographed dish in the world." The Tasmanian fish rests on a bed of fennel that provides complementary anise notes, and the kitchen scatters kombu seaweed around the centerpiece and accompanies it with a glass of Gewürztraminer and a small salad of mixed baby cresses and herbs with a hint of soy dressing. "Luscious," Cheryl repeats several times, "just luscious." Spanner crab ravioli follows, filled with bits of the crab and a smooth mousseline and covered with a fine chiffonade of fresh basil that helps to balance its East and West elements. It mates nicely with a lightly oaked Chardonnay.

On to meats and red wines, starting with slices of veal fillet dabbed with a pungent wasabi butter and a Pinot Noir, and after that, young squab on a "risotto" of buckwheat, chestnuts, and Lilliputian Japanese mushrooms matched with a deeply colored Grenache-Shiraz from the Barossa. Both dishes and drinks excel, particularly the deliciously gamy squab, the best rendition of it either of us has ever eaten, with none of the liver taste that often puts Cheryl off.

In the pause before dessert, we reflect on the courses so far, deciding the meal boasts about as much sophistication and refined orchestration as any we can remember. Bill says, "I can recall some dinners where I personally enjoyed the flavors and textures of the food more, but few that left me in greater awe of the talent and ingredients." Cheryl agrees.

Paired with a Tasmanian iced Riesling, the desserts do nothing to undermine the impression. Number one is a blood-orange-and-beet sorbet with petite cubes of beet gleaming like faceted rubies. The second reminds us of a strawberry shortcake float, with a pureed strawberry mixture and a layer of cream on a biscuit base. The next, a bite's worth of a blue cheese vanilla bean ice cream with a sauterne pear jelly, makes us frown a little dubiously at first but the components harmonize beautifully. The finale offers a soothing variation on a floating island, layering custard and intense cherries with meringue and a dribble of chocolate sauce. "I'm in total bliss," Cheryl proclaims as Bill forks over a credit card for the hefty tab, approaching U.S. $500.

"I suspect it'll be the most expensive meal of the trip," he says hopefully, "but it was worth the splurge."

Still satiated in the morning, we have a simple breakfast at our hotel before boarding the Bondi Explorer sightseeing bus for a tour of Sydney's shoreline. The route affords good, close-up views of coastal residential neighborhoods, which strike us as a Southern Hemisphere translation of British suburbia, with lots of solid brick homes as fully landscaped as similar ones in England except in a totally different, subtropical mode. The commercial strips along the way suggest much greater internationalism. A single block of two-story business buildings contains a Vietnamese restaurant, a pizza-to-go place, a Portuguese chicken diner, an Italian-style coffee shop, a Chinese acupuncture clinic, and a dental office. Our intention was to get off at famed Bondi Beach for a walk, but the day turns out cool and windy and Cheryl now has the sniffles, which develop into a full-blown cold by late afternoon.

Lunch is at Sailors Thai Canteen, back in The Rocks almost directly across the street from the Russell. David Thompson, a renowned chef, still owns this and its sister restaurant downstairs, though he no longer does the cooking. The hostess escorts us through the main dining room, a long, dark space just wide enough to hold a single galvanized-metal communal table, and seats us on a small balcony overlooking the harbor. "A beautiful view again," Bill says. "I wonder if Sydney residents get jaded about it?"

The menu includes a range of Thai favorites, such as green papaya salad studded with peanuts and prawns, pad thai, and beef and chicken curries, but we choose two deep-fried dishes—salmon with lime, mint, and chile; and chicken with rice, chopped peanut balls, and an herb salad. "That sure cleared some nasal passages," Cheryl says in one of her favorite compliments.

"Are you up for a walk around The Rocks, then?" Bill wants to check out three pubs that each claim the honor of being the oldest in Australia. The Fortune of War Hotel authenticates its position with a framed license dating to 1830. "The document looks official to me," Bill says, "but the best proof of seniority may be this carpet we're standing on, at least as old as the country itself." Contrary to his careful scholarship, historical purists point out that the pub went out of business for a year and only moved to its present location in 1921. The Lord Nelson Hotel avoids those embarrassments but didn't open until 1841. The Hero of Waterloo Hotel, which appears to be the most ancient, was founded by a man who got a license in 1831 and then opened a pub at the current site at a later disputed date. Our sleuthing yields no ultimate answers, but our votes go to the Fortune of War because it's the closest to our hotel, where Cheryl needs a nap.

By the time of our dinner reservation at est., Peter Doyle's restaurant in the stylish Establishment Hotel, Cheryl is feeling worse than Bill, sinking fast into a deep chest cold. "I don't think we should cancel," she says, "but let's not linger late over the meal." Even skipping an intriguing tasting menu and dessert, we still spend well over two hours savoring various specialties, including an icy platter of juicy oysters, garlic-infused sweetbreads, juniper-crusted venison saddle, a comforting side of creamy mashed potatoes to soothe our sore bodies, and—the highlight of the evening—pork belly and scallops with a salad of jicama, apples, walnuts, and cress.

On our last full day, Liz wants to take us to her favorite breakfast spot, Bathers' Pavilion Café, the casual half of Serge Dansereau's Bathers' Pavilion Restaurant, both lodged in a renovated seaside swimmer's bathhouse directly on pretty Balmoral Beach. Everything on the menu sounds good, but Liz settles on the Gruyère soufflé with shallots, mushrooms, and heavy cream. Bill opts for the fillets of smoked trout on brioche with spinach, fennel, and Nashi pear, while Cheryl chooses a poached egg tartlet with pea and leek puree, sugar snap peas, and scallion sauce, which she pronounces on arrival "a lovely spring symphony in green." The dishes taste as bright and spirited as they look, bringing us all alert, colds be damned.

While we're eating, Liz asks how we've liked Sydney. "Most important, what did you think about Tetsuya and est.?"

"Wonderful restaurants," Cheryl says, "truly terrific. The striking thing about their food and the other fine meals we've had in Australia is the willingness of the chefs to be adventuresome with flavor combinations. They take risks and challenge expectations without falling into the trap of silly mishmash dishes."

"Yeah, you're right. I guess they're literally changing the tastes of Australia, moving us beyond a stale, inherited food tradition to a wide-open frontier. It's an exciting time here."

"Sure seems like it," Bill says. "I doubt that the best Australian chefs are more talented and creative than the best American chefs, but they push the boundaries much more. A lot of our top chefs are satisfied with putting a good, standard dinner on the table, because that's what sells, even though the food is seldom much better or different than a skilled home cook can make. These guys act like they should be culinary leaders, blazing new trails rather than catering to conventional tastes. I'm impressed—in a big way."

Liz drops us at the nearest ferry stop for a leisurely boat trip back across the water as she zips off to work. These outlying ferry piers are pleasantly civilized, with little shops offering coffee, dry cleaning, shoe repairs, key cutting, and other same-day services. Out on the harbor, the boat passes some of the suburban inlets that make up the area, where all the residences face the water and enjoy some kind of access to it. Many of the homes along the shore have docks for boats, usually sailboats, and even some high on the hills flaunt funiculars to get down to a berth. Sidneysiders obviously love their harbor.

At Circular Quay we switch ferries to go to the Darling Harbour development, a huge complex of shops, restaurants, and other attractions geared to locals and tourists alike. Our interest is the Sydney Aquarium, which disappoints us a little given its international reputation. It's so cramped in its space, and so crowded even on a weekday, we don't get a good look at the tanks featuring sharks and giant rays or at the display about the Great Barrier Reef. "At least we saw some of Nemo's family," Cheryl says, sighing, as she puts stamps on postcards of the orange clown fish to send to our grandkids.

To conclude our sightseeing, we do another full circuit on the downtown tourist bus, stopping only at the Sydney Opera House for a closer peek. After walking around the marvelous structure, it becomes clear the building shows its best face from a greater distance, like on the harbor, where you can catch the full sweep of the cantilevered, soaring rooflines. Curiously, the Danish architect, Jørn Utzon, has never seen it from any perspective. He quit the project before its completion in a dispute about cost overruns and refused to return to the city.

Back again at Circular Quay, we walk down the waterfront a short way to make dinner reservations at Wildfire, owned in part by American chef Mark

Miller, who also consults with the kitchen. The *Good Food Guide* calls the restaurant "a party girl." It's certainly big, boisterous, and flamboyant, more so than we usually like, but we're curious about Miller's take on Down Under dining and find parts of the menu appealing, especially the wood-oven-roasted fish with bouillabaisse sauce, the Asian fish preparations, and the various chilled seafood platters with combinations such as lobster, crayfish, crabs, king prawns, bay bugs, and scallops. Unfortunately, we have to cancel our date later with the party girl. By dinnertime, Cheryl is running a fever of 102 degrees and can't budge from bed.

Despite this setback on our last night, both of us feel thrilled about our food and wine experiences in Australia. The country's Mediterranean-like climate, fabulous vineyards and winemakers, strong Old World roots, and growing love affair with Asia clearly give Aussies the genes and means for culinary genius. Our greedy mouths yearn for additional tastes, but we're content for the present at least to relish a small bite of this new brand of Continental cuisine.

THE NITTY-GRITTY

ROCKFORD ADELAIDE
www.rockfordhotels.com.au/go/
south-australia/rockford-adelaide
164 Hindley Street, Adelaide
61-8-8211-8255   fax 61-8-8231-1179
*Small, moderately priced
downtown business hotel with spacious
"corporate" rooms.*

BAROSSA FARMERS MARKET
at the corner of Stockwell and Nuriootpa
Roads, Angaston, Barossa Valley
*Saturdays year-round,
7:30–11:30 in the morning.*

MAGGIE BEER'S FARM SHOP
www.maggiebeer.com.au
Pheasant Farm Road, between the
towns of Nuriootpa and Tanunda,
Barossa Valley
61-8-8562-4477
10:30 A.M.–5:00 P.M.

YALUMBA WINES
www.yalumba.com
Eden Valley Road, Angaston
Barossa Valley

PETER LEHMANN WINES
www.peterlehmannwines.com
Off Para Road, Tanunda,
Barossa Valley

ADVENTURE CHARTERS
www.adventurecharters.com.au
Kangaroo Island
61-8-8553-9119   fax 61-8-8553-9122

BRIDGEWATER MILL
www.bridgewatermill.com.au
Mount Barker Road, Bridgewater,
Adelaide Hills
61-8-8339-3422
lunch only, Thursday to Monday

HUGH HAMILTON WINES
www.hamiltonwines.com.au
McMurtrie Road, McLaren Vale

CORIOLE VINEYARDS
www.coriole.com
Chaffeys Road, McLaren Vale

D'ARENBERG WINES
www.darenberg.com.au
Osborn Road, McLaren Vale

THE RUSSELL HOTEL
www.therussell.com.au
143a George Street, Sydney
61-2-9241-3543   fax 61-2-9252-1652
Enough said.

THE WHARF RESTAURANT
www.wharfrestaurant.com.au
Pier 4, Hickson Road,
Walsh Bay, Sydney
61-2-9250-1761
lunch and dinner

TETSUYA'S
www.tetsuyas.com
529 Kent Street, Sydney
61-2-9267-2900
dinner and Saturday lunch

SAILORS THAI CANTEEN
106 George Street, Sydney
61-2-9251-2466
lunch and dinner

EST.
252 George Street, Sydney
61-2-9240-3010
lunch and dinner

Barossa-Style Breakfast Sandwich

SERVES 4

Pickled Onions
- 1   medium red onion, sliced ⅛-inch thick
- ½   cup cider vinegar
- ¼   teaspoon salt

- 4   extra-large farmers' market fresh eggs
- 2   to 3 tablespoons butter
- Salt and freshly milled black pepper
- 4   soft egg rolls or buns, 4 to 5 inches in diameter, preferably just baked, or at least warmed
- Pear, peach, or other fruit chutney
- 4   slices top-quality smoky Canadian bacon, such as Nueske's (www.nueske.com), seared, or 4 thick-cut slices hearty country bacon, such as Allen Benton's, cooked just short of crisp

Prepare the onion at least an evening before you plan to serve the sandwiches. Bring salted water to a boil in small pan, enough to cover the onion slices. Add the onion and blanch for a quick minute. Drain onion and place in a small bowl. Pour the vinegar and 2 tablespoons of water over the onion; stir in salt. Cover and refrigerate until shortly before serving the sandwiches.

Crack each egg into a cup or ramekin. Warm butter on a griddle over medium heat. Nudge the eggs one by one gently onto the griddle, side by side. Cook the eggs for 1 minute, sprinkling with salt and pepper while they fry. Gently turn the eggs, puncturing the yolks so that they run a bit as they finish cooking "over hard," another 1 to 2 minutes.

Slather each roll with chutney, then arrange bacon and an egg on each. Top with pickled onions to taste and serve right away, preferably with a cup of steaming hot chocolate.

OUR COLDS GET WORSE ON THE FOUR-HOUR FLIGHT
from Sydney to New Caledonia, leaving us exhausted and feverish when we land. Alighting on terra firma lifts our morale slightly until a greeter from our hotel, the Novotel Surf, summons us outside the airport terminal with a placard: "Mr. William Jamison." He politely informs us in practiced English, "The Novotel Surf is closed because of a strike"—this is a French island, after all—"but, no worry, we have moved you to the Nouvata Park at the same rate." Bill saw a photo of this substitute spot once on the Internet, and rejected it as a lodging option right away because it looked large, impersonal, and graceless. This is the nastiest shock yet on our trip, and it comes on a day when we feel as sturdy as Jell-O and our skin color smacks of chicken soup.

Piling misery on misery, a gloomy tourist bus provides the only transportation from the airport to our destination, the capital city of Nouméa, and it's on full stall, sitting sans driver for more than an hour waiting for all the passengers on our flight to claim their massive loads of luggage and then collect their wits enough to climb onboard. The drive to town takes another hour, and after that the bus stops at every other local hotel before reaching the Nouvata Park, where our worst fears about the place are immediately confirmed. Dozens of people are trying to check in at once, and the reception staff dawdles along like mules on a mountain climb.

After Bill gets to the front of the line, he says snappishly, "Our original reservation assured us a room with an ocean-view balcony," the major consideration for us at any tropical seaside hotel. "Are we getting the same kind of room here?"

That's going too fast for her; she needs five minutes just to find the paperwork, sitting in several unorganized stacks behind the long desk that keeps customers at bay. Finally she answers, "Oui," but we remain skeptical, taking the elevator up with jaded expectations of foreboding.

When Bill opens the door, we gasp in disbelief. The balcony alone could hold a small island and it affords a splendid view over the hotel pool to the beach, sea, and sunset. From here, balmy tropical temperatures and gentle sea breezes assure us succor from our colds. The enormous bed faces the same scene through sliding glass doors, and the curtained windows behind the bed provide an identical vista from a circular Jacuzzi tub and shower. The huge room borders on Vegas flash, but of all the places we stay on our entire trip—including some much nicer quarters—none is better suited for rest and recuperation. Over the next few days, we learn that most of the Nouvata Park rooms fall well below this level of comfort, as do all the accommodations at the closed Novotel. Our good fortune results from making a reservation specifically calling for an ocean-view balcony, available at the Nouvata Park only in the most expensive doubles and suites, normally priced considerably higher than we're paying on our Novotel rate. The hotel is bigger and busier than we prefer, and not within walking distance of as many restaurants as the Novotel, but hey, we're slower than we prefer and temporarily more concerned about our congested chests than our taste buds.

Cheryl collapses right away onto the bed, unable to manage much of anything except to confirm that her temperature remains 102 degrees. She says, "I think we should have the hotel call the doctor on duty," something neither of us has ever done in decades of travel. "I must have a bronchial infection."

"What are the chances of good health care," Bill asks, "out here at the end of the earth, marooned on a speck of land in an immense ocean? We could try the antibiotics we've brought for other purposes."

"No, as a French territory, New Caledonia must have decent medical resources."

"You're probably right."

Bill sucks in a lungful of willpower and returns to the crowded reception desk to try to convey an urgent need for a doctor. Although it's late on a Saturday afternoon, within a couple of hours the promised physician appears at our door carting a bulging black bag. "Hello," he greets Bill in cheerful English. "Am I at the right room?"

"Yes, come in," Bill says, leading him over to the primary patient. As the doctor listens to Cheryl's raspy breathing with a stethoscope and takes her temperature, Bill asks, "How did you get to New Caledonia?"

"I grew bored with my practice in Paris and wanted a change of scenery. I had visited here before and knew it would be a big break from city life." To Cheryl, he says, "You've definitely got a bacterial infection. I better check you, too," he tells Bill, and goes into the same diagnostic routine. "I'm not sure you have the bug yet, but I'll write an antibiotic prescription to cover both of you, just in case.

"Only one pharmacy is open in town at this hour. Do you have a rental car?" Bill tells him we don't. "In that case, I better give you some samples of the medicine to hold you until Monday. Everything closes on Sunday, the pharmacy open now isn't within walking distance, and believe it or not, buses stop running in the late afternoon, when taxis tend to disappear, too." The suggestion of samples pleases us, but not the prognosis on dinner-hour transportation.

"What else have you been taking for the colds?" Bill shows him our decongestant pills and a bottle of Australian cough syrup called Chesty Forte, a name that sounded to us in Sydney like a marketer's worst nightmare until the doctor suggests we also pick up some Mucomyst, an expectorant powder sold in sachets. For the emergency weekend house call for two patients, lasting a half hour plus travel time, the bill comes to U.S. $80, about the cost at home for a ten-minute office visit on a normal Tuesday to inquire whether a vaguely described miracle drug advertised on TV is "right for you."

For dinner, we resort to room service. Some people consider this option attractive, but it seldom appeals to us. The food always sits around longer than it should in the delivery process and you usually dine in a setting poorly designed for the enjoyment of eating. The menu in this instance looks bleak as well, featuring dishes in vogue at chain restaurants around the world. Our interest in eating local leads us to order the closest approximations possible to South Pacific specialties—

tagliatelle à la carbonara, a hamburger with fries, and a bottle of wine. Much of the chow gets left on the plate, but the wine slowly disappears in full.

The next morning Bill urges Cheryl to take a walk with him. "The exercise will be good for us, and we should see more of our surroundings." She hugs her pillow in protest, but in the end goes along to check out nearby restaurants, which now sound like our only dinner possibilities. A stroll along the length of Anse Vata, the beach our hotel is on, takes us more than an hour even though it's only a mile and a half up and back. Since it's a weekend, lots of local families and couples show up to frolic or unwind in the long but narrow stretch of sand. Across the unhurried street, there's a scattering of hotels and other businesses as well as lots of open land. New Caledonia doesn't seem to be rushing into tourism, an impression reinforced during the rest of our week's stay.

Our only real meal today is Sunday brunch at the Nouvata Park's poolside restaurant, where we eat breakfast on other mornings. On the way out for our walk, Cheryl makes a reservation for noon and ends up committing a little linguistic faux pas. In her foggy state, she books *pour douze* instead of *à midi* and when we arrive at 12:00, the hostess escorts us to a table set for twelve. Figuring out the problem quickly, Cheryl groans out an apology and the hostess cheerfully moves us.

The expansive buffet provides plenty of agreeable food choices. We focus on the seafood starters, including oysters on the half shell, buttery yellowfin tuna sashimi with bronchitis-busting wasabi, and poisson cru (raw fish in coconut milk, lime, and spices), known in Nouméa as "Tahitian salad." For a main course, with our appetites askew, our selections tend to be side dishes, particularly haricots verts (thin green beans), French potato and vegetable gratins, and American-style deviled eggs. The dessert table offers simple sweets, such as paper-thin fresh pineapple rounds poached lightly in sugar syrup and fruit tarts that come out better than we expect in the tropical humidity.

Satisfyingly stuffed, we take a nap and then move out to the balcony in the late afternoon for a light supper of wine and olives. Even at this time of the day, when insects get the most active, no flying pests bother us in the least. A deep red sunset keeps the sky aglow until a bright quarter moon takes on the night-lighting duties. Cheryl says, "You know, everything seems to be perking up. We've got drugs to cure us and a relaxing spot perfect for our recovery."

Bill concurs. "Maybe I'm already feeling a little better." As convalescent wards go, New Caledonia ranks with the best.

> >

That wasn't our reason for picking it as a destination, of course. The idea of the French tropics has intrigued us for many years, since our early experiences in the French West Indies researching *Best Places to Stay in the Caribbean*. Surely, it seemed to us, islands with a similar heritage in the South Pacific would embrace the same kind of sensuous joie de vivre and enjoy a sophisticated cuisine as heady with equatorial spice as the Creole cooking of the Caribbean. Early in our planning for this trip, we made French Polynesia a priority stop, but the logistics for getting anywhere near the region proved unmanageable. Much more easily accessible, New Caledonia seemed like a reasonable substitute, a part of Melanesia instead of Polynesia but still in the vast South Pacific.

Viewed from this perspective, it disappoints us more than any other place on our itinerary. Our illnesses deserve some of the blame, to be sure. They leash us to Nouméa, preventing us from exploring more of Grande Terre, the main island, and from flying to smaller, more remote isles. The congestion also undermines our appetites, sense of taste, and willingness to walk much distance for dinner, a necessity for diversity of choice given the lack of nighttime transportation. Still, even at our healthiest, we're sure New Caledonia would leave us wanting. It's not, as we had hoped, a South Seas version of Guadeloupe or St. Barthélemy, and Nouméa falls far short of its self-proclaimed billing as "the Paris of the Pacific."

The city is closer in spirit to a serene, sprawling provincial French town, pleasant in all respects but not exactly exotic or exciting. Beginning on Monday, we travel around the main streets daily, starting on tourist excursion buses to get our bearings and then graduating to public buses. Our most frequent route takes us from Anse Vata around a rocky promontory to Baie des Citrons, the best beach for swimming, and then passes a yacht harbor and the Port de Plaisance shopping and residential complex before reaching Moselle Bay, site of the municipal market, and the adjacent downtown. Along the way, several vestiges of the American presence here during World War II pop up, from an old hospital barracks still in use as a clinic to a major memorial of appreciation, the latter conveniently located by a McDonald's.

During the war, many of the millions of Americans involved in the Pacific campaign spent time in New Caledonia, one of the main military staging bases for counterattacking the Japanese forces that had overrun much of the region. The central square downtown today, the Place des Cocotiers, named for its palm trees, used to be the army's vegetable garden, and the navy made the port, a mile farther away, one of the busiest in the world for a brief period. Apparently, judging from the reactions of residents, we're some of the first Americans to venture here since then. Almost all visitors come from Australia, New Zealand, Japan, or France.

The downtown doesn't offer much except small-town shopping and it closes for all practical purposes at dusk at the same time as the stores. Clothing and lingerie boutiques compete with electronics warehouses and tabac/presse businesses, much like in any French burg. The bookstore on Place des Cocotiers brims with *bandes dessinées,* the distinctive hardcover French cartoon-character stories, and an adjacent cookware shop features Provençal table fabrics. For dining and drinking, for biking or playing boules, everyone goes to the shore.

The produce and seafood market on Moselle Bay—in a half dozen interconnected, airy pavilions with bright blue tile roofs—opens at 5:00 A.M. each day and becomes the busiest place in the city within a couple of hours. The community living room, where neighbors come to chat as well as buy, it's also the only place where we see much mingling between people of European and Melanesian descent. The ethnic interaction seems normal on our first visit on Monday, but by our return at the end of the week, it's clear how rare it is in Nouméa.

The fruit and vegetable sections lack variety in this spring season, but tubers abound, from taro to the yamlike *igname,* and fruits as well. Two adjoining stalls must carry every variety of papaya on earth, along with bananas of all sizes and colors. Other produce includes limes, pineapples, oranges, scallions, small local shallots, eggplants, vanilla beans, mint, and basil. French and Asian selections often sit side by side, frisée with Chinese greens, for example, or in the prepared-food cases, Vietnamese pastries next to croissants, and quiche Lorraine surrounded by Indian samosas (fried turnovers) and Philippine lumpia (egg rolls).

The greatest diversity in stock shows up in the fish and seafood sheds, filled with mahimahi, tuna, salmon, marlin, rouget, oysters, calamari, shrimp, and *langouste cigale.* "These seafood salads look luscious," Cheryl says, surveying a display of chilled "Tahitian" and other similar salads accented with spices and little bits of vegetables. Bill is more fascinated with the fish treated like meat, such as *rillettes au thon maison,* shrimp-stuffed vol-au-vent, and tuna sausages.

Street markets pop up occasionally as well. On our last night in town, we happen on a music and food version near our hotel. A local group called Mahalo stages a hulalike dance show, and home cooks sell prepared take-out dishes, including the Melanesian specialty known as *bougna,* a combination of chicken and seafood steamed in banana leaves with yams, sweet potatoes, and coconut milk. Other stands boast a range of snacks and sweets, from cotton candy to West Indian salt-cod accras, so unfamiliar here that the Caribbean entrepreneur labels them "samosas."

As in the French homeland, supermarkets flourish as well. A large one in the Port de Plaisance mall carries a good range of wines for our evenings on the balcony and also stocks robust quantities of both French and Asian foods. There's mousse de canard, Strasbourg terrine, pâté Breton, *lardons* (bacon), Toulouse sausage for cassoulet, and foie gras. As you would expect from an island with lots of cattle ranches, the meat cases hold plenty of local beef, often in steak cuts such as *onglet* and *bavette,* along with rotisserie chicken, *pintade* (guinea hen), rabbit, pigeon, and *andouillette* (tripe sausage). Down other aisles, shoppers get a choice of five varieties of rice paper for spring rolls, a dozen kinds of Asian noodles, and multiple variations on coconut milk, curries, soys, and fish and chile sauces.

The strengths in these market selections don't always carry over to restaurant menus. In many French colonies, such as Vietnam and the West Indies, a distinctive cuisine emerged from the interaction of European and local culinary traditions, but that didn't happen here, largely because of ethnic enmity. The dominant cuisine in Nouméa remains continental French, whether it fits the hot climate or not. The few restaurants with haute pretensions flaunt this disposition, making concessions to the weather only through an emphasis on cool, raw sashimi, tartare, and carpaccio preparations. Many smaller establishments, curiously, seek to disguise the French essence in their cooking by professing to offer a different kind of specialization, a conceit that seldom convinces.

The haute restaurants don't appeal to us, but we do check out the menus, always posted by the front door. At one place, Cheryl says, "What an odd selection of appetizers. The lobster carpaccio or the smoked swordfish spring rolls might tempt me here, but can you imagine starting with a lentil soup featuring foie gras and veal sweetbreads?"

"Yeah, on a winter's eve in Paris," Bill replies. "The same for the main courses. Grilled tuna steak with mushroom risotto and bacon cream? Beef tournedos Rossini? Pork loin wrapped in Parma ham served with truffled potatoes?"

The Texas Grill presents the strangest of the specialty menus we find. Billing itself as "The National Cowboy Restaurant," it allows customers to lasso a herd of unlikely Lone Star starters such as beef carpaccio, an *assiette* (plate) of smoked salmon, and mozzarella salad. The main-course steaks climb the scale in size to the "350 gram! Entrecôte de Cowboy," by Amarillo standards a rather puny twelve ounces of meat. The desserts range from poached pears "Abilene-style" to ice creams named Rio Grande, Fort Alamo, Fort Worth, Santa Fe, and Billy the Kid. "I wouldn't even expect a menu like this," Cheryl says, "at the Paris Disneyland."

A couple of the semi-ersatz places lure us in with mixed results. A cheerful Tex-Mex café on Baie des Citrons, La Paillotte advertises fajitas, enchiladas, tostadas, nachos, tequila sunrises, margaritas, and more. Cheryl orders a combination plate with a chicken taco and a beef burrito, both fairly credible except that the fillings are minced almost to a paste in each case. On the side, she gets a chopped tomato and avocado puree topped with crème fraîche, a fanciful French interpretation of guacamole. Bill's ceviche bears no resemblance at all to the real dish, but the strips of raw tuna and bell pepper taste good anyway. The owner stops by our table during the lunch and Bill asks, "How did you come up with the idea for the restaurant? Have you lived in Texas or Mexico?"

"No, I've never been near either place. I moved here from the south of France and opened a sandwich shop originally, but business was slow. My main cook knew a little about Mexican food so we decided to take a chance with it. It's definitely the best Tex-Mex food in New Caledonia because no one else does it."

The San Remo, near our hotel, claims in its name and a big sign to an Italian bent. Again, the proprietor is French and so is his sandwich-board pizza chef on the sidewalk, holding aloft a pie topped with a sunny-side-up egg, common in Nice but not in Naples. Whatever their nationality, the pizzas come straight from a hot oven deliciously crisp, enough so to draw us back for an encore. The salads offered on the other side of the menu, such as the warm goat cheese with lardons and greens, make no pretense at an Italian heritage, and neither do any of the wines available by the carafe or bottle.

Our best meals come at small restaurants with more faithful specializations. One is a mom-and-daughter Vietnamese operation in a strip mall around the corner from our hotel. While the middle-aged daughter handles the cooking in the kitchen, the elderly mother serves the patrons, seating us at one of the two simple tables on the sidewalk, actually more atmospheric than the brightly lit, larger tables inside. For starters, she brings us a platter of delightful fried crab spring rolls, which we wrap in lettuce leaves with pickled ginger and then dip in fish sauce. Bill moves on to a spicy fish preparation, with cubes of the day's catch stir-fried with vegetables in a piquant sauce that gets his nose running again. Cheryl opts for a vermicelli salad with grilled bits of pork and pork balls, served with lettuce leaves, carrot strips, ginger, and peanuts to bundle together for eating.

L'Astrolabe, on the Baie des Citrons, reminds us of numerous seaside bistros on the French Mediterranean, in its menu as well as the alfresco setting. For our lunch, Cheryl chooses the plat du jour, a seafood carpaccio combination. Paper-thin slices of giant clams, salmon, and tuna arrive with seasoning portions of astringent green olive oil, coarse sea salt, black pepper, and lime, all arrayed around a mound of garlicky slivered crudité salad. As terrific as this is, she really swoons over the accompanying vegetable side dish. "It's the sweetest pumpkin I've ever tasted, baked and then pureed with cream and some curry powder." Bill picks the house meat specialty, a steak tartare with frites called Le Gastrolabe. Chefs prepare it in the kitchen rather than at the table, blending local beef lusciously and richly with capers, tomatoes, onions, and gherkins, and flavoring the mixture with subdued but sound hints of parsley, chives, basil, egg yolk, brandy, olive oil, garlic, and Tabasco. The food punches out our congestion for hours.

La Fiesta Chez Alban, at the other end of the same shore, also packs a wallop. The theme here is Basque cooking, from both sides of the western Pyrenees border between France and Spain. The walls of the interior boast posters of d'Espelette peppers, sheepherders' flasks, and photos of Basque sports teams and heroes. On both visits, we eat outside on the street-front terrace, watching locals take their lunch break on the beach directly across from us.

The first time, our shared appetizer is San Sebastian–style *pinxchos,* in this case slices of country bread layered with soft, strong cheeses and then smoked salmon, anchovies, red peppers, and slivers of ham. Cheryl's main course Basque salad features authentic ewe's milk cheese from the region, *brebis,* along with ham, roasted bell peppers, greens, and a garlicky dressing. Bill savors the succulent meat in the plat du jour, lamb curry—not exactly Basque but hearty and tasty.

At our second lunch, Cheryl opts for the daily special, a *brandade de thon* that she labels "the best tuna casserole of my life," and Bill goes for the Basque omelet with piperade, served with a side of wonderful slow-cooked confit potatoes. To celebrate the success of the meal, Bill proposes toasting the chef with a *ti ponch,* our favorite rum drink from the French West Indies, made with stout rhum agricole, muddled lime, and raw sugar. "This seems an unlikely place for them, but they're on the cocktail list." The bartender surprises us with a superb rendition.

The most glaring omission on restaurant menus is Melanesian food, which we find only at the street market by our hotel in the take-home portions of bougna. Although many of the native dishes, such as the *civet de rousette* (bat stew), don't interest us greatly, it is disappointing to see such thorough separation between other residents and Melanesians, who call themselves Kanaks in New Caledonia. At 43 percent of the population, the Kanaks constitute the largest ethnic group in the territory, but French settlers (37 percent) and their allies among Polynesian and Asian immigrants outnumber them. The racial segregation favored by the majority extends well beyond the kitchen into almost all phases of life and is deeply rooted in a history of conflict.

The Kanaks, related to the Melanesians in Vanuatu and the Solomon Islands, migrated to Grande Terre several thousand years ago. Europeans first discovered the realm when Captain James Cook landed in 1774, but no one started settling in any significant numbers until Napoleon III claimed possession for France in 1853. The French envied the British use of Australia as a penal colony, and acquired New Caledonia for the same purpose, sending twenty thousand convicted criminals here in the late nineteenth century as well as four thousand political prisoners who played prominent roles in the Paris Commune uprising of 1871.

The French soon became more actively interested in Grande Terre when an engineer found large deposits of nickel. To abet mining interests, the government pushed Kanaks off their land onto "indigenous reservations" in areas without minerals or ranching potential, leading to a series of native rebellions and long guerilla wars. Following World War II, France relaxed its colonial policy and allowed Kanaks for the first time to leave their reservations without police permission. French settlers rose up in arms now, determined to thwart growing native sentiment for independence. Violence between the two groups peaked in the 1980s, bringing the territory to the brink of civil war. The Matignon Accord of 1988 calmed tensions by dividing New Caledonia into three semiautonomous provinces, two controlled by the Kanaks and the most populous one, around Nouméa, in the hands of French and other residents. Still, the underlying causes of conflict remain unsettled and both sides continue to be wary of each other.

Our original plans included visits to Kanak villages or outlying islands during our stay, but our poor health prevents us from taking the long day trips necessary for that. Instead, for any introduction to Melanesian life, we have to rely on two museums, virtually the only places in Nouméa that accord much recognition to Kanak culture. The traditional way of life, still widely practiced, revolves around clan membership and subsistence agriculture based on the cultivation of the yam, taro, and banana. Chiefs rule through their connections to clan ancestors, the most powerful of the many animistic spirits that influence all aspects of life.

The Museum of New Caledonia provides a historic overview of the carved-wood art that represents and propagates the status of chiefs, including prestige objects such as ceremonial axes handed down through generations and haunting, emotive masks used in funeral rites. The exhibits also cover items of everyday life from the past, including simple coiled pottery for cooking, nets and traps for fishing, wooden spades and stakes for farming, and stones in the shape of yams and bananas to bury in fields to give strength to crops. Before Europeans arrived, women wore short skirts made of coconut fibers or banyan-tree roots and men donned only a woven penis shield, less from modesty in both cases apparently than to protect their reproductive organs from the evil eye and other bad spirits.

While the museum offers an anthropological perspective on Kanak traditions, the Tjibaou Cultural Center celebrates them. Named for Jean-Marie Tjibaou, the Kanak leader who helped to negotiate the Matignon Accord and was assassinated the next year for his efforts, it evolved from the 1988 agreements as a way of honoring New Caledonia's indigenous people in the province where their presence is the least respected. Architecturally, it soars majestically in a contemporary interpretation of the conical style of a chief's house, providing facilities for research, exhibitions, and performances devoted to the Melanesian legacy.

The most impressive galleries during our stop deal with Kanak and other Oceanic artifacts as art rather than as historic relics. Dramatic masks, totems, ceremonial axes, and additional pieces—many of them on loan from the Museum of Man in Paris—show the expressive skill of Pacific carvers, a theme carried over into exhibits of contemporary work. Other rooms pay tribute to Tjibaou's life and tell the story of the Paris Commune prisoners sent to New Caledonia in exile.

Knowing the center has a restaurant and figuring that surely it must serve Kanak dishes, we time our visit to be here for lunch. No luck again. The menu offers croque-monsieurs, quiche, and even hot dogs, but nothing related to the culture being commemorated. That's the day we end up with a Tex-Mex lunch back on the Baie des Citrons, giving a nod to part of our own heritage at least in lieu of a more appropriate one.

After a week in Nouméa, we're ready to bail for Singapore, where we're looking forward to real food adventures. New Caledonia treats us well in many respects, allowing us to recover from our bronchitis in a fortuitously favorable clime. Both of us leave much healthier and happier than when we arrive, which constitutes a wonderful gift, but we also depart with new pangs of hunger.

THE NITTY-GRITTY

⊡ NOUVATA PARK HOTEL
www.newcaledoniahotelsresorts.com
Anse Vata, Nouméa
687-26-22-00   fax 687-26-16-77
The four-star Park Hotel wing,
containing 110 deluxe rooms and 6 suites,
is far superior to the other,
less expensive wings.

⊡ L'ASTROLABE
35 promenade R. Laroque
Baie des Citrons, Nouméa
687-28-44-44
lunch and dinner

⊡ LA FIESTA CHEZ ALBAN
5 promenade R. Laroque
Baie des Citrons, Nouméa
687-26-21-33
lunch and dinner

Poisson Cru ("Tahitian Salad")

SERVES 6 AS AN APPETIZER, 4 AS A MAIN DISH

    1   pound very fresh high-grade ahi tuna, diced in neat ½-inch cubes
    ½   cup fresh lime juice
    ½   cup coconut milk
    ½   cup diced peeled and seeded cucumber
    4   to 5 scallions, green and white portions, split lengthwise and minced
    1   fresh hot small green or red chile, seeded and minced, optional
Several tablespoons shredded coconut, optional
    ¾   teaspoon salt, or more to taste
Freshly ground black pepper
    1   medium tomato, seeded and squeezed to eliminate liquid, diced

Combine in a medium bowl the tuna, lime juice, coconut milk, cucumber, scallions, optional chile and coconut, salt, and pepper. Refrigerate 30 minutes to 1 hour. Mix in the tomato and serve right away.

THE APPROACH OF EVENING LURES US IRRESISTIBLY
into Singapore's red-light district, discreetly hidden in residential quarters among the street-side shops of Geylang Road, a major artery. If you know the city-state's reputation for paternalistic morality, you might be surprised to learn that the sex trade flourishes here. The government bans adult magazines such as *Playboy* and even requires ones with "mature content" like *Cosmopolitan* to carry a warning on the cover, but Big Brother approves of prostitution, as long as it isn't merely for oral sex (legal just as a prelude to conventional copulation) and doesn't involve sodomy, a heinous offense punishable by brutal and bloody caning.

Heedless on this sweltering night to any of these indulgences, our carnal cravings focus exclusively on crab. On September 10, 2003, about a year before we made final decisions on destinations to visit on this trip, the late R. W. "Johnny" Apple, Jr., published an article in the *New York Times* on Singapore's "endless supper." A renowned journalist equally esteemed for his political reporting and his discriminating gluttony, Apple claimed the crab *bee hoon* (a preparation with rice vermicelli) at Sin Huat Eating House on Geylang Road was "the best crab dish we tasted in a city famous for crab." He didn't describe the place or its location in any detail, but we know our lust for the bee hoon will lead us to the door.

Assuming it has a door, which isn't really the case. Approaching the area on foot, looking carefully for any sign of an "eating house," we finally come across an open-air sidewalk dive on a corner with a small sign announcing "Sin Huat."

"Surely, that's not our spot," Cheryl says hopefully. "Let's look a little further." Nothing about the neighborhood or premises seems promising except for rows of fish and seafood tanks, enough—after cleaning the grime off the outside—to supply a large aquarium. The tanks provide all the decor, and several dingy, rickety plastic tables on the sidewalk constitute all the dining accoutrements.

"I'm afraid we've found it," Bill says. "Why don't we sit down and at least get a beer?"

He leads the way over to a couple of short plastic stools, the only seats out at the time until a wiry spark plug of a woman rushes from inside to wrestle real plastic chairs from a tall stack in a corner. Bill orders a big bottle of Tiger beer for us to share, and as Spark Plug pours us glasses, she insists, "You eat some steamed scallops, too." Not quite sure how or why to refuse the food, we shrug our agreement to the order, and she disappears into the maze of tanks. Inspecting the Tiger bottle, Cheryl hands it over to Bill, pointing to a promise that drinkers will "Live Like a Rock Star."

"Yeah, right," he says. "So Jagger's going to join us at this dump any moment now?"

While we sip the refreshingly cold brew, a cook emerges from a kitchen at the rear wearing knee-high rubber boots, sloshes along the wet floor, reaches into one of the tanks, and grabs our scallops, still alive in their shells. Cheryl watches him intently. "I love the Chinese sense of fresh. None of this 'air-expressed daily' or even caught the same day. If it's dead when it reaches the kitchen, it might as well have been dead for a week."

"It's definitely a good omen."

A half of the bottle of beer later, Spark Plug delivers a big plate of scallops on the half shell, bathed in a rich, heady, oily sauce. "My God," Bill swears. "These are unbelievable—maybe the tastiest scallops I've ever had."

"And," Cheryl says, "I bet the menu"—which we never see, even if it exists—"doesn't blather on about diver harvesting, plumpness, provenance, or other things so common in American restaurant descriptions. You see them in the tank alive and know they're truly fresh."

After a few more bites, Bill pauses and glances around again. "You know, this place doesn't look so bad after all."

Pleasantly acclimated now, we order Chef Danny Lee's specialty, the crab bee hoon. To accompany the dish, a waitress brings us rolled-up washcloths, a welcome sight, since none of the other food vendors in Singapore so far has offered napkins or wipes of any kind. Later, when he gets the check, Bill sees the washcloths for a second time, listed as a one-dollar charge. He laughs at the fee for a service that keeps the table manageably tidy for the restaurant, but pays it happily.

When we're well into our second beer, Spark Plug returns with a brimming platter featuring a magnificent jumbo crab, broken into big pieces over a tangled pillow of vermicelli in a sticky broth flavored with oyster sauce, mushrooms, scallions, ginger, and red chiles. "Apple certainly didn't exaggerate," Cheryl says. "How could crab get any better?" Taking turns with the metal cracker, we shatter shells much of the evening, probably even in our sleep later. Our goal is to direct the juices into the noodles, enriching them further with briny sweetness, but the shells go in every direction—including, as she discovers the next day, into Cheryl's purse. She doesn't keep the mementoes, but we certainly remember the night and its delight. Rock stars got no glory on us.

> >

Johnny Apple's article convinced us to go to Singapore on our trip, despite many misgivings about the political climate and the antiseptic, Western style of the city. The clique of autocrats who govern every aspect of life seem a little silly at times—banning the sale of chewing gum for many years, for instance—but they are deadly serious about their multitude of rules. Amnesty International condemns the country for one of the highest execution rates in the world (usually for possession of drugs, including marijuana) and also for its cruel and degrading use of caning as a common punishment.

The courts sentence more than one thousand men a year to a varying number of lashes for many different offenses ranging from overstaying a visa (at least three strokes) to vandalism (up to eight smacks) and robbery (a minimum of six blows for an act committed before 7:00 P.M. and twelve for a later offense). The caning crew straps a fellow to a metal frame with his bare butt exposed and whips him hard enough with a rattan stick to leave permanent scars. To increase the pain inflicted, officials soak the rattan overnight in water. It makes you wonder what these guys do for entertainment after work.

Just saying that probably gets this book censored in Singapore, which puts it in pretty good company, alongside the *Asian Wall Street Journal* and the *Far Eastern Economic Review*. Reporters Without Borders ranks the nation 140th out of 167 countries in its 2005 index of press freedom. The People's Action Party (PAP), which has dominated the nominally democratic government for forty years, takes harsh action against political rivals, from denying them almost any opportunity for public visibility to jailing them without trial as threats to national security. The government controls all local radio and television programming, and the Media Development Authority rigorously monitors the Internet to block Web sites deemed a danger to PAP or public morality. Unless you're trying to summon the police, forget about private satellite dishes, peaceful demonstrations, strikes, and hanging out on the streets in groups of more than six, which is regarded as riotous behavior.

Some citizens poke fun at all the regulations. A widely sold T-shirt proclaims "Singapore is a fine city," and displays cross-slashed images of various actions punished by substantial fines, which include eating or drinking on the subway, jaywalking, littering, spitting, failing to buckle your seat belt in a taxi, and not flushing a public toilet. PAP runs costly public education campaigns about these behavioral norms, trying to instill them as private disciplines by making deviants pay heavily. The T-shirt protests the paternalism, but more amazing than that, the censorship-driven government tolerates the implied disdain, most likely on the theory that any publicity is good publicity, hoping that the shirt's message reinforces its own efforts to advertise the officially sanctioned code of conduct. You can bet they're not chuckling at the pop humor.

The authorities are easing up on the strictness, however. Among other changes, gum chewers can now buy their treat at pharmacies if they're willing to produce identification and sign a register. The government appears to be making small concessions to appease both citizens and world opinion, but PAP isn't likely to head down a path that will gradually loosen its tight grip on power and public policy.

Many will say that's a good thing. Unlike most cases where autocrats control affairs firmly and thoroughly, the leaders of PAP seem satisfied with their clout alone. They don't raid the treasury, abide any corruption, dream of territorial conquest, or otherwise act like self-aggrandizing tyrants. Probably, they truly care about the economic strength of their city and sincerely want to keep it clean, safe, orderly, and running on time. If you judge them by these results instead of their tactics and obsessions, they make a Bill Gates success story look as simplistic as a game of Monopoly.

Singapore works in almost all respects. It's clean to the point of pristine, as spick-and-span as a Disney theme park even without hundreds of sweepers constantly collecting the trash. People actually take pride in their public restrooms, invariably spotless and in good operating order. The crime rate ranks as one of the lowest in the world, a blessing for locals and travelers alike and a major inducement to foreign investment. PAP places a high priority on labor productivity, which translates to high-level attention to education and health. Public transportation covers every corner of the city and does it efficiently. The Housing and Development Board creates livable high-rise residential estates and new towns—home to 80 percent of the inhabitants—with easy access to schools, shopping, and employment opportunities.

Most impressive of all, Singapore stands out as a monument to multiculturalism. The British colonial roots remain entrenched in many ways—such as the use of English as the primary language of the realm—but the population is diversely Asian. Though Chinese descendants predominate, they come originally from a number of different provinces and still speak dissimilar dialects. Malays and Indians constitute significant minorities, and they, too, derive from various ethnic and linguistic backgrounds. In addition to English, the law recognizes Mandarin, Malay, and Tamil as official languages, and the major religions include Buddhism, Hinduism, Islam, Christianity, Confucianism, and Taoism. The government stalwartly maintains respectful tolerance of these differences and clamps down forcefully on anyone breeding ill-will.

The city means business, in virtually every way that you can interpret the point. Founded as an Asian trading post in 1819 by Sir Stamford Raffles of the English East India Company, it grew into one of the British Empire's great entrepôts. It remains an international market center, but government-guided development has also created powerful financial and industrial sectors, resulting in the most advanced economy in Southeast Asia. Everything PAP does ultimately focuses on success in this sphere: even the ban on chewing gum began largely because of incidents where discarded gum clogged the doors of subway trains, impeding the transportation system of the worker bees.

Many visitors come to Singapore on business, a better reason than pleasure travel in most respects. The authorities want to encourage conventional tourism, and have tried to do it with enormous investments in a great airport, large international hotels, and colossal contemporary shopping centers. Apparently, they hope your main interest in a destination is duty-free buying and seeing the beauty of efficient air transportation.

The other tourist attractions—described of course in glowing terms in guidebooks and travel magazine articles—just don't add up to much. The historic colonial area sounds impressive on paper, but basically it's full of intentionally intimidating, blocky nineteenth-century buildings. Visitors often end up spending much of their time on the "miracle mile" of Orchard Road, an orgy of a shopping strip featuring absolutely nothing distinctive. Our trip to the area lasts less than thirty minutes before we flee the massive malls in dismay.

The extensive Chinatown is the only area we enjoy for sightseeing. Despite considerable urban renewal, it retains a fair measure of traditional character. The Chinatown Heritage Centre illustrates both the changes and the constants. Political turmoil, natural disasters, and famine drove many thousands of Chinese settlers here in the late nineteenth century, all risking their lives on a monthlong boat journey in horribly overcrowded conditions to reach what they called Nanyang, a place of escape. Most planned to return home at some point, but few ever did, sometimes succumbing to the ready availability of opium, alcohol, and gambling. They lived generally in two- and three-story shop-houses, with businesses on the ground floor and a dozen or more tiny residential cubicles upstairs, barely bigger than the beds they held, as the Centre documents in replicas; forty inhabitants might share one toilet, bath, and kitchen, as well as some space on the street outside as their common living room.

Japanese occupation of Singapore during World War II brought the local economy to a standstill, forcing many people to create makeshift jobs for themselves. Large numbers set up street-food stalls, cooking and selling one or a few specialties from their region of China, India, or Malaysia. These small "hawker" stands continued to flourish after the war, when Chinatown entered something of a golden age in vibrancy and liveliness. Important elements of that spirit remain today, though the government in recent decades has moved the street-food entrepreneurs into market buildings and hawker centers, the very places that have enticed us to Singapore.

Apple's story in the *Times* grabbed our attention not for its comments on Sin Huat, one of many places mentioned, but because the journalist talks at length about K. F. Seetoh and his guidebook to hawker street food. Neither of us could track down the version of the book Apple cites, but Bill soon found and ordered a revised edition, named *die, die, must try!*, at an online Singapore bookstore. Don't be put off by the strange title if you're planning a visit. You should die, die to buy it. The tome sucks in many respects, particularly the design and the maps, but it's one of the most extraordinary eating guides ever written.

The city enjoys a worldwide reputation, at least in culinary circles, for its wealth of tasty street food. The possibilities appealed to us strongly, but how would we find our way among the roughly twelve thousand food stalls scattered around Chinatown and all the other neighborhoods of the city? The book provides the answer. Seetoh's publishing and broadcasting company, Makansutra (from the Malay word for "eat" and the Sanskrit word for "lesson"), sends out about thirty-five undercover "Makanmatas" ("food police") to locate and rate the best cooking in the one-hundred-plus hawker centers and markets. Their research, tidily packaged in *die, die, must try!*, convinced us that we could pig out grandly in Singapore even on a short stop, now knowing the right food centers to visit, the dishes we want to try, the stands that offer premier examples of the fare, and the open days and hours of our chosen vendors. Between bites, we can check out tourist attractions, but our mission is to revel in Asian street food.

Ironically, we have to thank the tight-assed rulers for this wonderful opportunity. Their obsession with cleanliness guarantees sanitary cooking conditions everywhere, unlike in many cities, and their subway system zips us effortlessly between different hawker areas. The government even played a role in providing us a good place to stay, the Albert Court Hotel, a block of former shop-houses renovated into a boutique business hotel under a public program. Bill picked it in part because of a bargain Internet rate on a large executive room, but mainly because of its location between major stations on two of the principal subway lines. The plan is to stay on the move most of the time, munching as we go, except, of course, on the fine subway trains.

> >

After a late-Saturday-night arrival, we're up and off early on Sunday morning for our first day of progressive grazing. Most of the hawker centers don't open until later, so our first stop is one that runs around the clock, just like McDonald's local McDelivery service ("for orders of any size," the ubiquitous posters say). Makansutra recommends nothing at the Lau Pa Sat Festival Market, but all the standard guidebooks mention it as a nonthreatening place for visitors to check out the street-food scene. It sounds to us worth a look, at least to get a touchstone for what to avoid.

It's easy to see why Lau Pa Sat appeals to tourists. It occupies a faux Victorian open-air pavilion full of gingerbread accents, whirling ceiling fans, and comfortable modern tables. Like spokes on a wheel, wide aisles radiate from the hub in a half dozen directions, leading to pods of attractive stalls with names such as "Fantastic Handmade Noodle," "Smoking Duck," and "Wonderful Vegetable Mixed Rice." Bill says on the way out, "This would make a perfect base for McDelivery."

Getting to-go drinks of mixed mango and kiwi juice, we wander a few blocks over to the heart of Chinatown. The walk takes us along South Bridge Road, the neighborhood's main street and the site of the Sri Mariamman Hindu Temple. Dating back to 1827, before heavy Chinese settlement of the area, it features an arresting sculpted *gopuram* (tower) rising high above the entrance, flanked by statues of Shiva and Vishnu. Just days in advance of our arrival, the temple hosted an annual fire-walking ceremony, when scores of the faithful lined up on South Bridge to prove their spiritual strength by striding across a bed of hot coals. Today is also busy, leading up to tomorrow's inauguration of the preparations for Hindu Diwali, the Festival of Lights, called Deepawali in Singapore. Staring at piles of footwear on the sidewalk by the door into the temple, Cheryl is perplexed. "There must be several hundred pair of sandals and shoes in those stacks. How would you ever find your own again?"

Side streets off of Bridge offer other diversions. Along Pagoda on the way to the Chinatown Heritage Centre, pedestrians get a good view of the temple grounds, where today prostrate men dressed in simple loincloths roll themselves around the property. Sago Street once brimmed with death houses, which provided rudimentary care for the infirm elderly who didn't want to risk bad luck for their family by dying at home. Attached funeral parlors prepared the deceased for last rites, including the burning of paper replicas of their favorite possessions and also plenty of simulated money for them to spend in heaven or hell. Shops on Banda sell similar contemporary items for incineration, such as cardboard credit cards, passports, computers, and cell phones, each presumed to be useful in the afterlife. "So, what do you want to take with you?" Cheryl asks Bill.

"The only thing that tempts me is the dim sum, but I'd prefer to have the real deal alive rather than a facsimile in my coffin."

On that note, we enter one of the most famous of the hawker operations, the Maxwell Food Centre at the end of South Bridge. The travel guides that tout Lau Pa Sat sometimes mention Maxwell as well, usually preceded with an adjective like "drab" or "old-fashioned." Nonsense, it's just functional, not dressed up for a social outing. The open-air concrete pavilion with a corrugated roof holds more than one hundred stalls, each about ten square feet and jam-packed with cooking equipment, ingredients, and one or more proprietors. The booths line both sides of three broad, tiled aisles occupied by basic tables and chairs. As in other centers, you order at a stand that specializes in one or a few dishes, take a seat, and when the food is prepared—it never sits out under a warming light—the chef-owner or an assistant brings it over, locating you among the multitudes by some kind of mysterious radar. Low walls at the stalls allow you to watch everything going on inside from your table. When you finish eating, you leave trays, plates, and utensils on the table—stacking or clearing them can violate religious taboos—and someone picks them up shortly for cleaning.

Our top priority at Maxwell is Tian Tian Hainanese Chicken Rice, a stall that Foo Kui Lian took over from her brother forty years ago. Makansutra's Web site ranks it as one of fifteen 2005 "Hawker Legends," the best in the city, the group says, for chicken rice, itself a Singapore legend created by immigrants from Hainan Island in the South China Sea. The booth proves easy to find from the vendor number listed in *die, die, must try!*, a relief to us given the crowded conditions and large number of stands. Waiting for the business to open at 11:00, we kill a little time looking at other stalls across the aisle. When we turn around again, a minute or so before the appointed hour, suddenly two dozen customers have jumped ahead of us into a line, which moves quickly because Foo rents an adjoining stall for prep work and employs a staff of five—both unusual signs of success in this field.

Chicken rice may sound a little dull—it's just steamed versions of the two basic components—but it abounds with flavor at Tian Tian. The order taker asks us, "You want skin?" and both of us nod "Yes." Otherwise everyone gets exactly the same thing, a big mound of high-quality rice topped with rich chicken gravy, several thick slices of buttery white meat, a bowl of broth fragrant with stock, vinegar-bathed cukes, sweet soy, and a fittingly fiery red-chile sauce seasoned with ginger and a bit of orange. Each plate costs about U.S. $2, the average for hawker food anywhere in the city.

Another Maxwell favorite, Lim Kee Banana Fritters, also attracts us, largely because of its top Makansutra rating for the stall's specialty, *goreng pisang* (batter-fried bananas). The owners grow the fruit on their own plantation in Malaysia, using only the prime Raja variety, and work with a special batter they created themselves. The plump bananas come out of the oil as sweet as honey, with a tempuralike coating that's crackly crisp. While the cook prepares them, we watch a young woman at another stand making fresh sugarcane juice, wrestling short stalks through a press that mangles the cane and releases its liquid. Intrigued, both of us get a glass. "I feared it would be cloyingly sweet," Bill says, and Cheryl finishes his thought, "But it's really light and refreshing. I love the green-fruit flavor."

From the Maxwell complex, we walk a few blocks south to Tanjong Pagar Plaza Market and Food Centre, on the fringes of Chinatown. On the way, along Tanjong Pagar Road, we stumble across Singapore's Bridal Row, where virtually every shop focuses on some aspect of wedding management: gowns, photography, etiquette requirements, invitations, even spas to relax and reward the wedding party. Bars and nightclubs with racy advertising in the windows constitute the only other common class of commerce on the street, leading us to ponder any possible connection between the two types of businesses. "Maybe," Bill says, "stressed-out brides need a couple of stout ones after visits to the etiquette planner."

The market portion of Tanjong Pagar takes up the whole of the large ground floor, crammed with stalls offering a stunning array of produce, including dragonfruits that look like artichokes dipped in Chinese red lacquer and rose apples that resemble a cross between a pear and a chayote. The upstairs hawker center looks shabbier, enough so to intimidate the squeamish, particularly if they get a whiff of the pig organ soup simmering in the stand at the top of the stairs.

The soup draws crowds of fans, but our sights are set instead on ice *kachang*, another popular dish with greater appeal to us. The two places that tie for Makansutra's highest mark for the treat in the city, Annie's Peanut Ice Kachang and Huat Kee Ice Kachang, compete here as next-door neighbors. Our intention is to try both versions, but Cheryl demurs after we share one from Annie's. "This is good, but two's too many." The personable proprietor shaves ice finely to snow consistency in a machine designed for the purpose—Makansutra raves about the blade she uses for this—and then mounds it into a large volcano-shaped pile. She pours a rich fruit syrup over the stack and adds jellied fruit squiggles and cubes, corn kernels, and sweetened red adzuki beans, showering everything at the end with finely chopped peanuts. Weird but tasty.

Rain starts pouring during our stay in Tanjong Pagar, so to avoid getting soaked on the trek to the subway station, we take a taxi to our next, across-town stop, the Old Airport Road Emporium and Cooked Food Centre. From the outside, the square, open-sided, three-story building looks like it could double as a parking garage. Food stands occupy the same space a car would, packed together so tightly that they leave minimal room for walking and eating in the aisles.

Makansutra likes many of the one hundred or so vendors in this old-style structure, though business is slow late on a stormy Sunday afternoon. Our goal is to sample several dishes, starting with fried Hokkien *mee,* a Singaporan comfort food that blends fried wheat noodles with seafood stock, prawns, squid rings, and strips of pork, often from the belly. Ng Hock Wah of the Nam Sing Hokkien Fried Mee took the 2005 Hawker Legend title for this specialty, which he has cooked for more than forty years. He stays open daily at the Emporium, but closes occasionally on an ad hoc, unannounced basis—like today, unfortunately.

Determined to try the mee in any case, we find another version nearby at a friendly mom-and-pop stall where the man cooks and the woman serves. He fries the spaghettilike noodles in a wok with the seafood, meat, lots of bean sprouts, and bits of scrambled egg, and puts everything together in a bowl of flavorful broth. The lady brings it out with a proud smile with lime juice and chile paste, and we devour it all down to the last lick of liquid. It's good enough to get addictive.

While we eat, Pop prepares his other forte, known variously as *or luak*, fried oyster egg, and oyster omelet. He spreads a circle of taro flour on a flat-bottomed wok, adds beaten eggs and a sprinkling of red chile, splashes in some oil, and then dexterously maneuvers this mixture to the side of the pan. With his other hand, he dips oysters into more of the same flour and fries them lightly on the opposite section of the skillet, scooping them up when just browned to scatter over the still-runny eggs. He's done in less time than it would take one of us to wash his wok.

Curry puffs, one of the few items that disappoint us in Singapore, come next on our list of things to sample. Wang Wang Crispy Curry Puff fixes a nice, buttery and flaky pastry shell, but the curried potato-and-chicken filling lacks flavor to us. Blandness doesn't worry us at our next stall, Mattar Road Seafood Barbecue, another of Makansutra's top fifteen Legends and its number one choice in town for chile crab, a Singapore icon usually spelled the British way as "chilli crab." Ng Hung Leng and his wife close two days a week, a long business break here, to make the red chile sauce, a robust concoction with coconut milk, ginger, tomatoes, eggs, and stock.

When the Ngs see us striding toward their out-of-the-way booth, they know we're coming for crab, which they have stacked all around them in plastic laundry baskets and burlap flour bags. As soon as she seats us, Madame Ng carefully selects two of the live crustaceans for our approval—both 2.2 pounds plump and as feisty as boxers going to the ring—and then hands them to her husband for cooking. "Both want chilli crab?" she asks.

Cheryl says, "Make one of them a pepper crab," another local specialty loaded with freshly ground Tellicherry pepper.

"Want greens, too?"

"Sure," Bill answers, unsure until later that he's ordered stir-fried greens with garlic.

The supper costs much more than other hawker meals, and takes much longer to prepare and eat, but it's worth all of that and much more. "The pepper crab really zings you," Cheryl says, "but I like the chile version better because the sauce gives it greater complexity."

Bill agrees. "The sauce must be invisible, too, because I don't see a drop on your blouse, messy one, even though we've trashed the entire table and my stomach is screaming 'burst, burst, must die!' Let's go hail a cab on the street and get drenched with rain instead." The downpour ends, of course, as soon as we reach our hotel, a good excuse for wrapping up the evening with an obligatory Singapore Sling in the Albert Court's bar.

Early the next morning, we walk to the Tekka Centre in the Little India neighborhood near our hotel for breakfast snacks. "What's going on?" Cheryl asks, baffled by the festive decorations that have sprouted overnight on Serangoon Road, the area's main street. A huge sculpted peacock spreads his feathers brightly over the entrance to a department store and giant images of lotus blossoms, parasols, and elephants drape from the lampposts. Neither of us has a clue about the meaning until we discover most of the food stands at Tekka shut down tightly, in honor, according to an apologetic sign, of the official beginning of the preparations for the local Deepawali celebration.

So we hop on the subway back to Chinatown to track down some vendors who had been closed yesterday. In the Hong Lim Market and Food Centre, the group includes Outram Park Fried Kway Teow, which gets Makansutra's highest marks for *char kway teow*, a dish that becomes one of our personal favorites in Singapore. The stand's cook wok-fries a combination of fettuccine-size rice noodles and spaghettilike wheat noodles with bits of Chinese sausage and pork (including a generous portion of cracklings), cockles, bean sprouts, other vegetables, and a thick soy sauce. Sitting across from Cheryl on a simple outdoors-style picnic table, Bill says, marveling, "What a fantastic blend of flavors and textures, the seafood with the pork, crunchy with silky."

"You're right, a winner for sure. It speaks of a culinary sophistication way beyond the bounds of this humble setting."

One of the Makansutra Legends, Ah Kow Mushroom Minced Pork Mee, operates in a dark back corner of the same building. Cher Hang Peng stands behind the stove, where he's been for fifty years since the age of ten, preparing *bak chor mee*, minced-meat noodles with black vinegar, dumplings, and vegetables. His wife sits at an unoccupied table when she's not taking orders, folding wonton wrappers around big balls of finely chopped pork to make the dumplings. Both are a joy to watch, Mom folding and stuffing as Pop dunks wheat noodles and then minced meat and dumplings into a boiling broth to cook quickly. He puts the core ingredients together in bowls and adds, over the top, bean sprouts, crisp fried shallots, cilantro, Chinese black vinegar, and chile sauce. A cup of the steaming broth accompanies the main dish. For a grand tasting and the show, the tab comes to U.S. $3 total.

Positively aglow from the day's two starter courses, we stroll several blocks to the large Chinatown Complex, which brings us down a couple of notches from our noodle high. To get to the second-floor food stalls, visitors have to dodge and weave their way through swarms of clothes saleswomen and shoppers on the street level. Once you locate the stairs, the steps lead up to a sprawling, drab quarter deserving immediate attention from the government's current renovation program for hawker centers. It takes a dedicated search to find the two stalls we're seeking, one renowned for sweet rice balls called *ah boling* and the other just as famed for *chai tow kueh,* misleadingly labeled "carrot cake" in English. Both are supposed to be open according to our usually reliable information, but neither is.

Set on having the carrot cake, we dash across South Bridge Street to return to the Maxwell Centre, certain someone in the compound makes a reasonable version. A circuit around the stands leads us to "Auntie," where the namesake cook works on her savory specialty, which contains no carrots and tastes nothing like the American dessert. She coarsely grates enormous daikon-style radishes, puts a mound of them into a flat-bottomed wok, cracks an egg over the top, and fries it lightly into a loose mixture. Both of us get black cakes, darkened by soy sauce and dried chile, but we take seats at a table already occupied by a local businessman eating the simpler white rendition.

He nods a welcome to us and watches us curiously, remarking after a few minutes in good English, "You must live in Singapore because you handle the chopsticks so well."

"No," Bill answers, "but we use them at home in the United States with some frequency. Do you eat regularly at the Maxwell Centre?"

"Just occasionally when I'm in the neighborhood. What brings you here? You must be the only Westerners in the building."

"We're on a hawker pilgrimage," Cheryl says, "sampling as many dishes as we can at a variety of centers. These simple cakes are delicious, as flavorful as any hawker specialty we've eaten."

Smiling broadly, he tells us, "You're getting a real Singapore experience. I eat hawker food every day and think it's the best thing about the city. I couldn't live anywhere else for that reason alone."

A little full now, still before noon, we decide to get some exercise walking around the historic colonial zone of the city. If Bill had only packed hiking boots for the occasion, the tall, turbaned-and-robed doorman at the fabled Raffles Hotel might have let him enter the lobby. Both of us are wearing open-toed sandals, like most people on the tropical streets, which the establishment's inspector general deems okay for a lady but not a gentleman. Cheryl goes in for a look while Bill hangs around the portico, trying to annoy the burly fellow, who he hopes is sweating profusely under his officious garb and bulky black shoes.

This bit of fun stirs our appetites again, so we take the subway to the main Malay sector of town, a predominantly Muslim area, for a visit to the Haig Road Food Centre. Several generations of the same family have operated Warong Sudi Mampir since the 1940s, settling in this location about thirty years ago. The current chef-owner and Makansutra Legend, Gunawan Baajoan, seems a little overwhelmed at present with take-out orders, telling us, "You'll have to wait about forty minutes before I can get to you."

He probably expects us to leave, obviously oblivious to our reputation for obstinate persistence. Instead, we find seats, get drinks from another stall, and track his progress, noticing that he cooks on small logs rather than charcoal, a sterling sign. He catches on to our frame of mind pretty quickly and comes over to tell us he can fit in a small order, just what we want. Within minutes he brings us ten skewers, equally divided between beef and chicken, both types succulently marinated in coconut milk and spices and then grilled perfectly. Cheryl pronounces the proprietor's chunky peanut sauce "the best I've ever had," and guesses he made it by hand with a mortar and pestle, crushing peanuts with finely minced ginger, shallots, and chile, and for the salty tang, adding pounded dried shrimp rather than fish sauce.

Concluding the evening with crab bee hoon at Sin Huat Eating House, we go the next morning to the suburbs in search of the Bedok New Town and Food Centre. The Makansutra map of the area really lets us down, suggesting our breakfast stop is much closer to the subway station than it actually is. After hoofing it for a steamy mile or so through a well-manicured industrial zone, Bill finally checks at the security gate of an auto parts factory to make sure we're going in the right direction. The guard comes out to the sidewalk and points down the street at a cluster of high-rise towers, saying, "Maybe a ten-minute walk." Onward we trudge in air that clings to us like a wool blanket in a sauna.

A big, bustling patio market sits in the center of the residential complex. At one end, hawkers offer prepared food to eat here or take away. In the other half of the space, a variety of vendors butcher meat to order, sell live fish and seafood, display fresh produce, peddle brooms and plastic pails, and parade clothes of all kinds and sizes.

If we've felt like maverick cattle in other centers—Westerners gone astray from our herd—the sensation strikes us here with the force of a branding iron. Everyone else on the plaza lives in elevator distance of where they're standing or sitting. Near to nothing of interest to other Singapore residents or visitors either, the Bedok New Town market exists for a self-contained community, all of whom seem to be eyeing us intently. No one is the least unfriendly—quite the opposite in some cases—but they clearly regard us as novelties.

Our reason for venturing this far from the heart of the city is to taste another version of char kway teow, this time from the wok of Makansutra Legend Ng Chang Siang of Hill Street Fried Kway Teow. Mom and Pop Ng are just setting up as we arrive, so Cheryl proposes getting an appetizer at another stand. One aisle over, the Yong Hua You Tiao stall fries long bread fritters called *you char kueh*. They look like small Mexican churros, and taste similar, but the dough contains leavening in this case. A dozen of them wash down smoothly with squeezed-to-order melon and pineapple juices from Heng Heng Fresh Fruit Juice.

Returning to Hill Street right before the opening hour, we find the Ngs eating some of the same fritters. They offer us tastes, but Cheryl declines on our behalf, explaining we just had a batch. The couple acts like they've never seen foreigners, at least at their stand, and they take obvious pride in presenting us with our plates of noodles. Their rendition of the dish is wonderful, on a par with yesterday's version except for fewer bits of sausage and crunchy pork cracklings. On our way out, Bill offers our thanks. "Magnificent. Really rich and flavorful. You are very talented."

Rather than retracing our hike back to the subway, we hail a taxi on the street to take us to Little India for lunch at Banana Leaf Apollo. The restaurant enjoys a reputation for one of Singapore's best fish-head curries, another of the city's many food favorites. Immigrants from south India created the dish as a way of promoting their curry to Chinese settlers, who they knew to be fond of fish-head preparations. Understanding from our advance research that the staff serves meals on banana leaves instead of tableware, we expect a basic street-front joint, but discover instead an upscale establishment, replete with welcome air-conditioning, our first experience of that in a Singapore eatery. Even so, both of us get cooling yogurt-and-fruit lassis to drink, ordering to the background tune of "The Sound of Music" as interpreted in an Indian instrumental style.

The waiter lays out our leaves, cut in large rectangular sections, in front of us, covering much of the tabletop. He spoons rice in the center of each and to the side, dollops of two vegetable relishes, a chopped summer squash with turmeric, tomatoes, and curry leaves, and another headier mixture of cabbage, curry leaves, and black mustard seeds. He brings the main course shortly, a colossal snapper head floating in an herb-and-spice-filled south Indian curry with the sheen of coconut oil. Hollowing out the huge, tasty cheeks and other portions of meat between the bones, we dig in, using the rice, pappadums, and onion kulcha bread to soak up the magical sauce, which builds in heat like a symphony in the back of our throats. Aficionados say to leave the fish eyes until the end, but by then, luckily, neither of us can eat anything more.

After spending much of the afternoon confined to our hotel room by heavy rain, we go for dinner to another regular restaurant, Blue Ginger. It serves Nonya or Peranakan cooking, a local tradition developed when early southern Chinese traders in these waters married Malay women. The men (known as

Babas) brought soy sauce, garlic, and onions to the pot, and the ladies (Nonyas) contributed coconut milk, tamarind, and lime leaves. Indian and Thai seasonings, including chiles, entered the blend over time, and centuries later the result is a cuisine distinctive of Singapore.

Unfortunately, Blue Ginger doesn't earn much distinction itself tonight. Founded by the niece of famous Peranakan cookbook author Leong Yee Soo, it succeeds sometimes but falls flat frequently. The only outstanding item is the constantly replenished pickles on every table—cucumbers, cabbage, and carrots in a light vinegar and citrus dressing, meant to accompany the savory courses. They redeem our *otak otak* appetizer, mild white fish pounded with galangal, candlenuts, turmeric, kaffir lime leaf, chile, and shrimp paste, then wrapped in a banana leaf to grill. Bland and spongy alone, it needs the pickles for balance. Nothing can save our main dishes, a beef rendang without any of the character of its potent seasonings, and a muddy, clunky version of the Nonya classic, *ayam buah keluak,* chicken chunks cooked with the nutlike fruit of the Indonesian kepayang tree. Needing dessert to clear our palates, we decide on two shaved-ice options, each topped with a fruit puree. The soursop cream is yummy, but its cousin made with durian—infamous for its odor—starts whispering ammonia more and more loudly after the first few bites. "The Nonya dishes should be much better than this," Cheryl says. "The kitchen is the problem, at least tonight." Both of us regret booking our only Peranakan meal here.

On our last morning, we return to the Tekka Centre in Little India. The stalls closed on Monday are now open again, including two that Makansutra recommends highly. Rong Ji Cooked Food serves us *chwee kueh,* savory steamed cakes with a gelatinous, chewy texture, like glutinous rice. Okay, but not nearly as tasty as the treats at Yan Seng Cooked Food, where the booth's only words in English are "black carrot cake." Each of us orders one of the advertised dish, a loosely formed patty of grated white radish, mushrooms, and garlicky Chinese chives bound with egg and dyed with a sweet, dark soy that leaves an appealing molasseslike undertone.

While we're eating the goodies, a young Chinese businesswoman approaches us to ask, "How do you like the cakes?"

"Wonderfully delicious," Cheryl says enthusiastically, and the lady pulls up a chair at our table to join us.

She points to the stooped, elderly woman, barely more than four and a half feet tall, who cooked our food and is now making two kinds of dumplings at the table next to us. "She is one of the rare masters left who do everything by hand. Her fans come here from all over the city. I want you to try her dumplings," she insists, going over to talk to the cook in Chinese and pay for a couple of both types.

Each contains a vegetable filling, sealed in one instance with a rice-flour wrapper tinted a traditional pink and, in the other case, with sesame-seed-coated yam paste. Handing us containers of soy sauce and chile paste, the business-woman says, "Dip the dumplings in these."

"Lovely," Bill acknowledges after a dunk and a bite.

When the older woman sees us using the paste, she smiles and says "Chile," apparently one of the few words she knows in English. Still grinning, she passes us a small piece of banana leaf holding a bright red dessert dumpling, plump with a sweet bean puree.

"My, oh my," Cheryl says. "How can a morning get more beautiful?"

The young woman excuses herself at this point—"Got to rush to work"— leaving us feebly unable to communicate the gratitude we feel toward both ladies.

With spontaneous experiences like this, Singapore startles us more than any other place on our trip. The people, the food, and the cultures of the city over-whelm our preconceptions about the institutional negatives. By our departure, we regret our reluctance to come and the shortness of our four-night stay. Talk-ing about this on our way out of the Tekka Centre, we stop for one more fresh-juice fix. "Maybe we should go savory for a change, with tomato or avocado perhaps," Bill says, but both of us fall back in the end on syrupy nectars: mango for Bill, and passion fruit for Cheryl.

"It's a sweet finish," Cheryl says, "for an exceptionally sweet time."

THE NITTY-GRITTY

⊡ ALBERT COURT HOTEL
www.albertcourt.com.sg
180 Albert Street
65-6339-3939   fax 65-6339-3253
*"Courtyard" Executive and Family
rooms in the low-rise wing are larger
and more stylish than the quarters in the
tower that rises above the lobby. Check
the Web site for special promotional rates.*

⊡ MAKANSUTRA
www.makansutra.com

⊡ SIN HUAT EATING HOUSE
(a.k.a., Sin Huat Seafood Restaurant)
659-661 Geylang Road at the
corner of Lorong 35
dinner only (no reservations)

⊡ TIAN TIAN HAINANESE
CHICKEN RICE
Maxwell Food Centre at the corner
of Maxwell and South Bridge, Stall 10
(no reservations)

⊡ LIM KEE BANANA FRITTERS
Maxwell Food Centre at the corner
of Maxwell and South Bridge, Stall 61
(no reservations)

⊡ ANNIE'S PEANUT ICE KACHANG
Tanjong Pagar Plaza Market
and Food Centre on Block 6,
Tanjong Pagar Road, Stall 02-36
(no reservations)

⊡ MATTAR ROAD
SEAFOOD BARBECUE
Old Airport Road Emporium and
Cooked Food Centre on Block 51,
Old Airport Road, Stall 01-131G
(no reservations)

⊡ OUTRAM PARK FRIED
KWAY TEOW
Hong Lim Market and Food Centre
on Block 531A, Upper Cross Street,
Stall 02-18
(no reservations)

⊡ AH KOW MUSHROOM
MINCED PORK MEE
Hong Lim Market and Food Centre
on Block 531A, Upper Cross Street,
Stall 02-43
(no reservations)

⊟ WARONG SUDI MAMPIR
Haig Road Food Centre on Block 14,
Haig Road, Stall 01-19
(no reservations)

⊟ HILL STREET FRIED
KWAY TEOW
Bedok New Town and Food Centre
on Block 16, Bedok South Road,
Stall 01-187
(no reservations)

⊟ BANANA LEAF APOLLO
54-56 Race Course Road
65-6293-8682
lunch and dinner

⊟ BLUE GINGER
97 Tanjong Pagar Road
65-6222-3928
lunch and dinner

⊟ YAN SENG COOKED FOOD
Tekka Market Food Centre on Block 665,
Buffalo Road, Stall 01-389
(no reservations)

Fried Black "Carrot" Cake
Chai Tow Kueh

½ cup *kecap manis* (sweet, dark Indonesian soy sauce)

¼ cup soy sauce

2 tablespoons toasted or dark sesame oil

1 or more very large mild radishes, such as daikon,
equaling 2 pounds, peeled

2 plump garlic cloves, minced

Peanut oil or vegetable oil

Several pinches coarse-ground dried hot red chile or dribbles of chile oil

6 large eggs, lightly beaten

Thin-sliced scallions

Make the black sauce by stirring together the kecap manis, soy sauce, and sesame oil in a small bowl. Reserve.

Grate the radish on the large holes of a box grater or using a food processor with a grating disk. Place the radish on a clean dish towel or several layers of paper towels and pat moisture from the radish. Mix in the garlic.

Heat a light film of oil in a flat-bottomed wok, a well-seasoned cast-iron or other heavy skillet of at least 10 inches, or on a nonstick griddle over medium-high heat. As soon as the oil ripples, make the cakes one at a time in quick succession like a short-order fry cook. Scoop up one-quarter of the radish mixture and mound it in the center of the wok. Cook for about 2 minutes, patting it down into a loosely formed ½ inch-thick cake, then turn the mixture over and cook another couple of minutes, patting it back down again with a broad spatula. Scoop and turn another time or two if necessary to lightly color (but not brown) nearly all the radish.

Sprinkle with chile to taste, then cover evenly with about one-quarter of the kecap manis mixture. Cook about a minute so the sauce can caramelize in a few spots, then turn over again, using the spatula to once more nudge it back into a loose cake form.

Spoon one-quarter of the eggs over the cake. The eggs will begin to set immediately, so use the spatula to nudge all the mixture back into cake form again. Turn over and continue cooking until the egg mixture has set. The cake will look a bit like a dark mini-frittata. Slide out onto a plate. Wipe out the hot wok carefully and repeat with oil and ingredients until all four cakes are complete. Top each "carrot" cake with a sprinkle of scallions and serve right away, offering more chile or soy sauce on the side if you wish.

"What do you think about a picnic supper?"

Vithi asks Bill.

Bill had been hoping for a more rousing way to kick off our first night in Thailand—maybe something like a curry feast at a special restaurant known only to local connoisseurs—but it seems rude to say so to a volunteer guide we've just met. Going with the flow, Bill replies, "Sure, great idea."

Before we left home, a Thai chef and friend put us in touch with Vithi, an art professor at Chiang Mai University who is a friend of hers. "He'll be very helpful," she said, "if he has time for it, because Vithi is an expert on Thai culinary traditions, ingredients, and techniques. He also did undergraduate and graduate work in the Los Angeles area for seven years, so he speaks perfect English and knows American institutions and customs."

Bill called him at home, as our friend suggested, and Vithi said, "My schedule looks fairly open during your time in Chiang Mai. I'll put together a plan of activities and take you around whenever I can," which turns out to be most of the time. He appeared a perfect match for us, at least before the picnic proposal.

Vithi extracts his car from the crammed parking lot of our downtown chain hotel, the Royal Princess, and the three of us take off to buy some provisions, the only thing he explains in advance about what we're doing. The first stop is a supermarket with a surprisingly large wine department, where Bill chooses a couple of bottles of a Languedoc red from the extensive selection of French, Australian, and Chilean imports. Vithi leads us through a few aisles in search of snacks to eat with the wine, saying, "Expats love the variety in this place, both local and international. Check out the different kinds of Cheerios, more than I ever saw in Los Angeles."

"Wow!" Cheryl exclaims. "Six types. I wouldn't want any of them here or at home, but I'm amazed to find so many choices."

Two aisles over, Vithi says, "Here we go," picking up a package of sausage. "This is a Chiang Mai specialty made with fermented pork." Then, commenting, "We must have this," he grabs a plastic tray of ingredients for *meang kum*. (Note that we give the Latin alphabet spelling of some dish names, though you seldom find these in Thailand, where the names usually appear only in Indic-style Thai script except on tourist menus that take the extra step of providing translations into English and other languages. No telling what a menu would call meang kum in English, perhaps Lots of Goodies Wrapped in a Strange Leaf with a Tamarind Dipping Sauce.)

Vithi drives us next to a nearby neighborhood open-air market, a place so unused to Western visitors that everyone stares at us. He gets a kilo of sticky rice—the style favored in the north—that the vendor scoops up hot from a bamboo steamer three feet in diameter. With us in tow, Vithi hops from there to a stand with prepared curries, picking out a traditional version combining bitter and herbaceous greens, spooned like everything else into its own plastic sack. Then he's on to a stall featuring steamed vegetables tied in pretty bundles. "What do you want?" Vithi asks Cheryl.

"The young eggplants look good, and so do the cucumbers."

"Okay, we'll get them with several kinds of greens, and also these fresh bamboo shoots, which taste a little like hearts of palm or artichoke hearts." Finally, he stops for *nam prik*, a distinctly Thai chile paste that takes many forms depending on the specific ingredients used. "I'm going to get us two local favorites," Vithi says. "This one is flavored with small field crabs and the second one with ground water beetles," maybe more information than the two of us need in advance.

Vithi stashes the food in the backseat and heads to the campus of Chiang Mai University, where he suddenly pulls off a central avenue into a field with no discernible tracks or trails for vehicles—or pedestrians, either. Bouncing up and down over ruts and holes, he pulls the car up to a small house, which we soon discover is a caretaker's cottage for a living outdoor cultural museum, a collection of traditional houses brought here from various parts of Thailand. A young couple greets Vithi, their boss who oversees the museum, and hauls our groceries inside. The professor, still explaining nothing, leads us through the dark over to the large terrace of a historic teak home, lighted beautifully with rice-paper lanterns, candles, and a stunning full moon. Cheryl says in awe, "Absolutely magical!" and whispers to Bill, "I feel like the governess in *The King and I*."

The host seats us on woven-rag cushions on the wooden deck, elevating us an inch or two above the floor to make cross-legged sitting more comfortable for a longer period. As we marvel at the surroundings, he tells us about the house. "It belonged to a country squire, who needed a spacious terrace for entertaining, always done outside." Pointing to the two high peaks of the roofline, he says, "Unglazed terra-cotta tiles cover the roof, but the construction employs no nails, glass, or stone. Wood pegs hold all the joints in place."

The elaborately carved lintels, representing the genitals of a water buffalo, ward off evil, Vithi indicates. Curious, Bill raises the logical question, "What's the correlation between gonads and goodness?" The professor ducks the details as the caretaker couple reappears with large banana leaves to serve as a table setting for us.

The pair spreads plates of food on top of the foliage and gives us, for napkins, a roll of toilet paper, also used for the same purpose in many homes and simple restaurants. Vithi demonstrates how to eat the delicious meang kum, wrapping bits of ginger, shallots, chile, toasted coconut, roasted peanuts, lime on its rind, and dried shrimp into a betel leaf, then dunking the package into tamarind sauce and downing it in one bite. He then illustrates how to roll the sticky rice into small balls, and tells us to dip them into the curry or one of the two nam priks, also used to flavor the vegetables and sausages. Always eager about food eaten with the hands, we dive in.

The chile pastes stun us with their unusual tastes, way beyond the realm of our experience even as dedicated chileheads. "Do you notice the hint of menthol in the beetle version?" Vithi asks. "That comes from the insect and adds a wonderful counterpoint in flavor." Both nam priks go well with all the food except dessert, which features langsats, a tropical fruit unfamiliar to us that resembles a leathery yellow fig. Vithi cracks open a shell to reveal teardrop sections of fruit with a lycheelike flavor that provide a luscious, refreshing finish to the fairy-tale picnic.

An evening that starts out seeming perfunctory becomes one of the most delightful of our entire trip. Thailand can jolt you in that way, setting you up for one kind of expectation and then offering the opposite reality. Like tonight, most of our experiences end happily, but the gears can slip just as easily and abruptly into reverse.

> >

On the way back to the hotel, Vithi drives through an enormous overnight wholesale street market, telling us, "Markets operate somewhere in the city around the clock." He screeches to a sudden stop in the flower section, several blocks of buds, petals, long stems, and short stems in a rainbow of colors, all looking dewy fresh from last-minute picking. He hops out and grabs Cheryl a huge bouquet of pink-to-red roses that she can barely wrap her arms around. When she arranges them in the room later, using glasses and even the wastebasket as vases, it looks like we're going into the bridal business.

The next day, Vithi picks us up early to visit another market. The historic center of Chiang Mai remains a walled city, and vendors set up in the morning just outside each of the old gates. Our destination is the White Elephant market on the north wall, held like most of its urban kin in a covered, open-sided permanent site. On the way, Bill asks, "How does this compare with the Warowot market, the only one mentioned in most English-language guidebooks?"

"We're going to a true food market. Warowot is like a giant grocery store, with most of the food prepackaged."

The variety amazes us again: heaps of brown tamarind pods, mushrooms, and greens; fermented fish and buffalo jerky; banana hearts and yellow-and-maroon banana blossoms; eggplants the size of capers and field crabs even smaller; bamboo worms and freshwater river seaweed; rough-surfaced cylinders of "long" black pepper and Thai white peppercorns; wing beans that look like caterpillars and huge cousins almost as large as baseball bats; curry pastes of all hues and dozens of different nam priks. Tallying time on her fingers, Cheryl says, "In seven waking hours in Chiang Mai, we've seen more bounty and diversity in markets than we've encountered in a week anywhere else."

Vithi leaves us to wander on our own while he attends a meeting at the university, but we get together again for lunch at Hong Tauw Inn, a simple, away-from-the-crowds café that Vithi likes for northern Thai fare. Along with the menus, the waitress brings us a platter of various nam priks, with flavors such as dried shrimp, dried mackerel, mango, tamarind, and salted eggs. The base of each is a pounded paste made with chile, garlic, palm sugar, lime juice, fish sauce, and finely sliced eggplant. Vithi goes over the Thai-script menu with us and we pick a couple of things to try, but ask him to choose the rest.

The waitress delivers the food family style, allowing each of us to serve ourselves. First comes a green mango salad, with shredded fruit, greens, tiny eggplants, and slices of white turmeric root that look like ginger. Wing beans show up next, cut in cross sections so that the ridges form starburst shapes. Slightly crisp and cooked in a sweet-sour tamarind chile sauce, they become an instant favorite of ours. For soups, we get a spicy broth with jungle leaves, rice vermicelli, and tomatoes, and another with a coconut-milk base containing freshwater shellfish resembling snails in tang and texture. A fried whole freshwater fish wraps up the meal, accompanied by spicy pickled shallots, sliced cucumbers, and tomatoes, and for seasoning, *nam pla prik* (chile in fish sauce). Not everything is equally enjoyable to us, but the kitchen produces a dazzling array of tastes, a dynamic illustration of the key Thai principle of balancing salty, sweet, sour, and bitter flavors.

During lunch, the three of us talk about Chiang Mai and Thai food. Vithi tells us, "The town has changed radically in the last decade, mushrooming from a small provincial city and cultural capital to an enormous metropolis stacked high with residential towers and packed tightly with tacky tourist businesses." He complains about increasing internationalism, citing as an example the way that university students flock to fast-food franchises of Pizza Hut and Kentucky Fried Chicken. On the other hand, he says, they don't have lots of choices. As in Bangkok and other cities, "People eat Thai food at home and want something different when they go out for a major meal, leaving us with a glut of foreign restaurants and a shortage of good local options." In a sentiment we hear several times, Vithi claims that virtually every middle-class to upscale Thai restaurant in the country caters primarily to tourists and dumbs down the food accordingly, convinced that outsiders cannot take the combinations of vibrant flavors. "The only places to get good, real Thai cooking are at simple cafés with home-style cooks, like this one, and street stands where Thais stop to snack."

Vithi asks us about our other plans in Thailand. "After three nights here, we go to Bangkok for almost a week," Bill says. "We had a great time there on a honeymoon visit twenty years ago. After that, it's Phuket for four nights before we fly on to India. In all, we're spending more time in Thailand than in any other country on our three-month trip."

"Good luck," Vithi says, "in finding real Thai food in Bangkok and Phuket," a comment that sounds unduly pessimistic at the time but becomes apropos.

After lunch, we wander down a nearby street to visit several craft galleries. Much of the work comes from hill-tribe artisans who live in the highlands of northern Thailand. Women in a number of the tribes weave beautiful textiles, sometimes with elaborate embroidery, while many of the men fashion functional and ornamental items out of wood, bamboo, rattan, and metal. The hand-crafted tribal fabrics and silver jewelry in particular appeal to us, but we're content to see rather than shop.

While admiring the goods, we're startled when a woman calls out "Cheryl?" Looking up, we find ourselves face-to-face with Jackie Imamura, whom Cheryl worked with four years ago at the Santa Fe Farmers Market. She'd told us back then she was moving to Thailand because her husband took a faculty position somewhere in the country, which turns out to be at Chiang Mai University. After the ladies catch up and part warmly, Cheryl tells Vithi, "The small-world experiences on this trip are getting eerie. Not only this stunning reunion with Jackie, but of the dozen or so Americans we've met so far, three of the couples live at least part of the year in New Mexico within sixty miles of us."

Back in the car, Vithi suggests we check out other area crafts, which sounds good to us. In one compound, artisans produce bamboo lacquerware, coiling strips of the plant into a variety of decorative forms before glazing the pieces in bright colors. In a woodcarving neighborhood, small shops lining the street brim with work of all kinds. "Many of the craftsmen started out carving gables and temple ornamentation," Vithi says, "but discovered that tourists pay big bucks for trophies of their visit."

"What's hot in that department?" Bill asks. Vithi points to a pair of wood elephants, displayed with the prominence and pomp of the royal guards outside Buckingham Palace.

He drives slowly down the street, to give us a lingering gaze at the pieces and also to exercise his own sharp eyes. He stops suddenly at one shop, where he spots, among hundreds of items, an antique carving that he wants for an exhibition he is organizing on craft traditions. He makes the purchase, assuring us he got a bargain, and then notices some handsome old spirit houses, which Thais place outside of homes and other buildings to shelter and appease animist spirits, who can be terribly mischievous if not coddled. Vithi says, "Flat Stanley"—the two met an hour before—"needs a photo beside a spirit house, a perfect-sized home for him." The idea seems slightly sacrilegious on the surface, but the shop owner agrees cheerfully and Cheryl snaps a shot.

This sets up poor Pheng for a similar fate. A friend of Vithi's, the eighteen-year-old Laotian novice monk arrived in town earlier today to get the professor's help in securing a student visa to attend college in Chiang Mai. Vithi makes a short detour to pick him up before heading out of town to the mountaintop Wat Phra That, the most significant of the city's three-hundred-plus Buddhist temples. We make quite a striking group: the dignified Thai teacher, a pair of rumpled Americans, a two-dimensional storybook child, and a saffron-robed monk with a shaved head and a bright-blue alms bag. Stanley fascinates Pheng and so Cheryl asks, with Vithi translating, "Would you like a photo with him? I can e-mail you a copy later." Pheng agrees and Cheryl starts to hand him Stanley before remembering that Buddhist monks in Thailand can't accept anything directly from a woman. Vithi acts as an intermediary and Cheryl takes several pictures of the young man gingerly holding the boy.

The temple dates back to the fourteenth century, when the discovery of a new relic of the Buddha required the building of a wat to honor it. According to official lore, the King of Lanna decided that a sacred white elephant should pick the proper site, so he sent one to wander freely with the relic. The elephant climbed to the summit of Doi Suthep mountain, trumpeted three times, and lay down, indicating his selection. The relic went inside the arresting gilded-copper chedi built on the center of the site.

On the drive back to town, Vithi notices an elderly couple on the side of the highway making traditional tubes of rice, an item he had pointed out to us this morning in the market. Unable to resist an instructional opportunity, he pulls over to show us how it's done. The man stuffs rice soaked in coconut milk into a bamboo tube, about eight inches long, sealing it at each end with coconut-husk plugs. The woman roasts the tubes in an upright row over a wood-coal fire. When the rice is cooked, she strips away the charred outer layer of bamboo, revealing a pretty green carrying case for the simple meal. Vithi buys one to share with us—a toasty and succulent snack—but we have to leave Pheng out of the tasting because his vows prohibit him from eating after noon for the rest of his life. "Yikes," Bill exclaims, "that's as tough a choice as chastity."

After a quick circuit of two other wats in the old walled city, Vithi drops us back at our hotel around sunset. He offers to take us along with him and Pheng tonight to a temple fair and a transvestite beauty pageant, which we should have done, but instead we want to see the Night Bazaar, always described as one of the city's main attractions, and check out the street-food stalls at the nearby Anusarn Market. Within five minutes, the stifling bazaar appalls us. Every vendor seems to be peddling the same T-shirts, pirated DVDs, and cheap trinkets, and the maze of narrow, crowded passageways is lined with small booths too tall to see over, creating a sense of confinement and leading to disorientation.

Lost after a while, we never find the food stands and finally stumble, as a last resort, into one of the touristy Thai restaurants Vithi has warned us about. From the English menu, each of us orders a whole deep-fried fish in different preparations. The "sweet, sour, and spicy" sauce could be better described as insipid, and the other dish's "spicy" mango salad fits its name only if you classify sugar as such a seasoning. "Ugh," Bill says. "That's one of the worst meals yet in a month of travel."

"And some of it even stuck with me," Cheryl complains, pulling a Tide to Go stick from her purse to dab a red spot on her blouse.

The next day is devoted mostly to visiting Lampang, Vithi's hometown, with an intermediate stop at the National Elephant Institute. For the road trip, more than an hour each way, Vithi recommends we rent a van, figuring it will be more comfortable than his small car for four adults, including Pheng. The rental agency is out of standard vans, but Vithi negotiates a deal for an oversized one, complete with driver, for the same price. Able to really spread out now, we can hardly even see one another.

Organized sightseeing excursions from Chiang Mai often take tourists to various elephant camps that offer a pony-ride atmosphere, but the government-funded institute exists for the benefit of the giant mammals rather than entertainment. The elephants roam freely in an enormous forest reserve, returning to the central area at regular times for food, health monitoring, and training. Many of them suffered abuse in the past from private owners, and others endured serious injuries in the wild.

Vithi, a patron of the program, shows us the elephant hospital, the first in the world. It reminds us of a do-it-yourself car wash with a dozen or so jumbo bays. These open-sided treatment rooms contain spray hoses for cleaning the animals, and in the case of the emergency units, a winch and pulley system for moving them around. A medical bulletin board indicates that one of the patients has gastrointestinal problems, two others are recuperating from land-mine explosions in Burma, and another lost part of his trunk in a jungle battle. In the nursery section, a new mom tends her baby. A foster parent plan allows people to adopt any of the elephants by paying for the expenses of their care.

As we leave the hospital, Vithi says, "You should see the ambulance that brings in the patients."

Bill laughs. "Maybe we have. Is that where you got our van?"

At the nearby training school a morning class is just ending. Professional instructors called mahouts teach the elephants vocational skills for working in the logging industry, and in some cases, also how to paint like an artist and play musical instruments. One talented fellow is just finishing a drawing of flowers, handling the brush expertly with his trunk. The center sells the paintings to raise money for its other activities.

Vithi asks if any of us want to ride an elephant, and Cheryl volunteers eagerly for herself and Stanley. Apparently the mahout allows the elephant to take charge of the trek rather than keeping him on the usual course. The four go galumphing into the jungle, wading through a river at one point and then splashing across the center of a lake. Cheryl raves about her romp, which she enjoys much more than Bill does his upcoming surprise.

As a last stop before leaving, our leader suggests seeing how the center recycles some of its elephant dung, dumped at the rate of fifty pounds per day for an average animal. He introduces us to the lady in charge of the dung-paper studio, where the staff produces stationery, note cards, and other items to sell in a nearby shop and online. Looking as honest and innocent as a holy man, Vithi tells the woman, "Bill here would like a hands-on lesson in the process." Feeling sand-bagged, Bill gamely follows her instructions, breaking up a massive dried turd into smaller pieces, kneading and whisking the bits around in water to dissolve clumps, smearing the liquid evenly over a screen, and then setting the screen in the sun to dry. While Bill washes his hands vigorously for five or ten minutes, everyone else looks at examples of the finished product, which resemble textured rice paper.

On the outskirts of Lampang, Vithi asks the driver to pull over at the popular Jungle Market. Much of the food here is harvested or captured wild in the hills, a respected tradition that goes back to the earliest settlement of the area. Locals shop here for snakes, lizards, insects, exotic mushrooms and other fungi, whole honeycombs, and more common groceries such as pig parts of every kind, dozens of leaves and herbs, and fried bamboo worms, which, we find with trepidation, taste like hollow French fries. When Pheng gets some sticky rice for his one meal of the day, Vithi grabs a bag of the worms for himself and hospitably shares them with us in a way that seems impolite to refuse.

Much better is the *khao soi*, sold at a roadside stand-cum-café a couple of miles farther toward town. The most famous dish of the region, it's a hearty noodle soup created, according to Vithi, by a Muslim Chinese street-food cook in Lampang in the 1920s. This small family-run place, he says, makes the best version in northern Thailand, and to us it's as good as anything we try in the country. Vithi directs us through a kitchen and takeaway area, near the entrance, to reach a back porch with picnic-style tables. Despite the utter simplicity of the building and furnishings, a scenic river flows directly below the dining room and twenty or so pots of flowering orchids hang at eye level from the eaves of the roof.

The khao soi comes with chicken, pork, or beef. The two of us opt for the latter and order lemongrass juice to drink. The husband of the cook brings out big, steaming bowls loaded with linguinelike wheat noodles suspended in a rich, curry-flavored coconut milk broth. Crispy fried noodles and lots of fresh scallion bits float on top. Served on the side, to customize the soup, are lime wedges to squeeze for juice, fish sauce, chopped shallots, minced red chile in oil, and cabbage pickles. Following Vithi's lead, we alternate between chopsticks, to slurp up the noodles, and Chinese ceramic spoons, to scoop up the broth. Restaurants in Thailand offer these utensils only for dishes of Chinese origin, mainly noodle preparations. To eat anything else, Thais use a fork in the left hand to place food in a spoon, held in the right hand, and take bites only from the spoon, never the fork.

That's the method we employ at our second lunch later in the afternoon at Vithi's ancestral family home, a large but not ornate wooden residence near the center of Lampang. His grandmother lived here for many years and then his aunt, who died recently. Now only servants stay full-time, and Vithi visits when he can. Within minutes after we pull up in our van, we see confirmation of a growing hunch, that Vithi comes from a patrician background. Neighbors start appearing at the front door individually and in groups to deferentially seek his counsel and support on various issues, particularly damage from a recent flood. He seats them in a parlor adjoining the living room where we're sitting, saying he'll talk with them after lunch.

The servants fix and serve the meal, under instructions from Vithi to focus on exotic northern specialties we won't find elsewhere. The dishes include tempura-fried pumpkin, fresh bamboo shoots, fried crickets with a sweet and tangy dipping sauce, pig brains wrapped in banana leaves, pork with lemongrass, water buffalo sprinkled with dried red chile in both tartare and sautéed versions, vegetable pickles, and a couple of nam priks for seasoning everything to taste. For dessert, we nibble on bright gems of *look choob*, a marzipan cousin fashioned from sweetened bean paste, and we wash everything down with Thai iced tea, a potent brew diluted with sweetened condensed milk. It's all splendid to us since nothing makes food more memorable than enjoying it at a friend's home.

On our return to Chiang Mai, we hit two more markets, as if we haven't seen nearly enough yet. The first is an evening event, set up to catch people leaving work. The vendors specialize in partially prepared foods that take less time and labor to finish at home, such as skewers of roasted tiny eggplants, shallots, and garlic to mash together as the base for nam prik. The second market features street-food stalls, where we pick up a couple of snacks for a light supper: pretty, crispy banana fritters made from fruit the size of our fingers and fried, pork-stuffed long green-yellow chiles that look like the chiles rellenos in New Mexico. Both taste great.

On our honeymoon visit two decades ago, we loved the Thai enthusiasm for eating, a facet of life that we see again in abundance with Vithi. He introduces us to an incredible range of new tastes, not all personal favorites for us, but each characteristic of northern cuisine and intriguing to sample. Some of the dishes thrill us with their complex and bold flavors, especially khao soi. Many others—such as meang kum, the roasted rice in bamboo, wing beans, lemongrass juice, stuffed chiles, and more—delight us in simpler ways. What matters most to us in the end, though, is the breadth and intensity of our Chiang Mai eating adventure, a truly Thai experience we feel privileged to share with Vithi.

> >

The gray skies of Bangkok pour rain during most of our visit, seriously dampening our spirits and washing away many of our plans. It's still the monsoon season, as we knew in advance, but our stopover falls at the end of the annual cycle, which leads us to hope that storms would be decreasing in frequency and intensity. This year, the weather turns worse instead.

On our arrival from Chiang Mai, the taxi ride from the airport to our first hotel, the Siam City, takes almost two hours due to the wet roads and Bangkok's usual horrid traffic congestion. Siam City, near a Skytrain monorail station in the central transportation hub of the city, serves as our base for four nights to save money for a splurge our last two nights at The Oriental, our hotel on our honeymoon visit. In an old travel folder of mementoes from that trip, Bill dug out a receipt for our room, a split-level mini-suite in the original midrise wing that cost U.S. $127 per night then and $400 now. Until we return there, it seems important to have easy access to the Skytrain, which links to the subway and the Chao Phraya River ferries, to avoid long, slow cab rides and excessive walking along hot, muggy streets.

Even if the climate were conducive to being on foot, shopping touts pester visitors on any sidewalk near tourist attractions, a nuisance we encounter at least a dozen times. It's always the same routine, developed originally by drivers of tuk-tuks, the open-air, three-wheel vehicles that used to greatly outnumber taxis. "Hi! You look like you're from America, such a wonderful place. If you're going to the Grand Palace"—or wherever you seem to be headed—"it's closed right now," an outright lie. "Before it reopens, let me take you to a special shop that has the best bargains in Bangkok." Thais think tourists are obsessed with buying stuff, making them fair prey for scams to get commissions on sales. Usually the touts pretend to be someone you want to know, perhaps an off-duty policeman or a student leaving shortly to attend college in your country. In one case a "nurse" at a hospital we're passing, in search of a restaurant, tells us all the hundreds of stores in Siam Square are shut except one where she can obtain big discounts for us. The charade gets so tiresome that when strangers approach us to chat, certainly a pleasure in most places, Bill makes it clear early that shopping of any kind doesn't interest us. "Better to appear cheap than be conned," he says.

The frequent downpours and the tribulations of walking limit our sightseeing, but despite Bill's street-side protests, we actually spend a fair bit of time browsing. Many of the most popular places in the city—such as the beautiful temples, the bustling Chinatown, and the Grand Palace, where King Rama I established Bangkok in 1782—retain us only briefly because we saw them when we visited before. Several of the major markets, on the other hand, have opened or grown in prominence since our previous visit, providing the chance for fresh experiences.

The big Aw Taw Kaw food market, the most appealing of the possibilities for us, is unfortunately closed in large part for a renovation project scheduled to take months. Smaller food markets remain active, of course, in other areas of the city. In one off of Yaowarat Road, Chinatown's main thoroughfare, stalls near the entrance feature pork rinds, more varieties than we ever imagined on earth, in pillow-size sacks hanging from the rafters and piled like sandbags beside booths. Other stands display live crabs ranging from the size of a quarter to a foot across, live chickens and roasted ones, steamed buns alongside brioche, pickled vegetables next to pomegranates, giant cauldrons of unidentifiable cooked foods, more intestines than we want to know about, even cotton candy on sticks that a vendor holds so high above the throngs that the pink orbs look like balloons.

The Chatuchak Weekend Market, near Aw Taw Kaw, also offers some edible goods on a lot larger than many small towns, with whole neighborhoods of narrow aisles devoted to particular kinds of merchandise, from Buddha images to books, pets, and plants. In an antiques section, Cheryl spots a case of petite carved-bone bottles. "Come look at these," she calls to Bill. "Maybe they're old perfume containers, or something like that, but catch the erotic etchings on them, barely noticeable unless you look closely." Bill sorts through the collection to find the most lascivious image and buys the bottle, our only purchase in several hours of wandering through the thick crowds.

The Suan Lum and Patpong night markets are also booming on an evening with clear skies. Newer than Chatuchak, and more open and festive, Suan Lum features a similar range of products. After picking up small purses decorated with sequined elephants for our granddaughters, and looking for other gifts, we settle in at a beer garden, under trees with twinkling white lights, for people watching. A relaxed two hours later, the subway whisks us one stop to the Pat-pong district, notorious for its sex clubs and prostitutes but also popular locally for street food. None of the varied treats tempt us, but the brazen lack of subtlety in some of the advertising evokes a few stifled laughs. Many of the ladies stand-ing in groups in front of bars actually wear numbers, marathon-runner-style, that cover their salient selling points almost as thoroughly as their skimpy dresses.

Most of Bangkok's museums disappointed us last time, so we return only to Jim Thompson's House. Born in Delaware in 1906, Thompson worked as an ar-chitect before volunteering for military intelligence duty during World War II, which brought him to Bangkok. He stayed, played a major role in the revival of traditional Thai silk weaving, and built a home out of six old teak structures that he dismantled in the countryside and reassembled on-site. Guides take visitors through the rambling residence, providing an intimate glimpse at Thai art and architecture. Thompson maintained the original style of most of the buildings and furnishings but added a few Western touches, such as an indoor toilet by his bedroom; guest rooms contained the customary chamber pots, in the shape of a Siamese cat for men and a frog for women. A framed numerology reading, done by a monk, hangs on one wall, advising Thompson to be especially careful in his sixty-first year, when he disappeared without a trace in Malaysia's Cameroon Highlands.

The house tour is more enjoyable than most of our sightseeing, but we save the best for last, arranging at The Oriental for a half-day excursion on the klongs (canals) off the Chao Phraya River. From our room at the grand old hostelry, in the six-story structure formerly known as the Authors' Wing, floor-to-ceiling windows survey the river and its constant boat traffic, a magnificent scene. The newer, maybe more prestigious Peninsula Hotel towers above us on the opposite side of the broad channel, but lacks our intimacy with the water and the thousands of people who travel it at any daylight hour. Our room is almost identical to the one that elated us on our honeymoon and still seems just as idyllic. Cheryl says gleefully, "Yes, we can go back again!" Sometimes at least; and in this case, to one of the most special spots we've ever been.

The klong journey provides similar delight. The hotel's dock manager gets us one of the ubiquitous, gondola-style long-tail boats, named for their pivoting shaft that raises and lowers the propeller in different water conditions. He sets us up with a driver and handsome craft used in one of Pierce Brosnan's James Bond films, telling us, "Brosnan returns frequently to take out the same boat." The helmsman heads to the Bangkok Noi canal, one of the main arteries through Thonburi, a part of the metropolis that maintains an age-old mode of waterway living rarely found any longer in Bangkok proper. Residences, interspersed with occasional businesses and temples, line both sides of the klong and provide direct access to the water for traveling around, buying food from paddling vendors, growing gardens of aquatic vegetables, and washing clothes.

The houses we pass range from ramshackle to palatial. Some creep to the edge of the bank, others stand on stilts above the flood zone, and the biggest ones sit back on higher ground. As we putter by, residents go about their daily lives, obviously conducted much of the time on terraces and docks by the klong. Our driver halts briefly to allow us to peer into the Royal Barge Museum, home to eight magnificent vessels used in special river processions, and Wat Rakhang, a temple known for its bells and chimes. The only evidence of tourism is a sign in makeshift English for the Bangkok Noi Village Restaurant advertising food with "good test."

Good taste isn't always easy to find in Bangkok, at least not if you're looking for the distinctive and characteristic flavors of real Thai cooking. The same friend who put us in touch with Vithi suggested that we seek eating-out guidance from Bob Halliday, an American who has lived in Bangkok for most of the last four decades. A food, film, and music buff, he studied Russian and James

Joyce at Columbia University before moving to Thailand, where he quickly learned the language with a fluency that startles locals. Over the years Bob has written extensively for the *Bangkok Post* about his favorite subjects, including modern composers and places to find good Thai food. During a long stint as the newspaper's restaurant reviewer, he worked anonymously under the self-deprecating pen name of Ung-aang Talay, meaning "Sea Toad."

Having read about Bob in articles on Bangkok, we knew him by reputation before our friend gave us his phone number and encouraged us to call, which Bill did before we left home. Friendly and down-to-earth, Bob said he would be happy to join us for a meal and talk about Thai food, but that he was tied up judging a film festival early in our stay. Bill scheduled a dinner with him for one of our last nights in town, and for our eating pleasure before then, confirmed that Bob still liked several spots that he had recommended highly in the past according to our research. He also advised us to try street-food stands, particularly in the evening, going to areas where they are concentrated, such as Chinatown. "Find the most popular vendors and get what the other customers are buying, even if you don't know what it is." We've been intending to do just that, but get waylaid by the rain in trying to follow the plan.

On the appointed night for our dinner together, Bob picks us up at The Oriental and takes us to Raan Jay Fai, a tiny, fluorescent-lighted eatery at the corner of two streets, completely open to the breezes on both sides. A few days earlier at lunchtime, we had searched in vain for this and an adjoining place, but neither was open then and even with the exact addresses, we found nothing to indicate the presence of restaurants. Bill asks Bob about the situation, and he says, "It's tough for a visitor, even the most intrepid." He agrees with Vithi that most restaurants with Thai menus serve bland tourist food, and for authentic fare, you have to seek out small cafés with home cooking. "Many of them are in out-of-the-way locations and don't even have names." But even if you make it to one despite the obstacles, if you don't know Thai, ordering becomes a problem.

At least we've found Raan Jay Fai with Bob's help and can place our requests through him. He greets the owner and cook, a wiry, elderly woman, and tells her we all want the house specialty, *pad khee mao*, broad rice noodles combined with a wealth of seafood. She takes several steps back to her kitchen—three fiery gas burners and a charcoal brazier just outside the building on the slower of the streets—and jumps into action with surprising speed and dexterity. She puts water in a wok and brings it to a boil over a burner, adds the noodles by themselves briefly, and then in stages, tosses in prawns, calamari, chunks of fish, fresh hearts of palm, and red chile. After a little simmering, she pours off the water into another wok, fries the noodle mixture a bit, places some of the cooking liquid back, and stirs in coconut water from a young coconut with some of its jellylike meat. That's it—and it's glorious. The noodles remain slightly chewy, the seafood shines, and the simple flavorings bring everything together in resounding harmony.

As we leave, Bob spots a street-food stand a few doors away selling sweets. He wants to get desserts for the three of us and selects a steamed rice-flour disk stuffed with banana custard and coconut milk, as well as a folded banana-leaf pouch filled with a steamed mixture of coconut, coconut milk, and palm sugar, the latter a particularly luscious combo. Pointing behind us, Bob says, "That's Thip Samai, the other place you were looking for earlier in the week." Busy as possible at this hour, Raan Jan Fai's neighboring noodle shop specializes in a definitive version of pad thai, probably the most popular dish at Thai restaurants in the United States.

Despite our failure to locate these two cafés on our own, we do find three others that Bob recommends. It takes a little diligence in each case. Som Tam Polo, aka Polo Fried Chicken, requires the least effort since it's near the large Polo Club grounds, marked on all maps. The problem for us, at least the first one, is picking the right side street, Soi Polo, not identified for the public in any way we can decipher. Our second guess turns out to be correct, evident only when Cheryl spots a painted picture on a storefront window. "That looks like a Thanksgiving turkey on a platter, but maybe it's a chicken." Walking over for a closer gander, we notice the place's English name in inch-high letters.

Bob dubbed it "Polo Fried Chicken" years ago when he raved about the three-table stall in his *Bangkok Post* column. Since then, the cook-owner has added a regular dining room of sorts down the street, a simple space with the "turkey" poster outside and glaring overhead lamps inside for a decidedly non-subdued style of lighting. In place of a drinks list, liter-size plastic bottles of Pepsi and water sit on the tables for guests to pick and pour at will. A waiter brings us a place-mat-size picture menu with the half-dozen dish options, which include shredded fried beef and *larb moo,* minced pork with chile and other seasonings. Both of us point at the fried chicken and a green papaya salad. He scribbles the choices on a pad and hustles out the front door, heading to the kitchen that remains in its original location.

The waiter returns shortly with a tray of condiments: an ample bouquet of fresh basil worth more in the United States than the entire $6 lunch, a cabbage pickle, and a couple of nam priks, one reminiscent of a Mexican salsa made with cascabel chiles. Next come generous plates of crispy chicken pieces showered with chewy fried garlic slivers. At home, we would eat this by hand, but instead we follow the lead of Thai diners by cutting off morsels with a fork and maneuvering them onto a spoon for munching, like a two-step country dance: first a taste of chicken, then a nibble of the intensely anise-scented basil. When Bill branches out to the fiery papaya salad, he almost detonates his mouth by chomping down accidentally on a whole chile, mixed freely into the fruit medley along with dried shrimp for salty tang and tomatoes and green beans for crunchy sweetness. Except for that inadvertent bite, everything glows with unmitigated goodness.

The same holds true at Rut & Luk, a seafood eatery in Chinatown near the intersection of Yaowarat Road and Soi Phadungdao, oddly nicknamed "Soi Texas." Our information puts the restaurant on one of the four corners, but no such luck. It turns out to be down a side street, a rudimentary kitchen on the ground level, completely open in the front, with big washtubs used for cleaning plates. Without any place to eat, it looks weird and bewildering, as our expressions probably do to the cooks staring at us from inside. One of them finally gestures to us to come in and go upstairs, so we tromp past the tubs, fish, and other ingredients to get to another brightly lit dining room.

Except for a couple at one table, we're the first to arrive on a Sunday evening, though the space fills up completely within thirty minutes. The menu is mostly in Thai but contains some pictures, allowing us to identify the specialty we want, a whole fish baked in foil with loads of black pepper and garlic. We each order one of these, a beer, and an oyster omelet, a popular side dish in Bangkok. It's a hearty bellyful for both of us, wonderfully fresh and flavorful.

Chote Chitr impresses us even more. None of our maps show its street of record, Phraeng Phouthon, but we know the lane intersects the larger Tanao Road at some point in the neighborhood just east of the Grand Palace. In our search, we walk past the street once, decide we've gone too far, double back, and walk some more until we happen on it. Having allowed lots of time to locate the restaurant, we still arrive on the early side for lunch; the cook-owner is sitting at a table in front prepping vegetables by a small fountain. She scoots two bantam dogs off another of the five tables and seats us at it.

A delightful lady, we gradually discover, she speaks English well and offers to help us with her four-hundred-item menu, all in Thai. From online reports on the restaurant, we've decided in advance to order a couple of Thai classics, *mee krob* and banana blossom salad. Cheryl asks her, "What else would you recommend to fill out a little Thai feast?"

She thinks about the question briefly. "I would get a green curry with chicken and the eggplant salad called *makheua yao*." Everything astounds us, including the fresh lemonade, laced here with a little salt as well as sugar, which is common in Thailand. The eggplant salad, a gem, features slim, long slices of the vegetable, smoky and soft from the fire, in a light sauce with shallots, kaffir lime, palm sugar, cilantro, dried shrimp, bits of chicken, and slivers of incandescent fresh green chile. The lovely banana blossom salad comes with a tangy dressing of tamarind, coconut milk, and dried red chiles, along with shrimp and chicken.

A tangle of thin, caramelized rice noodles fried crisply, the mee krob arrives with shrimp seared perfectly on serious wok heat and a syrupy sauce enhanced by a rare, sour citrus known as *som sa*. Well balanced in all respects, it has none of the cloying sweetness often associated with the dish in the United States. The green curry inspires awe, dancing a tightrope of contrasting flavors high above any other version either of us has tasted. The tender chicken gives it body, and fantastically fresh Thai basil adds spicy anise undertones. Two kinds of round eggplants swim in the broth, one the size of plump peas to eat whole so that they pop in the mouth with zesty bitterness. Cheryl asks the owner what gives the curry its brilliance. "Just making the curry paste the traditional way, by hand daily. Not many people bother with that anymore."

They certainly don't seem to at many of the other Thai restaurants we try. The rain, forcing us to abandon the quest for good street food, drives us to seek inside shelter for most meals at places reachable by foot, taxi, or public transportation without getting soaked. Once each, we take a chance on the upscale Thai establishments at our hotels. At Sala Rim Naam in The Oriental, which excelled on our previous visit, Western sweet and salty tastes dominate the ersatz Thai dishes. In Spice and Rice at the Siam City, we enjoy only the bar's signature drink, the Red Elephant (watermelon juice with vodka and a splash of Curaçao), and the handsome table service, including a diminutive elephant hot-sauce holder that Cheryl manages to buy from the staff.

The kitchen comes closer to authentic Thai tastes at the Spice Market in the Four Seasons Hotel and Celadon in the elegant Sukhothai Hotel. The chefs at both, obviously talented, deliver a local riff on what the international hospitality trade characterizes as "fine dining." They translate Thai ideas and flavors in worldly ways, satisfying in many respects but ultimately lacking the robustness and complexity of the cuisine at its truest. Celadon's duck curry or the Spice Market's banana blossom salad might excite us in New Mexico, but not in Bangkok.

If hotels must cater to international interests, we wish they would handle it in a straightforward way, as The Oriental does at its bountiful buffet breakfast, served in a beautiful setting right on the river. Area growers provide the lusciously fresh fruit and other produce, and skilled bakers make a global array of breads, including croissants and pain au chocolat flakier and more buttery than most versions in France today. Depending on your nationality or just your druthers, you can load up on dim sum, fried noodles or rice, congee, yogurt, cheese, eggs, bacon, and more. Our two breakfasts here thrill us more than any of the faux Thai meals at fancier hotel restaurants.

Thais play metaphorically with food in many popular expressions and sayings. A *sen yai* (big noodle) refers to an important person, and *khoa mai plaa man* (new rice, juicy fish) describes the passionate early stage of a romantic relationship. We revel in some splendid Thai food in Bangkok, but too much of what we get is *manao mai mii naam* (like lime without juice), not worth the bother.

> >

In the few scant decades since a bridge first connected Phuket to the Thai mainland in the 1970s, the large offshore island has become a tourism phenomenon. It leaped quickly into worldwide prominence as a beach destination, brought economic vitality and jobs to southern Thailand, and spawned a flock of copycat resorts in the region. Since our days of writing travel guides to the Caribbean,

Hawaii, and Mexico, we've been curious about the prodigy and eager to see it. The devastating tsunami during the Christmas season in 2004 cut sharply into the local boom, leaving Phuket desperate for visitors and temporarily bringing prices down, other lures for us on this trip.

The fabulous Amanpuri resort slashed its rates for the first time ever by 50 percent for most of 2005, reducing the cost of its entry-level Garden Pavilion rooms from U.S. $800 to $400. It's long been a yearning of ours to stay at one of the Aman properties—particularly this one, the first of the elite chain's hotels and a model for the rest. On Bali, we had dinner at the Amandari, a close cousin, and now we're digging deep into our travel budget to indulge in a one-night, half-priced stay here.

An indulgence it is. Our bungalow sits among forty others of various sizes, all shielded from one another by lush vegetation, on a hillside overlooking the restaurants, bay, broad and sandy beach, and large, blue-tiled infinity pool. After leading us up several tiers of stairs to reach the room, the receptionist introduces us gradually to the amenities, starting with the two private outdoor lazing spaces, one in the sun with a couple of chaise longues and the other a covered pavilion, or sala, with a ceiling fan and a low Thai-style dining table with comfortable cushion seating. Bill says, "Add an outhouse and this area alone would shame most hotel rooms."

But there's more, of course, inside, all exquisitely understated in the hotel's gracefully unfussy way. Stunning woodwork in macah, which resembles rosewood, envelops us everywhere, on the floors, shutters, desk, night tables, beams, and a planter in the sprawling bathroom holding probably the largest, most effusively blooming orchid either of us has ever seen. To keep us from getting crosswise, we each have our own closet, luggage stand, vanity, toiletries, even phones if we wish, plus a choice of a shower or a soaking tub in case we want to wash our pampered bodies at the same time. "How come there's only one toilet?" Cheryl asks Bill. "I'll take it and you can have the outhouse."

One night for us equals four meals, including a simple pre-departure room-service lunch in our swimsuits at our sala. Our other lunch and a dinner feature Thai specialties, better prepared than at any of the Bangkok hotels where we tried similar dishes. Since Phuket is known for glorious seafood, both of us order *lab talay* for our introductory repast shortly after reaching the Amanpuri.

A chopped mix of small shrimp, calamari, scallops, fish, and kaffir lime, it comes with rice. The kitchen seasons the dish assertively, trying with some sincerity to follow our request to make it Thai-style.

At dinner, we stop first in the bar for the house specialty, a lime and lemon-grass crush with rum and orange liqueur. In the evening Amanpuri offers a choice of two restaurants, an open-air poolside pavilion for Thai food and an enclosed air-conditioned space for Italian fare, currently, of course, the trendiest of international cuisines. Opting as always to eat local, we take a front table overlooking the pool. The waiter presents us with a small menu and a large drinks list that includes some Thai wines promoted for their affinity with the dishes. After quizzing our server about the wine choices, we order a bottle of a red Monsoon Valley, a blend of Shiraz, black Muscat, and native *pokdum* grapes grown on floating vineyards in the Chao Phraya Delta.

The wine does make a good match for our food selections. To start, we share *yaam poo mim thod*, fried softshell crab, and a tangy green mango salad with shallots, chile paste, and lemongrass. A nearby aquaculture farm raises the meaty crabs, as briny and fresh as any just taken in the wild. For a main course, Bill gets *gaeng paad gai*, a spicy southern jungle curry with chicken, full of contrasting flavors and textures. Cheryl opts for *goong paad bai graprow*, stir-fried shrimp with hot basil, chile, and oyster sauce. Both light up our night.

Breakfast the next morning is almost as tasty. Inspired by a welcome gift of chocolate cookies that she devoured yesterday, Cheryl tries some of the other baked goods, a small sour-cherry muffin and a *pain au chocolat*, supplemented by a bowl of tropical fruits, red currants, and strawberries topped with yogurt. Bill considers the "Phuket" breakfast with rice porridge and Chinese sausage salad but chooses instead a hash of the local black crab. Baked rather than skillet- or wok-fried, as he thinks a hash should be, it's a little meek until he requests and adds the chile-and-fish sauce named nam pla prik.

Changing out of our swimsuits, we leave reluctantly after the lunch in our sala, taking a complimentary Amanpuri limousine from the quiet, relaxed setting to our next hotel, the Amari Coral in the much busier Patong Beach area. Our driver speaks English well, so we ask about the tragic tsunami's impact and the island's recovery progress. "Phuket is mostly back, and visitors are returning, but residents will never outlive their memories of the day." He illustrates by relating his family's experience. "My wife and I were both working at different hotels. I didn't find out for hours that she was safe. Amanpuri let me go home to check on our house and nothing was there. Nothing at all. Everything washed out to sea." Cheryl timidly inquires if the rest of their family survived okay. "No, two cousins died and also some good friends. Most people lost loved ones." Each of us expresses sympathy, but we feel feeble in our efforts.

A conventional beach hotel similar to thousands of others in the world, the Amari Coral sits at the south end of Patong on a sliver of sand not connected to the bustling main beach. The location allows us to walk at will into town—the restaurant, nightlife, and shopping headquarters of Phuket—but to escape the crowds at other times. The reception desk checks us in and escorts us through a maze of low-rise wings to our ocean-view deluxe room. With tsunami stories fresh in our minds, it's a little unsettling to see we'll be sleeping forty feet from the shore.

The tourist literature in the room informs us in detail about the activities available for guests, none in the least appealing to us. Many visitors apparently enjoy taking boat trips to secluded beaches and smaller islands, such as Phi Phi Don, where you will be "amazing" to witness monkeys "leaving" on the hillside, and Phi Phi Lae, the movie set for Leonardo di Caprio's *The Beach*. Others seem to seek out ATV thrills, diving, sailing and parasailing, sea canoeing, waterskiing, and touring underwater on a Yellow Submarine. None of the brochures offers anything remotely related to Thai life and culture.

After this dispiriting reading, we head into town in the late afternoon for a firsthand look at the hub of the hubbub. It doesn't set new standards for tacky—impossible to do any longer in a world awash in it—but it certainly reeks of banality. In most respects, it's Just Beach Town Anywhere, capable of being transplanted to Florida or Mexico without anyone noticing the difference. Scads of junky shops pack the main street that runs the length of the crescent coast, each with a hustler out front to tempt in the tourists. "Hey, Boss"—every man's name—"you want a Rolex?" "Please, Madame"—every woman's name—"try on one of my gold rings." In tune with the times, Patong flaunts a "Rock Hard Café" and a billboard-promoted show with Prasoot Srisatorn, the "Original Thai Elvis."

Only two features set the town apart from other beach burgs: a scarcity of restaurants with local food and the openness of the sexual lures. You can find huevos rancheros all over Puerto Vallarta and conch fritters anywhere in the Keys, but don't go looking for *kaeng tai plaa* or another southern Thai curry in Patong. Restaurateurs think visitors really want familiar food from home, so they offer plenty of what one sign calls "Euro Pian" dishes. Scandinavian places abound, but you won't be left out in the heat if you prefer a Hungarian goulash, German schnitzel, Italian pasta, or, from the bargain basement, a McDonald's burger.

Sex seems to sell even better than dinner, watches, and jewelry. In what local maps call the "Hot Zone," in the heart of town, tiny lanes branch off of Bangla Road, each lined on both sides with open-air bars with stool seating and names such as High Heels, Crazy Girls a Go Go, Luck Bar, Sex Stock Exchange, and, for more demanding patrons, Black Cat #1, with an image of a dominatrix on the sign. Notices often indicate "every body welcome," which we assume at first is another language oddity, like the restaurant claiming to be recommended by the "Fo Dor" guide, but we eventually decide they mean what they say, that everybody's body qualifies for action.

In another area, slightly less prominent, gay nightlife thrives in clubs such as Spartacus and James Dean, snuggled next to massage parlors announcing services "by men, for men." Farther afield, on the outskirts of town, the huge Simon Cabaret caters to all interests with a popular transvestite show. The brochure in our hotel room claims the performers are more male than any man and "more woman than you can imagine," perhaps like the attendant at the Amari Coral's business center, attractively feminine in all ways except for a voice deep enough to come from a subwoofer.

On our initial visit, it's still too early in the evening for the girls and boys to play, allowing us to explore their haunts without risk of untoward propositions. The poking around goes quickly because the same-old sensation takes over after a few minutes. By the third alfresco bar, they all begin to look alike. The search for a good place to eat takes much longer. Lots of restaurants serve fresh seafood, often displayed on ice in front of their large pavilion dining rooms, but they focus mostly on standard international preparations rather than Thai specialties.

Finally, our sleuthing brings us to a small, inviting spot called the Sea Hag. Maybe the name should have alerted us—or at least the clueless waiter standing outside by the posted menu, which appears Thai judging by the dish names. Before we go in, Bill asks the server, "Is your food truly Thai?"

"Oh, yes, in all ways."

Staring at him eye-to-eye, Cheryl says, "We want our food cooked Thai-style, like the chef would do for you. Understand?"

"Oh, yes, madam."

So our crab appetizer shows up without any seasoning at all, leading us to reject it as unacceptable and to reiterate our desires. When our two fish entrees arrive later, we simply give up, taking enough bites to stave off starvation but leaving the rest; one is insipidly bland and the other submerged in a sickly sweet chile sauce rather than the advertised red curry. Noticing we left a fair amount of food, the waiter says, "Oh, too spicy for you!"

Our dinners the next two evenings make up for most of the Sea Hag's deficiencies. After spending much of the second day in Patong reading by our hotel pool, we take a tuk-tuk south in the afternoon to the Karon and Kata Beaches. Unlike the scary three-wheel carts of the same name in Bangkok, the tuk-tuks in Phuket are small pickup trucks with bench seating in the bed for six or so people. Taxis and buses don't exist for transportation between beaches, so the uncomfortable trucks enjoy a monopoly on the traffic and charge accordingly. Dominated by a couple of mammoth hotels, Karon put us off, but Kata seems fascinating in a laid-back style. If we had a chance to choose again, this is where we would have stayed after the Amanpuri, probably at the hotel attached to our dinner restaurant.

Arriving early for our reservation at Mom Tri's Boathouse, we kill time across the street at the Cool Beach bar, which climbs up a hillside jungle on four small concrete terraces covered with tin roofs, punctured at points to allow palm trees to grow through into the sunlight. Portraits of the king and queen, found in most Thai businesses, hang on the walls of the upper level watching over a full-size pool table, where the women who run the place are currently teaching befuddled male opponents how to handle a cue stick. Bill orders a "Mai Thai," festooned with orchids, and Cheryl gets a frothy and cooling "SingaPore Sling." The drinks come with roasted peanuts and a choice of watching BBC TV or listening to Tracy Chapman songs.

The "Mom" in Tri's name is a title, like "Sir," rather than a shorthand form of "mother." His Boathouse restaurant enjoys a long-standing reputation as the best place to eat in Phuket and it sure shows us why. Executive chef Tummanoon Punchun skillfully steers a tough course, offering both classic French and Thai dishes, each prepared to complement the extensive, international selection of wine in the professional cellar. Our first night comes close to perfect as a dining experience, with superb food and wine in an enchanted setting, on a beachfront terrace with a gentle sea breeze and stars winking at us from above.

Cheryl starts with *poo cha*, deep-fried crab served in the shell with a sweet plum sauce, while Bill goes for *gung cha nam pla*, a rock lobster salad with a rich fish-sauce dressing laced with thin slices of chile and loaded with garlic and basil. The kitchen seasons both expertly, pumping up the heat in the salad but not so much that it overpowers the wine, a peppery, rustic French Mourvèdre. For main courses, we try *tom yam heng*, deep-fried garrupa caught just off the shore, and *gang phed ped yang*, pan-roasted duck breasts with a spicy curry sauce and lychees, which rates in the top ten dishes of our long journey.

Invoking her all-time favorite rationale for dessert—"since everything else was so good"—Cheryl suggests we share something, knowing Bill will leave most of it for her. Because we both want to sample a dish from the French side of the menu, she orders a *financier*, a warm almond-scented cookie-cake. The kitchen bakes a magnificent version and then takes tropical liberties with the idea, adding pureed fresh pineapple on top, and on the side, a creamy coconut sorbet and bits of luscious starfruit, mango, guava, and mint. An ideal finish for a dreamy meal, we feel like hitchhiking back to our bed on a cloud. Instead, we make a reservation to return tomorrow night.

A lashing rain wakes us the next morning, the last day of the official monsoon season. Brief showers have rolled past Patong earlier in our stay, but this is a black-sky drencher. The man who cleans the pool beside the breakfast restaurant appears bundled for a storm at sea in the north Atlantic, wearing a heavy, hooded, bright blue slicker and rubber boots. Given the dreary prospects for any time in the sun, we linger longer than usual at the breakfast buffet. Our waitress sympathizes about the weather but can't help pointing out the obvious. "We're still in our rainy season, after all."

A half-dozen serving tables offer the same selection each day, an international Who's Who of morning foods. Lacking anything better to do, we try to guess the guests' nationalities by their main choices, knowing most of them will stick with favorites from home. "That's an American couple for sure," Cheryl says, "because they got cereal first and then an omelet."

"I bet they're Scandinavian or German," Bill conjectures, pointing at a group loading up with cold cuts and cheese. Only the Japanese opt for miso soup, and only other Asians for congee. The fruit, sushi, and the various breads, ranging from croissants to scones, don't provide solid clues because a cross section of people pick them up. In case anyone else is playing the same game, we try to be tricky, eating a lot of the locally raised pineapple and a little of everything else except the tasteless boxed cereals.

The rain continues all day, driving us by the middle of the afternoon into the hotel bar. After surveying the worldwide list of possibilities, we order a margarita and a mojito, figuring Thais know a lot about lime and mint flavors. They do indeed, and the drinks go great with the snacks on the table, peanuts studded with garlic and cilantro.

Back at Mom Tri's a few hours later, we find the atmosphere gloomier than the night before, with the terrace closed and the windows shut tight against the storm. The cooking excels again, particularly the *pla tod ki mow*, a deep-fried sea bass topped with red curry, and the *goong sarong*, a Phuket specialty of shrimp rubbed with a paste of white pepper and cilantro, then wrapped in softened rice vermicelli and deep-fried. The food lifts our spirits, but not to the peaks of our first dinner.

It's still raining in the morning of day number one of the dry high season as we pack up to leave for India. By now, we're ready for a change of scenery. Our joys in Thailand certainly outnumber our disappointments, and guarantee to be far more memorable, but the up-and-down swings tire us in a way we don't experience elsewhere on the trip. Going from elation to frustration and back again requires a lot of running to keep up with the tempo. At this point, the soggy finish line ahead looks welcome.

THE NITTY-GRITTY

⊡ ROYAL PRINCESS CHIANG MAI
http://chiangmai.royalprincess.com
112 Chang Klan Road, Chiang Mai
66-5328-1033   fax 66-5328-1044
*Large, pleasant deluxe rooms, but the
hotel is too close to the madness of the
Night Bazaar for our tastes.*

⊡ HONG TAUW INN
Nimanhaemin Road near the intersection
of Huay Kaew Road, Chiang Mai
66-5321-8333
lunch and dinner

⊡ THE NATIONAL
ELEPHANT INSTITUTE
www.thailandelephant.org
Lampang
66-5422-8108

⊡ SIAM CITY HOTEL BANGKOK
www.siamhotels.com
477 Si Ayuthaya Road,
Phayathai, Bangkok
66-2247-0123   fax 66-2247-0178
*Classy for a moderately priced hotel and
near the Phayathai Skytrain station.*

⊡ THE ORIENTAL
www.mandarinoriental.com/bangkok/
48 Oriental Avenue, Bangkok
66-2659-9000   fax 66-2659-0000
*Once often ranked the world's finest hotel
and still as polished as ever.*

⊡ AW TAW KAW FOOD MARKET
www.talay.org
Bangkok

⊡ RAAN JAY FAI
327 Maha Chai Road,
Phra Nakhon, Bangkok
66-2223-9384
dinner only

⊡ POLO FRIED CHICKEN
137/1-2 Soi Polo
off Wireless Road,
Lumphini, Bangkok
lunch and early dinner (no reservations)

⊡ RUT & LUK
on Soi Phadungdao near the intersection
of Yaowarat Road, Chinatown, Bangkok
dinner only (no reservations)

CHOTE CHITR
146 Phraeng Phouthon,
Bangkok
66-2221-4082
lunch and dinner
Don't miss it.

AMANPURI
www.amanresorts.com
Pansea Beach, Phuket
66-7632-4333   fax 66-7632-4100
Absolutely lovely and restful.

AMARI CORAL BEACH RESORT
www.phuket.com/amari/
Patong Beach, Phuket
66-7634-0106   fax 66-7634-0115
Conventional in most respects,
but close to the water for Patong.

MOM TRI'S BOATHOUSE
www.boathousephuket.com
Kata Beach, Phuket
66-7633-0015   fax 66-7633-0561
Great ocean-front location for both the
hotel and the restaurant, which is open
for lunch and dinner.

Beef Khao Soi

SERVES 6 OR MORE

The Chile Paste

1 whole dried red New Mexico or ancho chile

2 to 4 whole dried chiles de arbol or japonais chiles or other small hot dried red chiles

2 teaspoons coriander seeds

½ teaspoon cumin seeds

½ teaspoon cardamom seeds

1 teaspoon freshly grated nutmeg

1 teaspoon ground turmeric

½ teaspoon ground cinnamon

3-inch chunk fresh ginger

½ cup vegetable oil

3 medium shallots, sliced into thin rings and rings separated

6 garlic cloves, chopped fine

Toast lightly in a dry skillet over medium-high heat until fragrant, first the New Mexico chile, followed by the chiles de arbol, coriander seeds, cumin seeds, and cardamom. As each is fragrant, dump out into a spice grinder or mortar and pestle and grind. Then add each to a food processor. Add the nutmeg, turmeric, cinnamon, and ginger. Pulse to combine.

In a small heavy skillet warm the vegetable oil over medium heat until very hot but short of smoking. Add the shallots, stirring them almost continually, until they begin to turn golden. After 5 minutes, add the garlic and continue stirring. Reduce the heat a bit if the oil is spattering or the shallots begin to brown darkly. Cook about 10 minutes longer, until both shallots and garlic are deeply golden. Pour the oil through a fine strainer into a heatproof container and reserve it. Spread the shallot mixture out on a couple of thicknesses of paper towels to cool briefly and crisp.

Add to the food processor and puree to a thick paste. The chile paste can be used immediately for the khao soi or refrigerated tightly covered for up to several days.

The Noodles
  1½   pounds thin dried egg noodles, about the size of fettuccine, Chinese or Italian
   2   tablespoons coconut milk, freshly made if available
   2   tablespoons coconut oil
  Reserved shallot-garlic oil and vegetable oil for deep-frying

Take one-third of the noodles (8 ounces), break them more or less in half, place them in a large bowl, and cover them with warm water. Let them sit in the water until they become pliable, about 30 minutes. Strain off the water and scatter the noodles on a clean dish towel to dry, patting them down a bit as you go so that all surfaces dry thoroughly.

While that batch of noodles softens, bring a large pot of salted water to a vigorous boil and in it cook the remaining 1 pound of noodles until quite tender, a bit softer and creamier than for al dente pasta. Drain the cooked noodles and place them in a large bowl. Toss them with the coconut milk and oil to help keep them from sticking together. Reserve them at room temperature.

Rinse out and dry the pan used for cooking the noodles. Add to it the shallot-garlic oil and at least 2 inches of vegetable oil and heat to 350°F. In several batches, deep-fry the 8 ounces of noodles that were soaked and patted dry. Fry until crispy and lightly golden, about 2 minutes. Remove with a slotted spoon or strainer to paper towels.

The Broth and Beef
  1½   pounds boneless top sirloin steak, sliced across the grain into thin strips, about ½ inch across and 2 inches long
  1½   teaspoons curry powder
   1   cup coconut cream (not cream of coconut), freshly made if possible
   3   cups coconut milk, freshly made if available

¼ cup plus 2 tablespoons soy sauce

1 tablespoon Thai fish sauce, or more to taste

2 tablespoons palm sugar, turbinado sugar, or brown sugar

½ cup sliced scallion rings, both green and white portions

¼ cup chopped cilantro leaves

2 teaspoons to 1 tablespoon fresh lime juice

Massage the steak pieces with the curry powder.

In a large heavy skillet with high sides, or a Dutch oven, bring the coconut cream to a boil over high heat. Stir in the chile paste and reduce the heat to medium. Cook for about 2 minutes, until the oil separates. Mix in the steak, stirring it into the mixture well, and cook until the meat loses its raw color. Pour in the coconut milk and cook the mixture another 10 minutes, adjusting the heat as needed to keep a bare simmer. Mix in the soy sauce, fish sauce, and sugar. Simmer for about 15 minutes longer, until the broth has thickened just enough to have some body to it and the steak is quite tender. Add the scallions in the last 2 or 3 minutes of cooking. Taste and add more fish sauce if desired for salty tang. Mix in cilantro and enough lime juice to balance the sugar and coconut. Keep the broth warm. If it thickens beyond soupy, add a little water to thin it.

Putting It All Together

1 tablespoon ground dried chiles de arbol or japonais chiles or other fairly hot dried red chiles, warmed in 1 tablespoon vegetable oil, then cooled

12 lime wedges, from 2 medium limes

About ½ cup finely diced shallots

Cilantro leaves

Thai fish sauce

About 1 cup packaged Thai or Chinese pickled cabbage or mustard greens, rinsed, patted dry, and chopped, optional

Chopped peanuts and/or shredded coconut, optional

Place as garnishes into individual bowls the chile in oil, limes, shallots, cilantro, Thai fish sauce, and optional pickled cabbage, peanuts, and/or coconut.

In soup plates or large individual bowls, arrange equal portions of the boiled noodles. Ladle broth over each portion, distributing the steak equally. Scatter with the fried noodles and serve. Guests garnish their bowls as they wish, from the selection of toppings. Start with chopsticks to slurp the noodles, then alternate with Chinese ceramic spoons or other soupspoons to finish the broth.

"WHAT THE HELL IS THAT?" BILL POINTS OUTSIDE, where explosions light the night sky on our plane's approach to the Mumbai airport.

"Good grief," Cheryl says, "it looks like Baghdad out there."

"Well, if crazies of some kind are firing at us, they must be poor shots. None of the blasts seem close."

Everyone has told us to expect the unpredictable in India, but this seems pretty extreme for an introductory howdy-do.

It is, as we soon find out. Our arrival coincides with the biggest night of the Hindu New Year celebration known as Diwali, the Festival of Lights. All the city is ablaze, though in a fashion as under control as anything ever gets here. A greeter from our hotel, the Taj Mahal, welcomes us at the airport and explains the occasion. "This is our biggest annual religious holiday and also the most jubilant night of the year, kind of like a combination of Christmas and New Year's Eve on the same day. The crackers"—fireworks—"will be going off all night and for the next couple of days."

His account continues while he escorts us to the hotel limousine for transportation into the heart of the city, provided as a part of our package for an executive-club-floor room in the Taj's original midrise Palace wing. With a special Internet rate, the deluxe room costs only a little more than a standard double in the same building, but the staff extends special attention and courtesies to the guests, including airport transfers, a club lounge with complimentary breakfasts and cocktails, in-room registration and checkout, and a private butler-cum-concierge. Even at a normal time, and especially now it seems, the city formerly known as Bombay can be as chaotic as any metropolis on earth, but we've ensured ourselves a means to retreat at will to one of its calmest corners.

"On the way to the hotel," the greeter goes on, "you will see lights everywhere because on this night the goddess Lakshmi, the provider of wealth, descends from the heavens to bless people with prosperity. Families put out lights so she will find their homes." When he turns us over to our driver, he tells us, "Ask him about anything you don't understand on your ride downtown, which will take a little longer tonight than the usual hour." Every neighborhood we pass through, even the slums, glows brightly, sparkling with candles, bonfires, lanterns of all kinds, and strings of twinkling white lights.

"Incredible!" Cheryl exclaims. "Mumbai looks beautiful, even though I know it's partially an illusion."

"Light in our religion," the driver says, "represents goodness and spiritual wisdom. Tonight, the light vanquishes wickedness, violence, and ignorance."

"What about the flowers?" Cheryl asks, peering out at houses and shanties bedecked with golden marigolds and other blossoms in red and yellow hues.

"They are offerings to Lakshmi. We also give flowers to friends and family at Diwali as symbols of love, along with sweets and other festive foods."

"The women and girls walking on the streets," Bill says, "look just as radiant, dressed in glorious silks."

"That's part of the celebration," the driver explains. "Families who can afford it make sure all mothers, wives, and daughters get new dresses and jewelry for Diwali."

"Oh," Bill mumbles, regretting that the notion came up with Cheryl listening so raptly.

Our car reaches the Taj Mahal right at midnight, pulling up to a small, private entrance for the Palace wing. When George Bernard Shaw stayed in this building not many years after the hotel's 1903 opening, well before the management added a conventional high-rise tower, he claimed that he no longer needed to see the real Taj Mahal in Agra. It's easy to understand the sentiment. The edifices differ substantially, of course, but both are architectural wonders; this one designed in an amalgam of Asian, Moorish, and Florentine styles. The other sports a more romantic origin, to be sure, but our nest sustains romance through sleepovers. Take your choice.

Our butler greets us in the reception area, escorts us to our room, expedites the check-in formalities, and gets us glasses of champagne as welcome drinks. "I can also bring you a deck of cards," he says, "if you want to celebrate Diwali that way."

"What do you mean?" Bill, the poker player, asks.

"It's a tradition to gamble on cards today. The goddess Parvati played dice with her husband Lord Shiva on Diwali night and decreed that people should gamble then, too. Winners are supposed to prosper in the next year and losers get another chance for success the following year. The real losers are people who don't try their luck, because legend says they will be reborn as donkeys in their next life."

"You better bring us a deck," Cheryl says quickly. Bill decrees we'll play two hands of Texas hold 'em for two rupees each, the equivalent of a nickel, giving us both a chance to win. Bill takes the first pot and then folds his cards on the second hand, forfeiting to Cheryl. Our mutual good fortune becomes instantly apparent, preceding even the fate of the deal. With pure good luck and no advance planning, we've arrived in Mumbai at exactly the right hour on the most exultant day of the year. If it's all about karma, as many millions of Indians believe, each of us must be starting with a full tank.

> >

In tourism circles, India is known as a tough nut. One of our most widely traveled colleagues, a master journalist at the *New York Times,* told us before we left, "No matter how much you like to chart your own course on a trip, India rules. It will always throw you tricky curves." In recognition of the difficulties, most Americans who visit the country come on a group tour or pay an expert to handle their planning in detail. Neither option appeals to us; we've never traveled like that and don't want to begin now. Perhaps we're too stubborn, a complaint each of us has made about the other a few times before.

As an alternative, after talking about the situation with Cheryl, Bill carefully picks hotel companies in our two destinations, Mumbai and the state of Kerala, that have the resources and experience to deal with all our local arrangements. Established places with a solid track record according to his research, they charge a premium for their accommodations and services, but that seems reasonable in India if they can deliver. The Taj Mahal certainly does, at least for guests on its executive-club floors.

In our room, swaths of silk in multiple shades of gold cover the bed, windows, and chairs, matched handsomely with carved-wood wall panels and accents. Bright sprays of orchids play counterpoint to the white-and-gray marble in the bathroom. For real executives occupying the quarters, the desk provides hookups for every imaginable electronic device, and for their downtime, a nearby cabinet holds a large plasma-screen TV. Surveying the gadgets after our poker game, Cheryl says, "We could probably launch the space shuttle from here."

"Go ahead. I'm stumped right now just by the master console for the lights."

Early the next morning, we're off to explore our neighborhood on foot. For many residents, the celebratory night continues. Crackers pop loudly all around us, and ladies parade past in their finery. Other locals go back to work. Crowds surround the massive arch in front of the hotel called the Gateway of India, waiting for boat transportation or trying to peddle goods to the captive audience. When Gandhi and his allies ended British colonial rule in 1947, the last of the occupying soldiers marched through the Gateway to waiting ships for the long sail home, leaving behind some institutional infrastructure and a widespread use of the English language.

While hawkers open stands on the sidewalks and a man ties a cow to a tree, traffic barrels through the streets, daring pedestrians to dally. Many of the vehicles are black-and-yellow Ambassador taxis made in India some thirty years ago. Rusty and battered, with meters welded on the top of a front fender, they look completely unreliable, but according to an English-language paper at the hotel, the drivers resist government efforts to modernize because they can repair the old cars themselves and fill them with the cheapest gasoline on the market. The taxis, as well as the buses and trucks, flaunt strings of marigolds and other flowers, palm fronds, and spirited ornamentation, often in gold, orange, red, and fuchsia shades.

Apart from seeing the city come to life, Cheryl wants to do a little browsing and Bill hopes to find a particular restaurant in the area, which turns out to be closed. No such luck for Bill on the stores, as open and abundant as any shopper might wish. Cheryl looks briefly in a number of places but gets engrossed for more than an hour in one warehouse-size emporium, a government-sponsored business selling handcrafted products from cottage industries across the country. She picks out some jewelry for herself, our daughter, Heather, and our granddaughters—"You've got to show respect for local traditions, okay?"—and together we round up a collection of festive Christmas ornaments for ourselves and friends, all small enough to fit in our undersized luggage.

With Bill's chosen lunch restaurant shut, we decide to eat by the hotel pool, keeping it simple with grilled pomfret and a fresh mango lassi for each of us. After a quiet interlude in the sun, sorely missed much of our time in Thailand, our butler arranges a driver and car for us to sightsee farther afield. Sebastian, the chauffeur and guide, takes us through the built-up and bustling core of the city, pointing out museums, government offices, and the main train station, the Victoria Terminus, a large and lavish nineteenth-century structure. He tells us, "Two and a half million commuters pass through those doors every day." Hundreds of beggars hang around waiting for them.

Sebastian pulls up eventually at Crawford Market (now officially Mahatma Jyotiba Phule Market), our first destination. Mumbai's biggest food bazaar, it operates in another colonial-era building from the 1860s notable for a bas-relief frieze designed by the father of Rudyard Kipling, a native son of the neighborhood. Sebastian stays with the car and hands us off to a Crawford guide who will show us around. Like a good leader, the guide asks, "Do you have any special interests?"

Cheryl immediately answers, "Dried spices." He escorts us first to that section of stalls, loaded with cardamom, coriander, turmeric, black mustard seeds, whole star anise, aniseed, ginger, cloves, canela cinnamon, Ceylon cinnamon, ground chiles, black peppercorns, and masala and tikka blends. At one stand, he asks the vendor to let us smell his tandoori mix, saying, "This man blends ninety-two different ingredients by hand to make it." The robust, freshly ground scent almost takes off our heads.

The extensive fruit selection also fascinates us. Alfonso mangoes, especially luscious when ripe, dominate in one area, and early picked green mangoes, eaten in that form, reign in another sector around the corner. Other stalls offer custardy cherimoyas, intensely orange persimmons, papayas, watermelons, plump heavy figs, and remarkable pomegranates, some shorn of their crown to display the glistening, voluptuous seeds. The market overall looks grittier and darker than others we've seen in Asia, but the produce is splendid.

Both of us regret what happens next as much as anything on the whole trip. As we leave Crawford, a guy tries to sell us a big, full carton of pomegranates. It's far more than the two of us can consume, and any kind of purchase seems likely to attract other sellers and beggars. As we refuse the offer and turn away, he pursues us with increasing desperation, almost hanging on to the car when Sebastian pulls out of the lot. Even as we write about this months later, we feel sorry about not responding to his pleas and buying the fruit to give to someone else. India isn't easy.

Sebastian heads next to the Jain Temple in the affluent Malabar Hills district. Although evidence of poverty abounds in Mumbai, as in all Indian cities, so do pockets of wealth derived from local industries, including the Bollywood movie business here. The Jain community practices a rigorously ascetic ethic prohibiting violence to any life-form—avoiding for that reason meat, wine, honey, and any fruits or roots that might harbor a living organism—but members contribute generously to the construction of beautifully elaborate houses of worship. This temple, usually regarded as the most impressive in the city, reflects the ideal with a vibrant and intricately detailed interior.

From the sacred to the profane, Sebastian brings us down from the heights to Chowpatty Beach. More of a park and fair than a spot for swimming or sunning, it spreads along the broad, sweeping Back Bay facing the Arabian Sea. Virtually empty during the day, Chowpatty comes alive in the evening, when hundreds of families gather to gab, gobble, and play. Musicians, trained monkeys, and contortionists, among others, provide entertainment, while kids chase after balloons and one another when they're not riding toy jeeps or merry-go-rounds. A couple of dozen *chatt* (snack) vendors sell popular street foods such as *dosas* (fried flatbreads) with various fillings, *kulfi* (Indian ice cream), and most famously, *bhelpuri* (crispy puffed rice, fried noodles, vegetables, and chutney scooped up with *puri* bread). The treats look good, but we're too wary to try them without good local guidance.

On the way back to the hotel, Sebastian drives us slowly along Marine Drive, which runs for several miles down the Back Bay shore from Chowpatty Beach to the upscale high-rise towers of Nariman Point. Nicknamed the "Queen's Necklace" for the way it's lit at night, the sidewalk promenade on the avenue attracts crowds of strollers, many of them young couples seeking a quiet, romantic spot to be alone in the city, probably as difficult in Mumbai as anyplace in the world.

Our choice of a dinner restaurant, after considering several respected places in the downtown area, is the Taj Mahal's Masala Kraft, highly recommended according to our research by Mumbai food authority Rashmi Uday Singh. It immediately looks like a good pick, filled on this holiday evening with multiple generations of local families dining together, as Americans might the day after Christmas.

The menu features dishes grounded in Indian traditions from around the country but prepared with contemporary urban flair. Cheryl starts with tandoori salmon marinated in a spice paste moistened with sugar cane vinegar and served with cilantro chutney. The crusty surface over the succulent interior carries a hint of smoke from the superhot, wood-burning clay oven. Bill opts for a cheese appetizer, cubes of simple, white *paneer* with pickled tiny whole purple onions in a sauce enlivened with freshly ground spices. "This idea works almost as well as *sag paneer*," he tells Cheryl, referring to a combination of the cheese with spinach that's our most beloved Indian dish at home.

For a main course, Cheryl gets griddle-cooked shrimp with toasted ground coriander seeds and Kashmiri chiles, served with a rich bell pepper sauce. Pomegranate seeds garnish the plate. It's a delight tonight but could have been a horrible mishmash in the wrong hands. Bill chooses a southern Indian fish curry, hoping for a foretaste of what we'll find in Kerala. Chunks of a firm, mild white fish float in a wonderfully complex sauce based on coconut milk and accented with chile, ginger, and curry (or *kari*) leaves, which look a bit like basil but boast a lemony bell-pepper flavor.

Crackling crisp *naan*, flecked with green olives and chile flakes, comes on the side, along with mango chutney fragrant with the fruit. The olives in the bread, certainly not customary, mimic the salty tang of pungent Indian pickles without their strident overtones. To drink with the dinner, Bill picks a Grover Vineyards Cabernet and Shiraz blend made in India in collaboration with a Bordeaux vintner. Both of us enjoy the wine, but while Bill finishes it, Cheryl switches to a first-flush Darjeeling tea, an earthy, full-bodied black brew made with leaves from the Himalayan foothills.

At sunrise the following morning, the hotel doorman hails us a cab to go to the Sassoon Docks, the likely source of our dinner fish and seafood. About a mile from the Taj, the driver leaves the main street and takes us into a maze of dirt alleys, increasingly muddy and packed with trucks and people as we creep along toward the shore. Finally, he creates a parking place for himself near a wharf and lets us out, indicating that he'll wait for us.

It's total bedlam in all directions. Vividly painted trawlers in the water jostle with one another for space to unload their catch, which they pile onto the docks in enormous stacks. Hundreds of women—often attired in silks and galoshes—sort through the mounds, slinging fish of different sizes and varieties into appropriate buckets of ice. Men and boys lift full buckets onto two-wheeled, wooden hand trolleys, heaping them precariously and then running with the trolleys in tow to waiting trucks that deliver the seafood around the city.

Not a single square foot remains unoccupied for more than a few seconds, leaving us no place to stand and watch. Our only recourse is to move around in tempo with the throngs, dodging and ducking obstacles constantly, including the swordfish on a man's head that combs through Cheryl's hair in passing. Everyone is working so furiously they barely notice us, even though we're the only observers and Westerners in the crowd. It's an exhilarating spectacle but soon tires us, so we slog back through the mud to our taxi—easy to find, since no one else arrives or departs this way. Cheryl jumps in the shower as soon as we reach the room, not bothering to remove her shoes, caked with muck.

After a breakfast of eggs and curry in the club lounge, a hotel limo takes us to the airport for our flight to Kochi (formerly Cochin), Kerala. Going along a four-lane boulevard jammed with seven sprawling, staggered lanes of taxis and trucks, the driver says, "Bet you don't see traffic like this in the United States."

"Not usually," Cheryl replies, "but here it seems part of the fabric of life, so it's not really bad. Mumbai just teems with everything—people and cars, vitality and chaos, joy and misery."

"That's all true," the driver agrees. "The airport teems, too. Good luck there."

> >

Poor Columbus. Even five hundred years after he stumbled across the Americas on a voyage to south India, we beat him to his planned and preferred destination, the fabled Malabar Coast, now in the state of Kerala. Black pepper, the dried fruit of a vine native to the area, made this Arabian Sea region a major world trade center starting as early as the reign of Ramses the Great in ancient Egypt. The Roman Empire sent fleets of more than one hundred ships on annual expeditions to collect the spice, the most pungent seasoning known anywhere on the globe then except in parts of the Americas, the original home of the chile.

When Rome fell, two of its conquerors demanded a ransom of more than a ton of peppercorns each, considering them as valuable as anything the citizens had. Arabs took over the spice trade during the Middle Ages, and when their cargo reached the Mediterranean, the savvy merchants of Venice and Genoa handled European distribution, using the profits to finance the rise of their city-states. The Arab-Italian monopoly and the exorbitant price of pepper inspired both Spain and Portugal to seek new, direct routes to the shores of Kerala. Columbus went west on his mission, but wiser Portuguese navigators realized the shortest route lay around the southern tip of Africa. Vasco da Gama arrived in India in 1498, ensuring Portuguese control of the trade for the next century and a half and leading to the establishment of the first European colony in Asia.

Even today, pepper remains, by monetary value, the most widely traded spice in the world. By weight, chiles enjoy a slight dominance in the market, but pepper sales account for 20 percent of the financial worth of all international spice transactions. Prices are still set largely in Kerala, in the small electronic trading office of the Pepper Exchange in Kochi—unfortunately not open to the public during our visit.

The fruitfulness of the land is visible from the air, as our flight descends toward the airport. Expansive waterways flow leisurely through fields astoundingly green and thriving. A woman from Mumbai sitting next to Cheryl, making her first trip to Kochi, gasps out loud and clutches her hands to her chest. "Pardon me," she says, "I just never knew the earth could be so lush."

A driver sent by the Brunton Boatyard, our Kochi hotel, meets us in the terminal and takes us into the city, pounding on the horn for almost the entire hour
we're on the road. Pastoral countryside lines the highway but actually increases
the congestion because hundreds of people, cows, and other creatures amble
along the shoulder, reducing the pavement available to cars, trucks, buses, motorbikes, and bicycles—all adept at occupying any empty space. As in Mumbai,
the concept of traffic lanes (despite frequent signs on the subject) appears to be
an alien principle, even less acceptable than allowing another motorist to pass
without a protesting honk.

A lineup of reception staff, awash in white linen, greets us at the seafront
hotel with necklaces of jasmine buds and marigolds. Previously a shipbuilding
yard, the gracefully nautical inn belongs to a small Kerala chain called CGH
Earth, founded by Dominic Joseph Kuruvinakunnel in 1957 and now run by his
six sons. The family also owns and operates our other two lodging choices in the
area, both an hour south of Kochi on the grand Vembanad Lake. As agreed in
advance, their managers are arranging all our local transportation and other logistics. The "Earth" in the business name denotes the family's commitment to
responsible tourism, a pledge to clients to respect and preserve the cultural heritage and natural environment in their work.

As an important aspect of the cultural and natural bounty, food figures prominently in this effort. The long menu at the History Café in Brunton Boatyard
incorporates dishes and influences from all the diverse people who have settled
in Kochi over time, including Hindus (vegetarian and not), Muslims, Syriac
Christians, Jews, and traders and colonial administrators from Arabic lands,
Portugal, the Netherlands (the country that ousted the Portuguese), and Great
Britain (which displaced the Dutch).

At a predinner cooking demonstration, a young kitchen assistant named
Anand discusses the comingling of these traditions locally. "Everyone shares
religious holidays. Yesterday was the end of Ramadan, and Jews, Christians,
and Hindus went with Muslims to the mosque. You will see Christian churches
around town right now still decorated with Diwali lights."

Anand starts his demo by telling us, "My name means 'making other people
happy,' which I hope to do for you today by cooking a Syriac Christian dish, fish
molee. It has lots of flavor, as you'll see, but requires fewer ingredients than spe-

cialties from northern India, where they season mainly with blends of lots of dry spices." He first heats coconut oil in a pan, then puts in black mustard seeds and, when they crackle, sliced red onions. Already the aroma tantalizes us. Next, he adds chopped garlic, small green chiles, ginger, ground turmeric, and at the end, enough fish stock to create a soupy mixture. Chunks of *seer* (kingfish) go in at this point and are simmered briefly to cook through; then Anand tops off the preparation with fresh curry leaves, thick coconut milk, and chopped tomatoes. The molee takes less than ten minutes from start to finish, and looks as vibrant in the bowl as it tastes, with white fish and red, green, and black ingredients floating in yellow gravy.

Bill asks Anand, "Do you have formal culinary training?"

"No, I learned to cook by experimenting with food as a child."

"Just like me," Cheryl says.

"I would like to go to the United States to school," Anand admits shyly. "I've researched the Culinary Institute of America and the chef's program at Johnson and Wales University. I dream about becoming a food writer, but my friends laugh at the idea."

"Go for it," Bill tells him. "Don't listen to naysayers."

For our dinner at the History Café, Bill orders a beef version of vindaloo, a Portuguese inspiration modified over time by Indian cooks. The hot, spicy sauce features freshly ground red chile and cloves, made tangy from a sour fruit called *kodumpuli*, or *gamboge*. Cheryl gets a green chicken curry known as *kariveppila kozhy*, containing cubes of chicken cooked with cardamom and tamarind. It reminds us of a Thai green curry without the basil. The paratha and naan breads on the side round out the meal perfectly.

The next morning, dismounting carefully from our high four-poster bed onto the coir (coconut fiber) floor mats, we go out to our ocean-view balcony to read the English-language paper hung on our room door in a pouch handmade from old newspapers, a crafty recycling touch. The sea traffic is heavy at this hour, providing a parade of harbor ferries, big commercial barges, container ships cruising the distant depths, a freighter that seems almost in touching distance, and lots of small fishing boats with flat nets, which are dipped into the water repeatedly to haul up accumulating catches.

Right down the shore, groups of other fishermen operate Kochi's famous

Chinese nets, the most photographed sight in the city. Erected between 1350 and 1450 directly on the edge of the harbor, the heavy, teak contraptions rely on a manual pulley system of cantilevers and counterweights—involving bamboo poles, stones, and the arduous labor of several men—to sink large nets into the sea and raise them out again. To get a closer look at the work, we walk along the coast, stopping to watch various teams in different stages of the process. "As rudimentary as it looks on the surface," Bill says, "it's a pretty sophisticated system." In a small outdoor market, vendors sell whole fish just hauled up.

Back at the hotel for breakfast, both of us get sweet lime juice to drink and a plate of papaya, pineapple, and *chickoo*, a fruit that looks like a tiny potato and tastes like a sugary pear. Cheryl follows with *uppama*, a local favorite made with *rava*, a couscous-type grain, mixed here with black mustard seeds, turmeric, curry leaves, broken pieces of dried small red chiles, peanuts, and vegetable bits. Bill opts for *uthappam*, a thick rice pancake prepared from slightly fermented batter, common in Kerala cooking. It comes with *sambar*, a spicy, soupy lentil concoction, and a southern-style masala, a relish of onions, tomatoes, and herbs rather than a northern Indian dried-spice blend. Fresh coconut chutney enhances both dishes.

In the historic Fort Cochin area of the city, where we're staying, tuk-tuks (also called "auto-rickshaws" and perhaps better named "auto-ricochets") provide most of the commercial transportation on the narrow lanes. Bill hails one after breakfast to take us a couple of miles to the Mattancherry business district, site of the Pepper Exchange, the Dutch Palace, the Paradesy Synagogue, and other visitor attractions. Built in 1568, the synagogue sounds fascinating, but it isn't open today. Spice shops and warehouses dot the district, mixed in with other stores selling Indian crafts, such as the quilted, sequined, and embroidered textile Cheryl buys for a dining-table centerpiece. As in Mumbai, women and girls on the streets dress for the holiday season, often wearing beautiful saris and, in the case of the young, floral garlands interwoven into hair braids.

Grabbing another tuk-tuk, we head to lunch at Malabar Junction, a restaurant in the simple but attractive courtyard of the Malabar House hotel. For a refreshing drink, the waiter brings fresh squeezed ginger juice for us to combine with simple syrup and sparkling water, like a do-it-yourself ginger ale. Cheryl orders honey-and-ginger marinated medallions of seer, sautéed and served on a bed of crab curry with batter-fried strips of okra. Bill chooses Kerala-style lamb, cooked in a sauce featuring black pepper. "The meat isn't much," he says, "but the sauce is a tribute to the potency of pepper, building bite by bite in glorious intensity." For dessert, we share chocolate samosas, pillows of crisp dough filled with melted chocolate and drizzled with mango puree.

A leisurely harbor cruise occupies much of the afternoon and early evening. Departing from the hotel, the boat takes us around the northern tip of the large, nearby Willingdon Island to see Kochi's extensive international port facilities, and then surveys the shore of Ernakulam, the city's main business and residential area. The captain pilots us by several smaller and relatively undeveloped islands, passing scores of other vessels, including navy ships, a tanker, many trawlers, and, around twilight, a two-level, Indian-style party boat named *My Heart*, which boasts a giant yellow duck head on the bow and an equally large duck tail on the stern. Everyone onboard is dancing as they wave to us, reminding us of one of the choreographed spectacles in a Bollywood movie. Right before we dock, a stunning sunset splashes the heavens with improbable shades of purple and fuchsia, providing a dramatic backdrop for photos Cheryl takes of the Chinese fishing nets.

The Brunton Boatyard staff has arranged a driver and car to haul us to dinner on Willingdon Island at the first CGH Earth hotel, the Casino, a name used in its earliest sense as "cottage home" rather than the acquired connotation of "gambling establishment." For decades, the Casino's seafood restaurant, Fort Cochin, has enjoyed a reputation for excellence, but we're skeptical because all our information comes from out-of-date and possibly unreliable sources.

The delightful dining terrace assures us at least of a charming evening. As you enter, the massive trunk of a banyan tree—so lovely it looks like an elegant piece of monumental sculpture—soars into the darkness above the romantically lighted patio. For taste teasers, the waiter brings us small plates of fried vegetable tidbits and addictive fried anchovies mixed with curry leaves. As we nibble on these and begin to think reports on the restaurant have some legitimacy, the waiter returns pushing a cart of fish and shellfish. "This is the menu. We don't put anything on paper because we only serve the catch of the day, which changes, of course." He points out the options, including two freshwater fish, mullet and pearl spot, plus seafaring creatures such as silver pomfret, seer, several snappers, rock lobster, and prawns of varying sizes. "The chef will prepare any of them in any way you prefer."

"Wow, what a responsibility," Cheryl says.

"While you choose," the waiter asks, "would you like bowls of seafood chowder, one of our specialties?"

"Sure," Bill responds, happy to see the fellow leave us alone for a moment to commune silently with the fish about their fate and ours.

"Maybe we should try the black pomfret," Cheryl says. "It's in the pompano family, I think, and it's considered the best fish in the area."

"Okay, but let's have it two ways, grilled with a spice coating and cooked in a curry."

Bill relays our decision when the waiter returns with the chowder, a creamy, substantial version flecked with bits of fish and prawns. The waiter flames it with brandy at the table and leaves us a bottle of an Indian hot sauce, Capsico, for seasoning the dish to taste. Yummy and unusual, it reminds us of a cross between a Manhattan clam chowder and a Charleston she-crab soup. The pomfret, rich and slightly oily, impresses us even more. "Remember the first time we had Prudhomme's own blackened redfish at K-Paul's?" Bill asks. "This expertly grilled version arouses the same sense of epiphany."

The curry is just as tasty, Cheryl insists. "The coconut flavor is subtly complex and it's fiery in an earthier way than Thai curries." The naan served with the fish flaunts the brawny chewiness of a proper pizza crust and comes with melted garlic butter, a combo good enough for a full meal in itself.

Under a dark night sky, the streets are deserted, except for a few wandering cows and goats, when we return to our hotel. Along the way, the taxi passes a sprawling residence sporting a sign saying Tourist Home. "What would that be?" Cheryl asks.

"Maybe," Bill says, "it's where old tourists like us move when we're too stuffed to get around on our own any longer. Should we ask the driver to stop?"

> >

The clear skies in the morning bode well for our most anticipated day in India, when we'll be spending much of our waking and all of our sleeping hours on a houseboat on Vembanad Lake. A driver is scheduled to pick us up after a leisurely hotel breakfast, which starts again with juice and fruit, followed today by a dosa and *idly*. Both local specialties rely on the same batter, traditionally made from a mixture of lentils, rice, and water allowed to ferment overnight. Cooked much like a pancake, the dosa comes off a big griddle thin and circular, whereas an idly is steamed in a mold to form domed patties of a few inches in diameter. Our waiter, Viju, brings us sambar and coconut chutney to eat with each, and asks, "What kind of Indian food do you find in the United States?"

"Almost all of it," Bill answers, "is northern Indian."

"Do you think Americans would like idly?"

"I definitely like it," Cheryl says.

"Maybe I will move to the United States and open idly restaurants, so I can get rich."

On the drive from Kochi, traffic thins out once our car clears the city limits, but even on the divided highway, a few tuk-tuks and motorbikes risk traveling for reasons of their own on the wrong side of the road. Lots of the people we pass are making coir, and others haul the finished product to markets stacked high on carts powered by three-wheel rickshaws. Elephants work in construction projects along the route; in one case, an elephant is clearing huge loads of palm fronds from a site. The long leaves stick out both sides of his trunk, making him look like a big grounded butterfly. Eventually, the driver turns off the highway onto a potholed dirt track that rambles three miles through thick vegetation to a clearing on the lakefront signposted Spice Coast Cruises, our CGH Earth home for the next twenty-four hours.

Vembanad Lake rests at the heart of the Kerala backwaters, a system of rivers, lagoons, lakes, and canals that covers much of the state. Vembanad alone extends sixty-five miles in length and broadens up to five miles wide at points. Of the thirty-eight rivers in the entire network, four major ones feed the lake and other smaller tributaries also connect into it. From the shores, you can navigate a thousand miles of natural and man-made canals. Villages and secluded farmhouses line the waterways, which have provided economical transportation for people and goods for centuries. An ancient lifestyle thrives along the banks, changed little by the recent arrival of scattered hotels and the conversion of old rice barges, or Kettuvalloms, into houseboats for visitors.

The receptionist leads us into a small office to register and pay the basic part of the bill. "If you want prawns, wine, or beer with your dinner," he says, "there is a supplemental charge the captain collects at the end of the voyage." He escorts us down a jungle path to the lake, where our boat sits at the end of a dock.

"Oh, my God!" Cheryl yelps in joy on seeing the stately craft. Bill tries to whistle his appreciation but releases more air than sound. About sixty feet long, the wood-and-rattan houseboat sweeps gracefully out of the water on both ends to open decks. A canopy of split bamboo covers the central guest space, featuring a lounging and dining salon, a small bathroom, and a comfortable bedroom with a king-size bed. Winged awnings rise rakishly along the sides, bringing in breezes and sunlight, and offering broad views to the outside.

Our three-man crew joins us on the dock and the receptionist introduces us to the captain, Sadasivum; the steward and engineer, Varghese; and a culinary-institute-trained chef, Rajesh Khanna, all dressed in cotton sarongs that can be tied up to shorts length or unfolded down to the ankles. "They sleep," our host explains, "on the open platform at the stern, by the galley kitchen, leaving you the rest of the boat at night. Each of them speaks some English, but only the cook is moderately fluent."

"We'll get by fine," Cheryl says confidently.

Pushing out of the shallow water with bamboo poles, the crew punts us toward the center of the lake, where the captain turns on the quiet engine. He sits at the point of the bow, navigating by memory rather than charts, and we stretch out behind him on the forward deck on pillows and padded mats, enjoying the sun and the serene setting. A few other boats putter by, mainly small fishing craft and less attractive (to us) houseboats, some containing two bedrooms. After an hour or so of cruising, Sadasivum pulls into a small cove for a lunch break, and we step back to the dining table in the covered salon.

Saying, "I always make lots of food in case you don't like everything," the chef brings out a local feast of seven dishes, mostly vegetable and grain preparations except for a spice-crusted seer topped with green chile, Bill's favorite among the array of choices. Cheryl prefers the sliced long beans simmered with garlic, turmeric powder, black mustard, black pepper, and chunks of toasted coconut. "Is the tanginess from tamarind?" she asks Rajesh Khanna.

"No, it comes from a native fruit called *cocuu.*"

Both of us also enjoy a red onion pickle dusted with black pepper, two vegetable mixtures, a *thoren* and an *aviyal,* and fresh pineapple for dessert. The food attracts a swarm of flies, but they disappear as soon as we're under way again.

After lunch, the captain guides us off the lake into a series of canals, some broad, others narrow, and we settle into lounge chairs in the salon to watch the languid world float by. A few people bathe in the channels, but many more work in rice fields along the banks, apparently using fertilizers that fuel a proliferation of water hyacinths, a pretty but noxious weed. Herons, ducks, and other water fowl greatly outnumber the human residents. Spreading her arms wide and smiling, Cheryl says, "I feel like Cleopatra sailing the Nile on my private barge."

In midafternoon, Sadasivum hands over the helm duties to Varghese and motions for us to follow him to the back. The captain leads us to the kitchen, where he grabs a stone mortar and pestle from a shelf, along with a number of fresh ingredients. Sitting cross-legged on the floor, he grinds grated coconut together with turmeric root, sprinkling in water when needed, then adds garlic, cumin seeds, and red chile, continuing to work the mixture until the puree is smoother than a blender version. "He's showing off," Rajesh Khanna tells us, "letting you know he's as good a cook as me, which he is. By the way, do you want prawns with dinner?"

"Yes, please," Bill replies, "and a bottle of wine, too."

An hour later, Cheryl returns to the galley, intrigued by the smell of toasting coconut. The chef has split open two extra-large prawns, almost the size of lobsters, and is coating them with a spice rub. Finishing that, he starts sandwiching cheese curd—like paneer cheese before it's drained and firmed—into rounds of bitter gourd. "These," he says, "will be deep-fried. In northern India, some meals include lots of fried items, but not in Kerala. We don't do more than one or two at a time to maintain a balance between different tastes. They also use more dairy products, like the cheese, than we do."

Just before sunset, the captain anchors for the night in a calm lagoon bristling with majestic palms on nearby shores. The chef delivers our wine, the same Grover Vineyards blend we enjoyed in Mumbai at the Taj Mahal, and starts laying out dinner. The prawns shine and so do most of the many other dishes, including local versions of two salads more commonly associated with Thai cooking, one based on green papaya and the other on banana blossoms. Rajesh Khanna chunks the papaya, parboils the fruit, and then dresses it with a mixture of heated coconut oil and spices to serve at room temperature. It comes out tasting like a wonderful summer squash. With the banana blossoms, he cuts them smaller than you see in Thailand, and whips them together with Sadasivum's hand-ground spice paste, cumin, freshly grated coconut, and lentils.

The stars of the table tonight, for our palates, are a chicken and fish duo. The chef massages the poultry parts over and under the skin with what he calls "chicken masala," a blend in which we can clearly pick out the tang of red chile powder, black pepper, coconut vinegar, garlic, and turmeric. He fries the parts deftly, producing a result that would shame many good Southern American cooks. The fish is a freshwater pearl spot—"My favorite from the backwaters," he tells us—that he rubs with spices, wraps in a banana leaf, and cooks on a griddle. "There's that sour tang again, like at lunch," Cheryl says. She asks Rajesh Khanna, "Is it cocuu this time, too?"

"Yes. You take the pulp out of the fruit, discarding the seeds, and dry it in the sun about a week, which turns it very dark. Then you hang it inside a fireplace to dry further and acquire a slight smoky flavor. I'll bring you some of the paste to sample by itself."

On tasting the paste, Cheryl calls it "Agreeably odd, like tamarind with lime and a hint of smoke."

A mosquito net hangs over our bed, but we don't really need it to keep away insects, which are not a problem at our anchorage. Another couple spending the night somewhere else in a houseboat complained bitterly to us the next day that mosquitoes practically devoured them. They could only escape the pests under the netting on their bed, where they had dinner and read. Apparently, not all captains are equally experienced in picking overnight stops.

Roosters on the shore wake us at daybreak, when the only things moving in the lagoon are several small fishing boats. The crew is already up, quietly preparing to take off. Back in the canals, people brush their teeth in the water in front of tidy stucco bungalows painted in pastel shades. All families have at least one dugout canoe, obviously the main form of transportation, and some demark their yards with fences of sticks or neat green hedges. A handmade sign on a log post in one channel declares in English, "A hearty welcome to backwater tourists in Snop Canal."

The famous spices of Kerala, as well as tea, grow at higher elevations in the distant hills, far from sight. The chef brews some of the local tea for breakfast, and serves it along with coffee, fruit, toast, and tropical jam. He steams some starchy plantainlike bananas, but we also eat finger-size cousins just out of the peel. When he arrives with a platter of eggs scrambled with tomatoes, onions, and bits of fresh green chile, he says, "Onions and tomatoes are not traditional ingredients for us. We've only used them for a few decades now."

Just before lunch, the crew drops us back on Vembanad Lake at Coconut Lagoon, another pretty CGH Earth inn. The trio of boatmen has treated us great and we part with warm farewells, but the new place looks fascinating, too. It's laid out like a local village, with cottages and larger two-story residences spread across twenty-two acres, everything connected by footpaths and mini-canals. While staff members whisk our luggage off the houseboat to our Heritage Bungalow room, a receptionist guides us over to the open-air lobby, where a flute player sitting cross-legged on the floor pipes us in. The manager who registers us provides a brief tour as he escorts us to our cottage, pointing out the library, restaurant, bar, and gift shop.

The large room offers a covered terrace by the front door, a pitched ceiling, red tile floors with coir mats, a king-size bed, and air-conditioning, a convenience we never missed on the breezy Kettuvallom. The best feature is a walled outdoor-garden bathroom with a palm tree in the center, a wide-open shower in one corner, and vines dangling everywhere. More than just an enticing courtyard, it turns out to be a terrific spot for washing and drying laundry, a big plus for us.

Lunch looms as soon as we're settled in, and the Kerala feasting continues in high gear for the rest of our two-night stay. Shortly after our arrival at the restaurant, the chef, Raju, comes to our table and says, "I've heard about your interest in our food. The manager of Brunton Boatyard called to let me know, and the cook on your houseboat stopped by, too, just a little while ago. Most Westerners want to avoid our dishes, afraid they're too spicy or weird."

The latter point strikes us as an exaggeration, but we see ample proof of it shortly in two different situations. In the first instance, a large American YPO (Young Presidents' Organization) group with name tags comes to the breakfast buffet and sticks strictly to boxed cereal, omelets, and white-bread toast; a single member of the troupe tries a dosa, and everyone else looks at him like he's scaling Mt. Everest. Why would they come this far across the globe to get together in a place where the cuisine repels them?

Another time, a regularly scheduled cooking demo somehow attracts a bunch of guests uninterested in food. They whine rudely throughout the presentation about all the spices used, causing Cheryl to uncharacteristically lose her cool and tell one of the bitchers, a fellow American, "They can probably make you some pabulum, lady, if that's more to your taste."

Regarding our lunch, Raju makes an offer we would never refuse. "If you will allow me, I would like to send out some extra samples of my local cooking."

"Certainly," Cheryl says excitedly, and he does this again at dinner as well. Over the two meals, the kitchen gives us tastes of four pickles, almost a dozen vegetable preparations, and, for comparison purposes, the same kind of bread made in both northern and southern styles. The pickles include a mango version enlivened with green chile and mustard seeds, but also more unusual takes on the idea, such as a mouth-puckering gooseberry variation and a scrumptious chunky beet rendition. Among the other dishes, the most appealing to us are a sambar with a bold turmeric and cumin taste; a cubed pumpkin with banana, dried garum beans, fried curry leaves, fresh coconut, and dried red chile; a beet and yogurt combo (*pachadi*) with black mustard seeds so fresh and pungent they taste like horseradish; a tamarind-accented chopped cabbage thoren dotted with more of the seeds and curry leaves; and a knockout ginger-tamarind chutney.

The buffets at breakfast and dinner provide many additional local choices. The curries run the gamut of possibilities, from a meatless sweet-sour green mango version to a "dry" chicken adaptation in which the poultry is fried in coconut oil with curry seasonings until little liquid remains. Chutneys come in tamarind-date, tomato, and coconut–red chile flavors, and desserts vary from a luscious coconut mousse made from young, semijellied coconut, to a less satisfying sweet custard of lentils and cumin. The morning spread features a made-to-order dosa station, where you can request fillings such as *ghee* (clarified butter) with black pepper, and the evening spread includes a naan cooking extravaganza, in which a staff member forms flat rounds of bread about the size of an old LP album, slaps them onto the inside wall of a blazing-hot clay tandoor oven, and removes them moments later with a poker.

At the end of our second dinner, Cheryl reflects on the food. "It's amazing that the same basic set of ingredients can yield so many different flavors and textures. Coconut in all forms, black mustard seeds, pepper, ginger, garlic, turmeric, chiles, and coriander, in one combination or another, produce incredible bounty."

"Yeah," Bill says, "and each is a bit player rather than a star, part of an ensemble rather than a show-stealer, like basil can be in Thai cooking."

"But, Bill, this is the closest relative to Thai food in the world, with similar seasoning elements, complexity, and robust flavor."

"Then why are Kerala cooks so happy and eager to share tastes with foreign visitors, without any compromises, and Thais so reluctant to do that? It doesn't make sense to me."

Between meals, we occupy much of our time with the swimming pool and long walks, unlike most guests, who mainly go on boat excursions in the backwaters and visit the hotel's Ayurveda center for massages or holistic health treatments. Our walks end up twice at Coconut Lagoon's butterfly garden, where dozens of varieties flutter by regularly, including, the signs say, Blue Tigers, Monkey Puzzles, Restricted Demons, Crimson Roses, and Chocolate Pansies.

On an escorted stroll, a sprightly staff naturalist named Munoj Junior—"Just call me 'Junior' "—takes us and two Scandinavians to the village of Kumarakom, just beyond some rice fields across from the inn. One dirt path runs through the community, right along the shore. Most residents get around in canoes, but we pass some on foot, a few on motorbikes, and about twenty kids crammed into and hanging outside a Jeep, the local school bus. Although the village is quite poor by Western standards, it shows no signs of desperation, squalor, or the crushing poverty of urban areas. The land and the water provide sustenance, and widespread education in Kerala produces a high literacy rate. As Junior puts it, "They have almost no money but are rich in family, culture, and religion. They live simply and happily."

The children learn English in school and always greet us with a big "Hello!" and an odd request for "One pen?" Junior isn't clear why they want pens, but the repetition of the plea makes us wish we had a box of them to pass out. One little girl, maybe four, picks a hibiscus blossom and gives it to Bill. Cheryl snaps a photo of the two and the flower, then gets her mother and brother, standing nearby, to join them for a family shot with Bill. He searches his pockets for anything to offer the girl and finds nothing except small change, which he hands her hesitantly, unsure whether it's a good idea. The news apparently spreads quickly because suddenly every kid in town has a flower for Bill.

Our departure from Coconut Lagoon and India involves most forms of transportation known to our species. A boat takes us from the hotel several miles to a river jetty, where a driver and car are waiting to haul us to the Kochi airport, where we catch a Jet Airways flight back to Mumbai, where a bus picks us up at the domestic airport to transfer us to the international field. Staggering finally into the latter after dark, we face a four-hour wait in an uncomfortable sitting area before our midnight flight to Hong Kong via Bangkok.

Indian ingenuity intervenes to save us from that fate. A young man in a suit comes up to us and asks, "Would you like to buy a pass to a first-class lounge with free food and drinks? I can sell you two for one thousand rupees," about U.S. $25.

A little suspicious, Bill says, "Show us." The man leads us past several lounges operated by major carriers to one that serves a bunch of smaller airlines. A concession operation, no doubt, owned by local entrepreneurs, it's virtually empty now, so the employees are taking the initiative to bring in paying customers. The notion sounds good to us, so we shell out and enjoy the filling food and cheering wine. It's a fitting finish to our visit, another oasis in the crowded, bustling nation, like the Taj Mahal in Mumbai and almost the whole state of Kerala. From India, of all places, we leave relaxed and rested. That's less important to us than feeling so well feted and fed, but it is certainly a blessing in the middle of our long journey.

THE NITTY-GRITTY

TAJ MAHAL PALACE & TOWER
www.tajhotels.com
Apollo Bunder, Mumbai
91-22-6665-3366
fax 91-22-6665-0323
For pleasure travelers, the extra expense of staying in the Palace Wing pays off. Look broadly for good deals, which are usually available.

BRUNTON BOATYARD
www.cghearth.com
Calvetty Road, Kochi
91-484-221-5461   fax 91-484-221-5562
A gem.

MALABAR JUNCTION
in the Malabar House hotel
Parade Road, Kochi
91-484-221-6666
breakfast, lunch, and dinner

CASINO HOTEL
www.cghearth.com
Willingdon Island, Kochi
91-484-266-8221
fax 91-484-266-8001
Not as good a location for pleasure travelers as the Brunton Boatyard, but its Fort Cochin restaurant is the best in the area.

SPICE COAST CRUISES
www.cghearth.com
Puthenangadi Jetty, Kottayam
(no phone or fax)
Highly recommended.

COCONUT LAGOON
www.cghearth.com
Kumarakom
91-481-252-4491
Serene retreat with good local food.

Fish Molee

When fresh curry leaves aren't available, we use a handful of cilantro leaves.
The flavor's not the same, but the herbal freshness is similar.

SERVES 6

¼ cup coconut oil

2 teaspoons black mustard seeds

1½ cups chopped red onion

1 cup diced red-ripe tomato

2 plump garlic cloves, minced

2 teaspoons minced fresh ginger

1 or 2 serrano chiles, split lengthwise and seeds removed (mince part or all of 1 chile for a spicier sauce)

1 teaspoon salt, or more to taste

½ teaspoon ground turmeric

½ teaspoon freshly ground black pepper

1½ to 1¾ pounds cod or haddock fillets, cut into 2-inch-wide sections

1 cup coconut milk

½ cup fish stock, clam juice, or water

10 to 12 fresh curry leaves, or a handful of fresh cilantro leaves

Lime wedges

Warm the coconut oil over medium heat in a large, deep skillet. As soon as the oil is fragrant, stir in the mustard seeds, and as soon as they begin to crackle and pop, stir in the onion. Once the onion has become limp, after about 2 minutes, stir in one-half of the tomato; add the garlic, ginger, chile, salt, turmeric, and black pepper. Fry, stirring up frequently, until the tomato has softened and begun to break down, about 5 additional minutes. Push the onion mixture to one side of the skillet and add the fish in a single layer. With a spatula, scrape up enough of the onion mixture to smear over the tops of the pieces of fish. Pour the coconut milk and stock around and over the fish; then scatter the curry leaves over everything. Cover and simmer

3 minutes; uncover and give the skillet a swirl, rather than stirring the mixture, which could break up the fish. Cook a few minutes more, uncovered, if needed to cook the fish through. The sauce will be fairly thin. Spoon into soup plates, garnish with the remaining tomato and lime wedges, and serve.

"DO YOU THINK WE OUGHT TO TAKE ALONG THE EXTRA bar of soap in the bathroom?" Cheryl asks as we're packing to leave India for Hong Kong.

"What for?"

"For the YMCA, of course. Do you think the rooms have soap?"

"Cheryl, we're booked into an executive suite, not a dormitory. No one in Hong Kong makes executives walk around the city stinky."

"I don't know about this," she says, going to the bathroom to grab the soap just in case.

On our one previous trip to Hong Kong, twenty years earlier, we stayed at the Excelsior Hotel, an upscale establishment that offered rooms with great views of the harbor and the city, including planes cruising by at eye level to land at the old downtown airport. No concerns about soap there. Now our Cathay Pacific flight goes into the mammoth but sleekly efficient new airport, far out of the city but a quick trip in on an effortless express train to the Kowloon station, where we grab a taxi. Cheryl carefully watches the reaction of the lady driver when Bill gives her our destination, hoping for a clue of one kind or another about the Y, but the woman doesn't look back at us or change expressions.

The lobby provides a mixed preview. Large, colorful paintings by children hang on two walls, cheerful in their welcome but definitely not luxe hotel art.

The café in one nook is a self-service, fast-food operation. No comfortable lounging quarters, concierge desk, Versace shop, or, of course, bar. But the reception desk brims with smiling young men and women smartly dressed in business attire. One of them registers us and gives us card keys for a room on the top, sixteenth, floor.

Bill unlocks the door and ushers Cheryl into a plainly furnished sitting area reminiscent of a Ramada. The sofa and matching upholstered chair look comfortable, at least, and there are little amenities like a TV, coffee maker, minibar, and fruit basket. Cheryl wanders to the other end of the parlor, opens the drapes covering floor-to-ceiling windows, and says, gasping, "God Almighty! Look at this." The view bowls us over, encompassing a vast sweep of the harbor and, beyond the water, the high-rise towers of Hong Kong Island and Victoria Peak. By the next day, we can even pick out the Excelsior Hotel in the panorama, where the view that stunned us before wasn't nearly this grand.

The wall of windows continues into the spacious bedroom, curving gently in an arc around to the far side of the corner suite, giving us in all about four hundred square feet of vista wrapping around the king-size bed. An IMAX screen pales in comparison. Next door, the opulent Peninsula Hotel, visible in full, rises above us, helping to inspire the Y's advertising boast that "The Neighborhood Could Not Be Better."

"Look at those puny windows," Bill says, pointing to the classy edifice, "and how much farther back they are from the water. The cheapest room over there with just a peephole view costs about three times what we're paying, and the penthouse, which seems to have the only comparable sights to ours, runs U.S.$5,000 per night."

"Be right back," Cheryl declares on her way to the bathroom. She returns momentarily with a wrapped bar of soap in each hand. "Not just one, but two. I think we'll be able to make do."

> >

Hong Kong doesn't excite us in advance as much as most of our stops. None of our memories of the city put us off, but as a fast-moving contemporary metropolis, it's less fresh and novel to us than other places. It probably wouldn't have made the itinerary at all except for being the best Asian transit spot to our next two destinations, the Chinese mainland city of Chaozhou, where we will visit friends, and Cape Town, South Africa. India is closer than Hong Kong to Cape Town, of course, but there aren't any ONEworld airline flights between them, the reason we're zigzagging east to west and back again going from Bangkok to Mumbai to Hong Kong.

Only two activities really interest us in Hong Kong: walking the streets, as much a priority here as in New York or London, and eating good Chinese food. After admiring our view for most of an hour, we go outside and head north on Nathan Road, the Kowloon Peninsula's main thoroughfare, sometimes called in tourism talk "the Golden Mile." The fancy shops don't entice us because our focus—other than stretching our legs and looking around—concerns practical needs: some extra microcassette tapes for our recorder, over-the-counter Excedrin migraine pills for Cheryl, and a computer center where we can burn our digital photos onto a CD for a backup copy. It seems as if all three should be available along the crowded commercial strip, but we find only the tapes.

Our walk takes us up to the Temple Street Night Market, where vendors are just beginning to set up for the evening. Most of the merchandise here wouldn't appeal to us, but the food stalls would. Not knowing when they'll open, though, we decide to catch a cab back toward the harbor for dinner at City Chiu Chow, which looked good earlier in the afternoon on a quick inspection. It promises a foretaste of the cooking of Chaozhou, which the Cantonese call Chiu Chow. The regional style is well known and respected in China but is much less commonly found in the United States than its Cantonese, Szechuan, and Hunan cousins.

A giant, one-story, free-standing image of a crab—covered with long, silky hairs that camouflage it in patches of seaweed—serves as a sign for the restaurant, as smaller drawings of crabs also do in Chaozhou. Shellfish and fish of all kinds are specialties of the cuisine, often served with zippy sauces. Other favorites include goose, frequently flavored with a garlic and vinegar sauce, duck, and shark's fin and bird's nest preparations. Chefs pride themselves on a variety of vegetable dishes, from deep-fried greens to sweetened taro, and also on elaborate vegetable carvings, which are used to decorate tables. Diners usually start and end a meal with an exceptionally strong oolong tea nicknamed "kung fu" and "Iron Buddha" because of its ferocious caffeine kick.

The waiter brings us tiny cups of the tea as soon as the hostess seats us. One large room, lively with conversation and laughter, the restaurant teems with businesspeople grabbing a meal between work and home. The menu doesn't prove terribly helpful to us, with just a few English descriptions of dishes and a smattering of photos, and none of the staff seems able or willing to speak English. By pointing to names and pictures, we manage to order deep-fried crab and shrimp rolls, a disappointment, and a "sizzling" freshwater yellow croaker that sounds like it would be fried but is actually poached in a light and delicate broth with toppings of Chinese chives, Chinese cabbage, fresh bamboo shoots, and bits of mushrooms. Our waiter demonstrates putting some of the fish in a small bowl with broth and a bit of chile oil, and then shows us a Chaozhou method of eating rice, pouring broth over it to make a soupy mixture to scoop up with a spoon. The standout dish of the evening, one of our favorite simple preparations of the whole trip, is wok-charred green beans cooked with bits of minced pork and black olives from China. "I'm going to make this when we get home," Cheryl says. "It's superb."

The stroll back to the hotel takes us along the promenade that fronts the harbor, where hundreds of people have gathered to watch the nightly Symphony of Lights, which the *Guinness Book of Records* lists as the world's "Largest Permanent Light and Sound Show." Thirty-three of the most prominent buildings on both sides of the harbor project a dazzling array of beams into the sky, carefully choreographed in a sequence of patterns converging into a blazing crescendo. After we watch it for about five minutes from the waterside, Bill grabs Cheryl's arm and says, "Let's get upstairs to our room as quickly as we can." Seen from our bank of windows, the spectacle sets the heavens aglow like a dancing rainbow.

Our walk the next day covers a bigger area, all of it on Hong Kong Island. The famous Star Ferry hauls us across the harbor to the Central District, the financial and governmental heart of the city. Architects come from around the world to see some of the contemporary skyscrapers—such as I. M. Pei's Bank of China Tower and Sir Norman Foster's Hong Kong and Shanghai Banking Corporation's structure—but we only glance at these briefly on our way to the historic and traditional Chinese warren of small streets called the Western District.

Our route along Des Voeux Road Central leads us to several pedestrian lanes, barely larger than alleys, packed with market stalls selling clothing, handbags, costume jewelry, and trinkets of all kinds. Deeper into the neighborhood, the businesses get more exotic, selling "chops," or personalized, carved stamps for documents or possessions, intricate bamboo birdcages, death money for the afterlife, antique snuff bottles, and an incredible range of food and medicinal items, including ginseng, preserved sea slugs, dried fish bladders, twigs, seeds, powdered horns of different animals, and live snakes (favored in a warming winter soup and in a rheumatism cure, where the patient swallows the gallbladder in a glass of Chinese wine).

Some of the same edibles—but not the snakes—show up in two major food markets, one in the enclosed Sheung Wan complex and the other outdoors around Graham and Gage streets. The first requires a strong stomach, particularly in the downstairs fish and poultry section, where the Chinese desire for freshness results in some on-the-spot butchering and cooking. The breadth of produce on the upper floor makes us stagger: perhaps all of the two hundred varieties of Chinese brassicas (cabbages, broccolis, etc.), tofu of a thousand nuances, eggplants of every color and size, grapes almost as big as golf balls, mountains of bean sprouts, and pyramids of eggs, oranges, and tangerines.

The street market features a similar range of vegetables and fruits, plus flowers—orchids, peonies, proteas, roses, daisies, mums, and more—tanks of fish and seafood to take home live, sausages, hand-size knobs of ginger, lotus seeds, gingko nuts, fresh water chestnuts in their dark brown husks, and, as a thoughtful accessory, lots of rolls of toilet paper.

In the same vicinity, Hong Kong has sprouted its own SoHo ("south of Hollywood" in this case) around the Mid-Levels Escalator, which carries residents between the Central District and the homes and apartments on the slopes of Victoria Peak. The trendy area abounds with international restaurants and watering holes with names such as El Taco Loco, Nepal, Pepperoni's, Phuket Thai, Archie B's New York Deli, and the Rendezvous French Café and Creperie.

Our taste buds yearn instead for dim sum. Interrupting our walk temporarily for lunch, we hop a taxi to the Wan Chai neighborhood, no longer the raunchy nightlife quarter of Suzie Wong and Vietnam War R&R. Two of our favorite food authorities, Nina Simonds and R. W. Apple, Jr., have both raved in print about Victoria Seafood in the Citic Tower, where the dim sum is made to order rather than prepared in batches to be carted around for diners to select. While this method is preferable for flavor, it taxes us more in this case because we come up short again on English-language help from the menu and staff. As a Chinese cooking expert, Simonds wouldn't have needed any assistance, and Apple arrived, most likely, announced as a writer for the *New York Times*. Our entrance, in contrast, suggests we're clueless tourists gone astray, because the restaurant isn't on the way to anywhere except perhaps a diving expedition in the nearby harbor.

The problem is compounded by the empty tables nearby, preventing us from falling back on the often reliable technique of pointing to indicate "I'll have what she's got." In spite of the constraints, lunch turns out great, lacking only in our imagination of other treats available to the cognoscenti. Hairy crab dumplings top the lineup. The waiter brings the plump, juicy little purses in a steamer but then spoons them into small bowls to eat with a vinegar-soy dipping sauce. Two types of shrimp dumplings follow, one with a chubby pink shrimp glistening visibly through the sheer, pleated wrapper, and the other with tiny shrimp, greens, and Chinese chives in rice-paper rolls. The baked barbecued pork dumplings, next on the card, completely outshine the more common steamed pork buns offered on dim sum carts the world over. "This has to be lard pastry," Cheryl says about the flaky crust holding the scrumptious meat. Sweet egg-custard tarts, just a single, ethereal bite each, provide a divine finish with a pot of jasmine tea.

"Good thing the cooks knew more about what we wanted than we did," Bill says.

Unlike City Chiu Chow last night and the dim sum spot at lunch, our dinner restaurant, Hutong, deals with English-speaking tourists regularly. A strikingly handsome space, it gleams in the dim light from sleek ebony furniture, old Chinese objects displayed as contemporary art, and celadon-glazed porcelain tableware. Many people probably come for the view, similar to ours at the Y except a couple of blocks more distant and twice as many stories high. "From here," Cheryl says, "the boats on the harbor look like bathtub toys."

The food, on the other hand, is huge in flavor. Cheryl orders radish-wrapped crab rolls for an appetizer, which the kitchen prepares by cutting a daikonlike white radish lengthwise into paper-thin strips and wrapping them around Alaskan crabmeat and black sesame seeds—an elegant idea with a tasty result, as is

Bill's salad of raw scallops sliced finely and topped with pomelo, a grapefruit relative, pulled into its tiny individual sacs, a delicate combination served with a robust house-made chile paste.

The main-course presentations practically knock us off our ebony chairs. The waiter delivers our crispy lamb ribs on a section of banana leaf over a long wooden plank. The cooks have boned out each rib individually and reassembled them side by side like a rack. Every bite mingles the crusty surface meat with melting fat and succulent rare lamb, enhanced beautifully with a sweet soy sauce. If that has us leaning back in our seats in appreciation, the fried baby soft-shell crabs kick the legs out from under us. They show up perched dramatically atop at least one hundred stir-fried dried red Szechuan chiles (the "looking to-ward heaven" variety) in a round, dark bamboo container an arm's length in di-ameter. Neither of us can remember at first how to close our gaping mouths, but the reflex comes back with the initial taste of the luscious morsels coated in rice flour and ground red chile. On the side we get another stellar version of long beans, this time cut in two-inch pieces and stir-fried with garlic, ginger, bits of fresh red chile, minced pork, and dried shrimp.

"I can't imagine we'll have a finer or more artfully staged feast in China," Cheryl says sensibly but ultimately in error.

Our flight to mainland China the next morning concerns us a little, for rea-sons of check-in rigmarole rather than safety. Everything goes quickly and pro-fessionally, though, on China Southern Airlines, leaving us plenty of time for breakfast in a fast-food court. Hoping for dim sum, we discover an irresistible anomaly and wind up with Louisiana red beans and rice, southern fried chicken, and biscuits at a Popeye's, a chain based in New Orleans. Not bad at all for air-port fare this far from the roots.

On the way to the gate for our nonstop hop to Shantou, the airport city closest to Chaozhou, we wander through the mall-like shopping arcade, heavy on inter-national designer names with cookie-cutter purses and perfumes. There's even a Ferrari exhibition with a doll-size replica of a red Testarossa, where Flat Stanley poses as the driver for a photo op. When we're finally seated in the departure lounge, Cheryl looks around at the surrounding group of Chinese passengers. "No one else is wearing these goofy tags they gave us at the check-in desk," a round stick-on label for our shirts with the airline logo and flight number. "I guess in their eyes we're like unaccompanied minors, at risk of getting lost."

"Probably so," Bill says. "They don't realize we've put Stanley at the wheel."

> >

Where else in the world would a city of three million people not qualify for an airport of its own? And, for that matter, remain unknown to most of humankind? In China, numerous other cities simply outrank Chaozhou in population, political clout, industrial strength, and international contacts and recognition. That's basically why the local Communist Party wants us to go on TV.

Bill's college friend, John Oliver; his wife, Patty; and a ramrod straight Chinese gentleman with a seriously squared-off flattop meet us at the Shantou airport, an efficient if plain facility. John introduces their companion as Ziggy, explaining that it's their nickname for him based on the local Chinese dialect word for "driver," a respected title in Chaozhou. "Ziggy won't say much, but he knows English moderately well. He learned it during a long stint in the PLA"—Chinese People's Liberation Army—"in circumstances he doesn't discuss with us. The car is ours, but we don't dare drive it ourselves, because if one of us got in an accident, all the blame would be put on us and the penalties would be harsh."

A modern divided highway runs between the airport and Chaozhou, about forty minutes away when traffic flows smoothly. Cars, trucks, and motorbikes crowd the road these days—a development, Patty says, of the last decade. "There used to be protected lanes for bikes and motor scooters, but with the rapid expansion in the number of cars, they got taken over for parking spaces." Driving is something of a free-for-all, but no crazier than in Rome. Ziggy handles the job confidently and often aggressively, sometimes more so than the Olivers prefer.

Within an hour, he reaches the historic center of the city and turns down a narrow alley, barely one car wide, to get to John and Patty's residence and principal offices for their Calabash pottery business. They own multiple units in a seven-story building formerly occupied by the Chaozhou Chamber of Commerce. The Olivers take us first to their home, two apartments combined into one spacious and comfortable abode, and then call their marketing office downstairs to ask a couple of their key employees to come meet us. Two young women, both initially shy, show up shortly. "This is Simin," John says, nodding toward a perky lady in her early twenties, "and the one with the big smile is Vicky," who is a decade or more older. "Remember the e-mail I sent you about doing a little interview for our local TV station about your cookbooks and your visit to Chaozhou? That was Vicky's idea, and she is acting as a liaison on it. Is it still okay with you?"

"Sure," Cheryl says, "we do short TV spots all the time in the States."

"It'll be fun to see the setup here," Bill adds.

"What's the status of that now?" Patty asks Vicky.

"The producer is still trying to figure out exactly what he wants to do and when. I'll phone him again this afternoon."

When she and Simin return to their jobs, John tells us, "We helped to teach them English, and both of them handle it pretty well now. Vicky has a connection at our single TV station, operated under the auspices of the Communist Party, because she works part-time for the Chamber of Commerce, also tied into the Party power structure."

"Let me show you our kitchen," Patty says, "and then we'll take you up to the guest apartment." She has good reason to be proud of the light-filled space, probably one of the largest and most modern kitchens in the city. The Olivers enjoy cooking themselves but also have a cook, "Aunty Jane," who takes care of much of the marketing and meal preparation.

"Notice," John says, "we don't have an oven, because no one uses them in China. We do have a rice cooker, of course, like everyone else, and a dish sanitizer, because the water doesn't get hot enough to kill all bacteria."

Patty walks over to a small refrigerator. "This is our most unusual appliance. It doesn't hold much by American standards, but the whole idea of storing food at home is new here. Typically, families buy just what they'll eat at one meal."

"Let's head upstairs," John suggests. "This building, like many others, is seven stories because higher structures must have elevators. You're staying on the top floor so you won't need to worry about extra exercise." The Olivers bought the two-bedroom apartment several years ago in part for guest use and also for the access it provides to a large rooftop terrace. Patty decorated the flat in an attractively simple Chinese style and has placed orchids in the living room and fragrant tuberose in the thankfully air-conditioned bedroom. Water for showers, as John demonstrates for us, is heated on demand by igniting a gas burner before turning on the faucet. The windows on one side overlook a sprawling old family compound, once widespread in the neighborhood, where several generations lived in different quarters but shared a single kitchen and bathroom. A few centuries of weather have faded the terra-cotta roof tiles almost white.

"Farther out," John says, "you can see a slice of the mighty Han River and a part of the walls that encircled the ancient city, which dates back to the first century BC. It's been officially designated a 'Famous and Historic Cultural City.' We get lots of Chinese tourists, but few visitors from other countries."

"Chaozhou has long been known for porcelain and other ceramics," Patty adds, "because the area is full of good kaolin clay. That's why we built the factory here for our Calabash pottery. Would you like to visit the plant this afternoon?"

"Let us freshen up," Cheryl replies, "and we'll be ready to roll."

Ziggy drives the four of us, and Simin follows on her motor scooter to act as an interpreter. As soon as we arrive, Ziggy jumps into a routine that becomes common over the next few days, immediately brewing and serving Iron Buddha tea to the group as a ceremonial welcoming gesture. Calabash makes mostly landscaping ceramics, both slip-cast and jiggered pieces. Many of them are flower and plant pots of various sizes and styles, glazed and unglazed, designed to specification for American clients such as Lowe's and Kmart's Martha Stewart Enterprises line. In showing us some examples, John says, "Martha's buyers ordered these for the next season. No photos, sketches, or descriptions of any kind are allowed until they reach stores in the spring of 2006."

Parts of the production process are automated, but much of the tooling is still done by hand, often by couples working together, with the man handling the heavier labor and the wife doing the trimming. Lacking piped natural gas, the Olivers truck in huge tanks of propane to fuel their two kilns, one configured for specialized situations and the other a large, fully mechanized device that moves pottery through different temperatures over a nine-hour period.

"Many Chaozhou factories," Patty tells us, "house migrant workers in dormitories at the plant, but that violates good labor practices so we don't do it. We do feed our employees, however. I'll show you the kitchen." As immaculate as the rest of the operation, it features industrial-dimension woks, about three feet in diameter, and a rice cooker the size of a bathroom Jacuzzi. The company chefs, who prepare two meals a day for eighty people, are currently stir-frying chicken with loads of garlic and red chile over leaping flames.

"That looks tasty," Bill said.

"Want to come back for lunch on Monday?" John asks.

"It's a date," Cheryl answers, unaware yet that all of us will be eating elsewhere.

"Speaking of food, let's go see a Chinese version of a megastore," Patty says. "When Wal-Mart started opening outlets in China several years ago, they inspired local clones, like our Fu-Mart." She decides to ride with Simin on the back of the motor scooter, against John's objections, and the rest of us pile into the car with Ziggy.

On the way there, John tells us, "Locals dismissed this place at first because they're used to shopping on a day-to-day basis in small quantities. Then they came in on particularly hot days to take advantage of the air-conditioning, still rare in the city. They liked the constant music the store plays and also the discounted specials. Now it's busy all the time."

Several stories high, Fu-Mart stocks a range of goods, from auto parts to mattresses, but the grocery section is enormous. Patty guides us up a moving ramp walkway connecting floors, lined on both sides with bins bulging with bags of potato chips for impulse buying. Upstairs, a wall of packaged teas extends at least seventy-five feet and large baskets nearby hold twenty-five varieties of loose floral and herbal tea leaves. Banks of tanks display live fish and seafood, and rows of tables parade fresh produce of all kinds, including shiitake mushrooms for forty cents a pound and porcinis for even less. An aisle of soy sauces offers the various kinds in gas-can-size containers, and the shelves of MSG boast a hoard of the seasoning sufficient to supply every Chinese buffet restaurant in the United States for a year. In-store bakers make Western breads and pastries, previously rare in Chaozhou; Simin admits to liking some of the cookies, but even the baguettes and doughnuts look decent. The wine department carries both Chinese and French selections, the latter in locked cases. Prepared take-home food ranges from chicken feet to whole medicinal chickens (cooked with healing herbs) and dim sum to potsticker dumplings. Some things entice us more than others, but we definitely leave with an appetite.

In the store, Cheryl mentions to Patty and Simin that we looked without luck all over Hong Kong for someone to burn our trip photos onto a CD. Simin says, "Oh, I can do that. It will just take a few minutes before we go to dinner." The pictures intrigue her when she loads them into her computer and she requests permission to make copies for herself, too, so she can dream about traveling someday to all the places we have visited. "Who is the little guy in these shots?" she asks about Flat Stanley. Cheryl introduces the two and they become instant friends, posing together—and with the rest of the Calabash office staff—for their own photos.

The Olivers have planned dinner at an upscale establishment they call "the Door Man's Restaurant," a nickname derived from the owner's skill in making handsome carved doors. "It's right on Chaozhou's version of Tiananmen Square, built as a new city center for government offices just five years ago," John says. "Since then, the whole town has shifted in that direction. The old center, where we live, will be historically restored and made into a pedestrian-only zone."

Simin's parents—introduced to us only as Mr. and Mrs. Wu—join our entourage at the restaurant. When John and Patty first moved to Chaozhou, they rented rooms in the Wus' home, where they began teaching Simin English when she was just twelve. Mr. Wu is a highly regarded sculptor, currently working on a piece commissioned by a Chinese peace organization to present to President George W. Bush on an upcoming visit.

The Wus and the Olivers order for the table, just discussing the possibilities with the waiter rather than studying a menu. In halting English, Mr. Wu says, "The Chinese always try to get balance in a meal between the yin and yang, so we talk it through."

Patty mentions that Chinese restaurants dominate the dining scene. "So far, there are no Western places at all. Occasionally, you see a menu offering a 'Western dinner,' usually something odd like Salisbury steak over spaghetti."

The dishes tonight, roughly in order of service, include a warm soup; steamed vegetable dumplings; turnip cake similar to the carrot cake we had in Singapore; oyster omelet; stir-fried leafy greens; stewed sweet potatoes; and tender strips of beef with green and red bell pepper, tofu, and shiitake mushrooms. Dessert combines crisp apple slices and tiny tomatoes. John complains that the kitchen is off-key this evening and the Wus agree. Mr. Wu comments he can tell from the texture that the dumplings were refrigerated before cooking, clear evidence of a deficiency in freshness. When Cheryl compliments the turnip cake, Mrs. Wu says, "You will like mine better. I'll send some over to you with Simin." No one objects to the price: U.S. $20 total for eight people with tea and Chinese wine.

After dinner, we walk over to the huge square across the street, where hundreds of people are watching the Saturday-night entertainment. A group from the Chaozhou opera company performs in one corner, and in another, fountains on a pond splash towering columns of water skyward, forming a screen for projected scenes from the movie *Finding Nemo*. Neon lights outline the mid-rise buildings surrounding the square and some feature additional neon images, one an elaborate rendition of a pagoda and bird. Grinning children and teenagers rush up to practice their English on us, repeating after one another "Hello," "Welcome to China," and "Good-bye." A number of them and their families gather around Cheryl for photos with a blue-eyed blonde, like she's from Mars or maybe even Hollywood.

On the way back, Ziggy drives us through a night market jammed with stalls specializing in clothes, and then down another lane lined with new upscale boutiques that John and Patty have dubbed "Hong Kong Street." Near their home, John points out the Friendship Store. "When we moved here, that run-down place was the only department store the Party would authorize in town. Now there are modern, 'bourgeois' shops everywhere." Ziggy has to stop twice in the alley leading to the Olivers' apartment building to get other residents to move their motor scooters so he can get by. Old and new, traditional and trendy, Communist and entrepreneurial, Chaozhou flaunts it all at once.

> >

Vicky calls John on Sunday morning about TV taping plans. "The producer would like to take Cheryl and Bill, with the two of you, me, and a video crew, on a one- or two-hour tour this afternoon of historic Chaozhou, where they will film the Jamisons' reactions. He wants to know if they would be willing to sample street food from some of the most popular stands." John frowns at the last part, but poses the question to Bill while Vicky holds.

"Sure," Bill replies. "When we've got reliable local guides, we'll try anything edible once."

John relays the information and works out a time and place to meet Vicky and the producer. After hanging up, he says, "You're braver than us. We've always been curious about the street food but have never had the guts—pardon the pun—to eat any."

Patty proposes that we walk to the nearby Kaiyuan Temple, Chaozhou's main attraction for Chinese tourists. As we leave the apartment building, she points out across the alley a small barbershop and a house where a woman sews sequins and beads on wedding gowns and evening wear. John spots an older gentleman outside his home and introduces him to us as a tailor. He's obviously fond of John in more than a neighborly way, and invites us to come into his studio, where he replicates costumes of the Peking Opera and makes elaborate ornamental pieces such as fans and headdresses. He picks items for each of us to model for photos and takes care to pose John in a properly theatrical manner.

On the main street of the area, Patty shows us a curbside stand that specializes in medicinal herb drinks for motor-scooter riders, who pull up, place their order, chug it down, and putter off again. The business reminds John about a time when Mrs. Wu came down with a back ailment, in the period when they lived with the couple. "Her doctor made regular house calls on his motorbike. He always brought a live snake in a basket, killed it on the spot, and made a potion from it. The back problem went away. Just the thought of that drink would cure me."

The twelve-hundred-year-old temple, one of the oldest in Guangdong province, is beautifully serene, despite its location in a bustling area, and artfully adorned with elaborate wood carvings and lovingly sculpted images of the Buddha. More people, mainly adults today, want photos of themselves with Cheryl, not even usually bothering to pose with the striking architecture or landscaping in the shot. Before we leave the grounds, Patty gives each of us coins to pass along to the beggars outside the gates, many of whom suffer from severe physical deformities.

Vicky joins us at a vegetarian restaurant across from the temple, one of a breed that attempts to make its dishes look like meat and fish preparations. "The idea," Patty says, "is for vegetarians to be able to enjoy their food without any sense of deprivation." To further that illusion, we get tofu in two principal forms, as pretend pieces of calamari, beef, and bacon on a kebab, and as faux fish fillets topped with greens and carrots, both reminding Cheryl of the similar "mock chicken legs" served in her junior-high cafeteria. A crispy potato bowl plays the role of a bird's nest in a more earnest and effective performance. The cooks don't disguise mushrooms, presented in two tasty preparations, or the stir-fried rice-flour noodles with bits of fresh and pickled vegetables, a good foil for the house's red chile paste laced with Szechuan peppercorns and fermented black beans. As is the custom, rice arrives as the final course after other dishes are done.

During lunch, Vicky fills us in on the TV station and program we're appearing on. "In English the station name is Chaozhou Broadcast, or CZB. The program name translates as 'Eating Is Everything.' Almost everyone in the city watches it because it comes on three nights a week right after the evening news on the only station we get. I guess I'm going to be your translator because they don't have any English-speaking staff. I've never done that before on TV so I'm nervous."

"You'll do great," John assures her.

The producer, Mr. Lin, shows up with cameramen, a quiet young lady who turns out to be the show's hostess, and a team of bicycle rickshaws or pedicabs. Two to a carriage, we head out into traffic with as much safety protection as a troupe of naked Rollerbladers. The first stop, less than a mile away, is a stand known for spring rolls. The family proprietors are offering two versions today, one filled with mushroom and baconlike pork, the other with beans and herbs. They make the wrappers fresh at the stall, add the stuffings, and fry them in large woks. Light and crispy, the spring rolls trump any of the lunch dishes, but we would have cooed for the cameras in any case. "If you can't act better than tofu," Bill says, "you should stay away from TV."

From there, Lin leads us across the street to a cart with giant steam cookers. The vendor-chef is pouring a soupy rice-flour batter into tiny teacups placed in appropriate-size holes on the lid of the steamers. The batter firms in a few minutes; then the cook tops it with chopped, sautéed turnip, making it a nice two-nibble tidbit. As we sample the treat, the crew tells us through Vicky that these are popular after-school snacks for children, and a growing band of waist-high kids nods vigorously in agreement. The vendor also sells a loose-textured link sausage of rice, pork intestines, other pork, and seasonings, which he simmers first and then finishes in a wok. It looks and tastes much like a Louisiana boudin.

By this point, the TV action has attracted quite a crowd, with the children swarming in as close as possible and the adults hanging around the fringes. Traffic on the street has slowed to a crawl—luckily for the drivers of a motor scooter and a car who run into each other while craning their necks to see what is going on.

This seems to be our cue to move ahead. The producer hops into the lead pedicab, and the rest of us climb into others to head down to the section of city wall along the broad Han River. The crew films us admiring the ancient main gate into Chaozhou, and just across from it, the reconstruction site for the Guangji Bridge, originally built—some say by a supernatural being—during the Song dynasty as a floating bridge supported by boats, which made it one of the earliest bridges in the world capable of opening and closing for big river craft. The restored version will have stationary supports at both ends, but twenty-four boats serving as pontoons through the center. Lin signals us, in what becomes a continuous refrain, "Just one more hour."

A half-mile walk along the river promenade takes us to another historic temple, one that did double duty as a lighthouse for night navigation. As the group gathers to leave here, we learn that all the pedicabs have disappeared because their shift ended during our sightseeing. The producer summons their replacements on his cell phone and soon new bicycle rickshaws appear, racing each other down the street to get first dibs on the stranded customers.

The winning drivers pedal us less furiously to Fu Ron Chuan, a street-side snack shop more than one hundred years old. Vicky tells us it's famous for spring rolls, dumplings, and moon cakes, and stays busy at all hours. After samples of several goodies, Lin invites everyone to join him in an upstairs dining room for tea and a meeting. The producer indicates he has talked with the station's director and given him a good report on the day. Together, he says, they decided that if we could give them one more hour of time, they would like us to come to the studio the next morning to make one American dish and watch their show chef prepare one Chinese dish. Then the hostess, now introduced as Miss Cheung, would do a short, formal interview. Sounds fine to us.

Patty says, "Let's do something relaxing. I know just the thing, a head massage."

"What on earth is that?" Bill asks.

"Come see."

Vicky backs off after an afternoon of translating, an exhausting job, but Simin joins us again. Ziggy, apparently used to going all kinds of places, drives us to a slick, contemporary hair salon. The five of us sit down side by side, and different masseuses deal with each of us simultaneously, shampooing our hair thoroughly while massaging our scalps, necks, shoulders, and arms for about forty-five minutes. Patty encourages the two of us to get a trim, too, if we want, and since both of us are getting shaggy, we do. It's easily the least likely spot where either of us has ever had a haircut.

"There's more in the neighborhood for Cheryl and Simin," Patty says. "The boys can wait with Ziggy." She takes the ladies down the street to a shop called Happy 2000, her favorite girly tchotchke store, loaded with Hello Kitty, Mickey Mouse, and Winnie the Pooh toys plus an international array of makeup products, accessories, and hair doodads.

Cheryl tells the guys, "Most of the merchandise is cutesy, sweet, and plain fun. Our granddaughters would love it."

Back at the Olivers' home, the two of us wash our laundry in a machine—a Little Swan—for the first time on the trip, and hang it out to dry on the balcony like everyone does in the neighborhood. John fries Mrs. Wu's turnip cake for a light supper, getting it extra crispy as she instructed. It comes out luscious, crusty on the surface and as creamy inside as a good gratin. While he plates the treat, we discuss a dish for us to demonstrate at the TV station. "We've got to keep the ingredients and kitchen tool requirements simple," Cheryl says. "Most American TV stations are poorly equipped for cooking demos, and who knows what we'll run into here." One or another of us brings up gumbo, crab cakes, Texas chili, succotash, and apple pie, but all seem to present possible problems.

Finally, Patty suggests southwestern salsa. "They can easily get the ingredients, you won't need much more than a knife, and you can show it served both as a dip and as a sauce for a steamed fish."

"Good idea," Cheryl says. "That's perfect."

The next morning, Vicky calls John early. "Last night the TV chef came up with a different plan for the show. Now the producer wants us to gather at the Shengle Hotel, that fancy businessmen's and dignitaries' hotel between

Chaozhou and Shantou." None of us knows any more than that before we arrive. On the way, Vicky tells us about the "Eating Is Everything" star, Chef Fang Shu Guang. "He's the most respected authority anywhere on our local cooking, famous in Chaozhou and Hong Kong, too. He has a very popular and expensive restaurant, with a name that translates in English as 'Tasty and Happy.'"

Two Mr. Lins greet us in the hotel lobby, the second the head of the TV station. Vicky proudly admits her name is Lin as well. The male Lins usher us into the employee-only inner recesses of the hotel to a corridor leading to the kitchen. Inside, three dozen cooks look up briefly at our group as we enter, and then return their rapt attention to Chef Fang, presiding over an enormous prep table. The producer introduces all of us to the Emeril of Chaozhou, causing Vicky to get as flushed as a schoolgirl meeting Bobby Flay. Through her, Fang tells us, "Since you have come from halfway around the world to enjoy Chaozhou food, I'm going to prepare you a proper banquet." He then presents the hotel's executive chef, Su Pei Ming, who has brought in his entire staff to help in the effort and learn from the master.

Fang says he has looked at a map of the United States and knows that New Mexico is a large state. "How many people live there?"

"Less than the population of Chaozhou," Bill says.

When Vicky translates this, everyone in the room acts astonished. She pauses herself, thinking about the facts, and asks with wonder, "So you can have a very big house?"

While one of the assistant cooks brings Fang a live slipper lobster—a clawless but sizable langouste—for his next dish, we take a lingering look around the immaculate kitchen. The only obvious things that would rile an American health inspector are trays and bowls of some prep ingredients sitting on the clean floor and the wood cutting boards, all round cross-cut sections of giant trees, usually about six inches thick. A couple of sous-chefs are intently carving squashes, making methodical, intricate cuts into the surface with the tiniest of knives. They fasten two pieces of their vegetable sculpture together, one on top of the other, to form a two-foot-high golden dragon destined for the center of the banquet table. Another squash, the size of a Halloween pumpkin, is being hollowed out to make a soup tureen. The carver selected it for its delicate shades of green, yellow, and pale orange, which he uses in incising images of birds in flight to highlight their graceful shapes and movements.

Fang holds the scrambling lobster firmly and splits it down the center, removing the meat meticulously by hand so that the shell can be reassembled. He picks up a handful of ginger and scallions and squeezes them forcefully to drip the juices on the meat, which he then sprinkles with a little rice wine. He allows the lobster to marinate briefly in this mixture before draining and cubing it to make wrapperless dumplings. After topping each neat cube with a sliver of ham and a perfect cilantro leaf arranged to look like a flower on a stem, the chef swathes the pretty packages in lacy-thin pork caul fat, a prized fat from the abdominal cavity that will nearly melt away during the steaming process. "Damn," Bill whispers to Cheryl, "that makes our salsa seem ridiculous."

Next, Fang squirms his right hand into a large, pastel spiraled shell, wrestling out a foot-long live whelk. He gives it a quick bath in a rice-wine marinade and tucks it back into its former home, placing the shell over the fire of a small charcoal brazier to roast slowly for two hours. At this point, the action and cameras switch across the table to Chef Su, who is cutting into a whole fish flopping around on the counter. It looks like the pomfret we saw in India, but no one knows the name of the fish in English. Su slices the meaty white flesh into plump rectangles, lays the pieces on a platter, and adds between each slivers of dark forest mushrooms, lard, ginger, and Yunnan ham, similar in smoke and salt flavor to an American country ham. He puts the platter into a large steamer to cook, later restoring the fish's head, tail, and top fins to the serving plate at mealtime so that it looks whole again.

Fang draws our attention to cooks working on shark's fin soup. "One of them," he says through Vicky, "got here hours ago, in the middle of the night, to start the broth," which contains at least chicken feet, pork, beef, scallion, and ginger from what we can gather. Neither of us would order the soup in a restaurant—because of the brutal way the fins are harvested from live sharks—but we won't refuse it in this situation because the Chinese regard it as a delicacy to give to honored guests. The cooks eventually remove the long-simmered fin from the broth, pull it into hundreds of gelatinous bits, and serve it in bowls topped with cilantro and black vinegar. It tastes like a meaty version of bean-thread noodles.

Moving into a more instructional mode, Fang shows us and the assembled chefs how to slice and cross-hatch squid steaks to make them resemble a ginger flower when steamed. He does it a dozen times, but the technique sails over our heads. Explaining that a garlic-vinegar sauce goes with the squid blossoms, he demonstrates how he wants the garlic sliced into tiny bits rather than mashed, and passes around tastes of it in vinegar treated both ways to illustrate the subtle difference. Grabbing a couple of tail-on shrimp, he talks next about cutting them to achieve the desired presentation effect. If you want them to curl up, he indicates, slice them down the top side; but if you would prefer them to lie flat, as he does today, cut them lengthwise on the bottom side. "I never knew that," shrimp-whiz Cheryl admits.

The cooks eventually flavor the shrimp with ginger and fry them in batter to go around the base of the dragon centerpiece along with two kinds of fried balls, one of fish and the other combining shrimp and pork. As the banquet time approaches, four hours after our arrival at the hotel, Fang extracts the whelk from its shell, slices it paper-thin with his cleaver, lays it out in a fan pattern, and glazes it with oil. He adds carved vegetables to the plate plus a section of the shell that shows the beautiful spiral pattern.

The producer escorts Patty, John, Vicky, and us upstairs to a private banquet hall and seats us at the larger of two round tables. The Olivers ogle the china, claiming it's some of the finest from the area. Chefs Fang and Su join us, and everyone else takes a chair at the other table, where our leftovers go when we've had our fill of the fifteen or so dishes. The servers bring us Iron Buddha tea first, to sip with stir-fried peanuts with a crackling sugar glaze and tangy, spicy pickles of cabbage and other greens with black olives. Then comes a Chaozhou specialty we didn't see in the kitchen, goose braised in black vinegar, soy sauce, garlic, cinnamon, star anise, and ginger. The skin-on slices taste overly fatty to us, but the vinegar makes a superb foil for the rich meat and the aromatics in the braising sauce have fully permeated the goose.

Our favorites among the dishes are the flowery squid, the simple lobster dumplings, and the fish with the ham and mushrooms. Both the lobster and the fish have absorbed a surprising amount of their gentle seasonings without losing any of their own delicate character. Steamed, vividly green baby bok choy decorate the fish platter, and the intact lobster shell, along with a garnish of orchid sprays, sits beside the dumplings. Cheryl says, "I swear the lobster antennae are still wiggling." A halo of deep-fried morning glory leaves surround the pristine white squid, now topped with fried garlic as well as the garlic vinegar, making it a garlic lover's dream.

The whelk is also tasty, but both of us have trouble holding the large, slick slices with our chopsticks and decide that restraint is the better part of valor in this case to avoid making a mess. An oyster omelet, cleverly arranged to display the yin and yang signs, arrives near the end, moist and creamy with just a touch of crispness on the edges. It's good enough for a full meal, but we can't manage more than a few bites each. Bill sums up our feelings when he tells Fang, "This is one of the most incredible experiences of my whole life."

It's our turn to perform, however, and the salsa idea, so brilliant last night, now looks like a recipe for cultural disaster. To offer it as any kind of counterpart to the Chinese feast seems totally insulting, so we start trying to weasel our way out of it, saying there isn't enough time to do both the demo and a formal interview, the more critical element to them. After all, what was planned as a short morning appearance has already taken us into the middle of the afternoon, leaving us scant hours with our friends before our departure early the next day. The producer pleads, "One more hour," even though he knows the taping would take longer. John and Patty come to our rescue, promising that they will come back to the station another day and prepare an entire American Thanksgiving dinner for them. The compromise satisfies everyone, and the TV crew starts setting up for the interview.

The producer seats us and Vicky at a round table with Miss Cheung and a gentleman in a suit who does nothing except serve us Iron Buddha tea. Demure to the point of silence up to this point, Cheung suddenly shows a confident, assertive charm, reminding Cheryl of Katie Couric. While her sidekick constantly refreshes our tea, and Vicky scrambles successfully to handle the back-and-forth translation of everything, the interviewer probes our responses to Chaozhou and its food more deeply than we expected. She questions us as if we're representatives of the Western world, seeking acknowledgment from us that Chaozhou deserves global recognition as a special city. The TV station's interest in us clearly revolves around this desire for outside approval of the widespread hometown pride. As enthusiastically as possible, we give them what they want, which is easy to do because we feel genuine gratitude about their generosity and goodwill.

Who knows what the viewers think we said. After our return home from the trip, Patty and John get us a video of the show, which has us talking in English with Chinese subtitles rather than Vicky's oral, on-the-spot translation. The Olivers report that the station promoted the program extensively for two weeks before airing it, often with shots of the four of us together, making them local celebrities for a while. Neighbors and strangers on the streets greeted them regularly with the Chinese phrase for "Eating Is Everything."

Whether Chaozhou itself is truly exceptional—and a good case can be made for that—certainly our experience of the city is. The whole visit, however brief, fascinates us completely with different and unexpected pleasures, from the wonderful people we meet to the offbeat things we do. The banquet alone ranks as the most extraordinary treat of our whole three-month trip because of the combination of watching the preparation, relishing the food, and sharing it all with friends. It's such fortuitous good fortune that makes travel one of the most marvelous and meaningful joys of life.

THE NITTY-GRITTY

The Salisbury YMCA
www.ymcahk.org.hk
41 Salisbury Road,
Kowloon, Hong Kong
852-2268-7888 fax 852-2739-9315

City Chiu Chow
98 Granville Road,
Kowloon, Hong Kong
852-2723-6226
lunch and dinner

Victoria Seafood
Fifth Floor, Citic Tower
1 Tim Mei Avenue,
Central, Hong Kong
852-2877-2211
lunch (dim sum) and dinner

◧ HUTONG
www.aqua.com.hk
Twenty-eighth Floor
One Peking Road,
Kowloon, Hong Kong
852-3428-8342
lunch and dinner

◧ SHENGLE HOTEL
www.shenglehotel.com
North Hengli Road, Chao'an
86-768-6669338   fax 86-768-6617567

◧ CHAOZHOU BROADCAST
www.czbtv.com
Chaozhou

Wok-Charred Long Beans with Black Olives

SERVES 6

1½ pounds fresh long beans or other green beans, tipped and tailed,
    and cut into 2-inch lengths

3   tablespoons vegetable oil

4   ounces ground pork

1½ tablespoons minced garlic

1½ tablespoons minced fresh ginger

1   fresh, small, hot red chile, seeded and minced, or 1 teaspoon dried
    hot red chile flakes

¼   cup plus 2 tablespoons salted chicken stock

2   tablespoons Chinese black vinegar or balsamic vinegar

1   tablespoon soy sauce

½   cup halved, pitted dry-cured black olives

Blanch the beans: Bring a large saucepan of water to a boil, immerse the green beans, and boil them for 1 to 1½ minutes. Pour off the water and then plunge the beans into a bowl of ice water to set the bright green color. Drain when cool.

Heat a wok or large heavy skillet over high heat. When hot enough to evaporate a bead of water, swirl the oil around in the wok. Add the pork and fry it, breaking it into tiny bits. When all the pork has lost its raw color, stir in the garlic, ginger, and chile, and keep stirring for 1 minute. Add the green beans and stir-fry for several minutes until just tender. Pour in the stock, vinegar, and soy sauce, and toss the beans until the liquid is mostly evaporated. If the beans are not yet fully tender, add a little water or additional stock, cover them, and reduce the heat to medium. Uncover again after several minutes, and if liquid is left, return the heat to high and toss the beans until they are nearly dry. Mix in the olives and heat through very briefly. Turn out onto a platter and serve hot or at room temperature.

EIGHT OF US, ALL THE GUESTS AT THE TREE TOPS Lodge, pile into the safari-modified Land Rover, open on the top with rising levels of backseats to assure everyone a good view of the terrain and wildlife. The young ranger Juan MacDonald, in his early twenties, takes the wheel and Bill sits next to him in the front. Juan barely gets beyond the lodge grounds when his radio crackles with news about the lion family. The male, female, and two nine-month-old cubs are nearby, resting in a shaded thicket.

Juan soon leaves the dirt tracks that serve as roads at the Lalibela Game Reserve, and drives carefully through the brush upwind of the lions to avoid startling them. On the way, he tells us, "Remember to keep silent and don't stand up or move around much. The wildlife views the Rover as a single, nonthreatening animal, but hearing voices or seeing movement can make them curious in an undesirable way. The worst thing is for anyone to get out of the Rover, because that signals it isn't one individual animal. In this case, the lioness still feels especially protective of her young cubs and will for several months longer. We've got to be wary of her."

Bill says, "The male didn't seem nervous or threatening yesterday. He was just lying lazily on that hilltop gazing into the distance and yawning occasionally."

Juan wrestles with the steering wheel to avoid a bush before responding.

"The lioness is much more dangerous. She's the hunter of the family, even though she lets the male eat her kill before taking a turn herself. Lalibela released a new male lion just this week, and no one knows yet where he's hanging out. At some point before long he will probably try to kill the cubs, because that puts the mother in heat again, and then the males will fight for dominance and the right to mate with the lioness."

A vivid image of that ritual jolts Cheryl, who read a magazine article a couple of days earlier describing the mating routine. The author reported that the sexual carousing lasts about five days at intervals as frequent as every fifteen minutes. When she showed the story to Bill, he said, "That would give you and me both a headache pretty quickly."

Juan pulls into the thicket, stopping about twenty yards from the family. The male reclines peacefully by himself under a tree and the mother sits between her cubs a few feet from each, all of them facing away from us but certainly aware of our presence. After we watch them for five minutes or so, Juan backs out and tells us, "I'm going to move to the other side to get better views. We'll be looking directly at the lioness, who will always give us clues if she's getting irritated. Watch to see if she lays back her ears, grunts softly, or flicks her tail, ways she warns off bothersome animals before attacking. Usually lions aren't too interested in people unless they appear simple, helpless prey, like someone walking through the veldt alone."

Juan parks in a grassy area a little closer to the mother and cubs than we were before. She stares at us intently but stays still for a couple of minutes before suddenly whipping her tail into the air. Bill, ready to jump out of his skin, nudges Juan, who whispers to him, "One more flick and we're out of here." Right on cue, she does it again, and the ranger backs the Rover away slowly.

"Yikes," says Annette, the lady in an Irish couple. "That was edgy."

Anna, a jocular young Swedish woman—who, like all Swedes, speaks English well, along with some fifteen other languages—agrees quickly with a little laugh. "I'm going to have to wash my underwear tonight."

For the next half hour, Juan drives around in search of an African buffalo, sighted nearby recently. "They are mighty creatures," he says. "They even scare and sometimes kill lions. It takes at least two lions to down a mature buffalo." Bill spots the broad, arching horns of a buffalo deep in the brush, too distant to see clearly. In trying to find a better perspective, Juan encounters a group of giraffes grazing on treetops. Juan points to one of them. "Look at the scratches on his hindquarters. A lion tried to jump him from behind, but the giraffe kicked him away. Antelopes, zebras, and other animals like to hang around giraffes because their height gives them an advantage in spotting approaching predators early."

Ranger Darrell, a good friend of Juan's, calls on the radio at this point to relay that the lion family has moved into open grassland. Juan takes off in that direction slowly. "We want to give him time to clear out of the area before we go in. Two Rovers at once might make the lions nervous. Darrell and I grew up together as local farmboys, learning with each other how to hunt and how to track animals by their spoor and the freshness of their dung. We know every inch of this land." The latter seems a slight exaggeration when we cross paths with Darrell as he's leaving the lions' roost and we're heading in. Darrell plops his Rover into a big pothole, causing Juan to snicker and say, "I'll give you some driving lessons later today."

So begins the longest fifteen minutes of our lives. Juan pulls up about the same distance as before from the lioness and cubs, who are spread farther apart from one another this time. The mother glares at us, stands up slowly, and takes a few steps toward us, settling down again when she's clearly closer to us than we are to either of her cubs. The unexpected advance rattles everyone except maybe Juan. No one utters a sound, but at least sixteen eyes grow to the size of saucers.

After giving her a minute to relax again, Juan puts the Rover in reverse and starts making an arc through the tall grass around the lioness and cubs toward the more tranquil king of the jungle, slouching around in the rear of the pride as if he's waiting for his wife to bring home dinner and a six-pack. She watches us keenly every foot of the way, never even blinking, it seems. When Juan is around to her right side, ninety degrees from where we were and only several yards more distant, he hits a deep hole hidden in the grass that brings us to an abrupt halt. Normally when something like this happens—we get marooned in mud another day—the passengers hop out and help push if necessary. Not a good idea just now.

Juan kicks the Rover into its most powerful four-wheel-drive gear and rocks the vehicle back and forth aggressively, but we're dead stuck. Again, everyone remains silent, with at least two of us thinking about Juan's earlier offhand comment about "helpless prey." The ranger loads the rifle that's always secured to the dashboard and rests it in his arms pointed toward the lioness, who has craned her neck around to maintain the fixed stare. He then quietly calls Darrell on the radio to ask him to come tow us out of the jam, puts the rifle in firing position, and takes aim at the huntress, who, he tells us later, would reach us if she wanted to in about two seconds, time for one quick shot. The five-minute wait for the arrival of the other Rover seems longer than the process it took to produce the two cubs.

Darrell positions his vehicle, full of other alarmed guests, directly in front of ours, supposedly conveying an image of a single, extra-large benign creature. All four lions watch us now, wondering no doubt, What the hell? Darrell loads his rifle and directs it at the lioness, after which Juan climbs out of the doorless driver's seat—leaving Bill openly exposed to a bounding leap—and connects a tow rope between the Rovers. He gets behind the wheel again, relieves Darrell from the sharpshooter role, and his buddy floors the accelerator, bouncing us out of our black hole. The lions, never moving, keep looking as the tandem Rovers return to the road and disappear out of sight.

When we're safely away, Juan and Darrell stop to disconnect the tow line. "About those driving lessons," Darrell quips, "I think I better teach the class."

In the first words any of our group has spoken in some time, Anna the Swede says, "Now I'm just going to have to throw these panties away. And they used to be so sexy."

> >

The rest of our three-day safari is less traumatic on everyone's nerves and underwear. It starts for us with an early lunch in the Cape Town airport before our noon flight to Port Elizabeth. The terminal's featured eatery is Spur Steak Ranches, a member of a local chain that boasts about being "the official restaurant of the South African family." A caricature of an American Indian chief serves as the logo, cowhide cushions line the booths, and a neon saguaro cactus flashes green in a corner. The menu offers burgers, steaks, and Buffalo wings as well as our choices, fish and chips and calamari and chips. Sitting on the table, handy for splashing on anything, are bottled sauces, including two barbecue versions (original and spicy) and another labeled "Salad and French Fry Dressing." The serviceable food sustains us until dinner, and Bill actually enjoys his lime milk shake.

At the Port Elizabeth airport, a driver meets us in the baggage area to take us to Lalibela, about one hour northeast. As he maneuvers through the oceanfront city toward the highway, he points out different residential neighborhoods, some affluent, others "shack towns," as he calls them, where people still have no electricity or running water. He praises Nelson Mandela's initiative in building modern homes for the poor, and says the national government has constructed a million and a half houses in just over a decade since the country's first real democratic election in 1994.

"What other South African languages do you speak besides English?" Bill asks.

"There are eleven official languages, you know. I also speak Afrikaans, the local variation on Dutch, and my native tribal tongue, Xhosa, which is full of wonderful click-clack sounds." He rattles off a few sentences in Xhosa to illustrate his point, producing tones that range from something like an English "tsk-tsk" to a booming pop reminiscent of a cork pulled from a bottle.

"I'm sure you are going to love Lalibela," he says. "But do you mind if I ask why you chose it for your safari? It's just a few years old and not well known."

"I'm the one who pushed the safari idea," Cheryl replies. "Bill agreed to do it if we could find a reserve easily reached from the Cape Town area that has the 'Big Five' game animals and reasonably affordable rates."

"Affordable is relative, of course," Bill says. "Many of these places pride themselves on grand European luxury and charge prices approaching U.S. $2,000 per night for a couple. Lalibela offers what seems to be a less snooty but similar safari experience for one-third to one-half the cost."

"We like the emphasis at Lalibela on African food and atmosphere," Cheryl adds. "Besides, I want to stay in a tree house."

The driver drops us at a check-in office just off the highway, where the staff loads us and our luggage into a Rover for the fifteen-minute ride to Tree Tops, one of four lodges scattered around the 18,500-acre private reserve. Cornelia Stroud, the lodge manager, greets us and introduces us to ranger Juan. "Normally, my husband, Mark, serves as the ranger for guests staying here, but he's away on family business and Juan is subbing for him. As you'll notice, raised boardwalks connect our dining-room-lounge area, the pool, and the four guest quarters, with all the structures elevated on platforms above the ground." Grabbing a handrail, Cornelia goes on, "Locals call this 'sneeze wood' because when you cut it, it gives off little fibers that make you sneeze. It's virtually indestructible."

Like the other accommodations, our spacious room is framed and floored in wood but contains a pitched thatched roof, zip open-and-shut canvas sides, a contemporary bathroom, and a covered viewing deck about twenty feet above the lush vegetation. Kilim rugs cover much of the floor, hand-printed African fabrics swathe the king-size bed, and carvings decorate the end tables and a storage chest. Conveniences include air-conditioning, heating (useful at night this spring), a phone, and, for dire emergencies, an air horn that would probably wake people as far away as Port Elizabeth. "At night," Cornelia tells us, "a ranger will walk you to your room, just in case you have any unexpected visitors."

Like most safari reserves, Lalibela includes two game drives a day in the price, along with all meals and drinks. Cornelia gives everyone a wake-up call at 5:30 in the morning; we gather for coffee, tea, muffins, fruit, yogurt, and cereal around 6:00; and Juan takes us out promptly at 6:30 for about three hours. On our return, the cooks lay out a prodigious brunch buffet, after which we're on our own during the heat of the day, when most guests laze around the pool, read in the central lounge or on their deck, or, in our case, do little maintenance chores like trying to stitch together our pants sufficiently so they will last another month. At British teatime, around 4:00, the lodgemates assemble again for tea, coffee, or wine and substantial snacks such as sausage rolls, lemon meringue pie, and on one occasion an excellent carrot-and-beet cake. The ranger loads us up in the Rover at 4:30 and we're off again until 8:00 or so, with only one sundowner stop for drinks along the way. When Juan delivers us home, another large buffet awaits, ensuring that everyone waddles to bed with their ranger escort as a fully stuffed prize treat for any predators in the area.

On our six game drives, we enjoy good sightings of four of the "Big Five" African animals—lions, buffalos, rhinos, and elephants—but never see any leopards, who Juan describes as "hide-and-seek artists," active mainly late at night. Once, Darrell gets the guests in our Rover excited by calling to report a "leopard in its shell." Juan knows his friend is teasing us, but takes us anyway to see a leopard tortoise, speckled like the namesake cat.

The buffalos are more elusive during our visit than usual, the rangers tell us, but we have one great encounter. As Juan drives us back to dinner one pitch-black night, Bill sits beside him scanning the brush with the ranger's powerful spotlight, looking for reflected glare from animal eyes. Suddenly, two small headlights gleam back at us from a buffalo standing near the road. Magnificently muscular, he looks as big as the Rover, a hulking black beauty with glorious upward-curling horns and flaring nostrils. Set one of these creatures loose in a bullring and the bullfighter would faint on his sword. Irish Annette laughs softly, whispering to us that she expected to see the curly-haired head of an American bison.

Bands of rhinos pop up regularly around the reserve, particularly the larger and more sociable white rhinos. "They aren't really much different in color than black rhinos," Juan says, "but these are the big boys, weighing in between two and three tons each at maturity. They had dwindled in population to around thirty-five at one point, due to hunting, but are coming back slowly. The females produce only a single calf every three or four years, probably because it's not much fun to give birth to a one-hundred-pound baby." Our group sees an infant once, wallowing playfully with his mother and other adults in a mud hole on a warm, sunny day.

Most of the elephants hang together in a herd that the rangers never find during our stay. "How can a bunch of elephants hide from experienced trackers?" Cheryl asks.

"They're clever," Juan replies. "There are young calves with them now, whom they want to keep out of sight from the big cats." Males tend to be more solitary than females, and we do come across two of them frequently, always alone. "These guys are really unpredictable," Juan says. "All of us fear them more than any other animal, because of their size, strength, and erratic behavior."

"Has an elephant ever injured any guests?" Bill asks.

"Yes, killed two as a matter of fact. A pair of women friends insisted on going off by themselves on walks, despite repeated warnings about it. They ended up a mess, I hear. Those are the only deaths we've had at Lalibela."

The two males are called Floppy and Gaadjie, the latter earning his Afrikaans tag from a hole in one ear. "The rangers rarely name animals because it breeds a familiarity that may make you less cautious around them," Juan says. "These boys are so distinctive, they've become exceptions." Around us, Floppy is the more aggressive of the pair. He ambles toward us once, getting too close for comfort, and another time he trumpets loudly and digs his tusks into the ground as if he's ready to charge us. "They are much faster than you think," Juan tells us. "And nothing stops a rushing elephant, even the high electrified fence around the property line. One male got his kicks by knocking over the fence. He wasn't trying to escape because he never wandered away. He just liked to attack it for fun."

In addition to the "Big Five," hundreds of other mammals, birds, reptiles, and amphibians roam around Lalibela. Just on the trip from the check-in desk to Tree Tops, before any of the game drives, we spot hippos resting in a pond, with just their bulbous eyes and the top of their heads protruding above the water. "They may weigh three or more tons," our driver says, "but they can outrun people. They also cause more human deaths than any other animal in Africa, because they're extremely territorial in rivers, frequently upending boats and canoes that cross their turf."

Zebras, warthogs, and many kinds of antelope graze all over the reserve, often darting off when a Rover approaches. Warthogs may look ferocious, with warts on their faces like those of a fairy-tale witch and tusks protruding from the side of their mouths, but they sprint swiftly on their toes in a hilariously dainty fashion, holding their tails straight up. The antelopes—including wildebeest, blesbok, eland, nyala, impala, kudu with beautiful spiraled horns, different duikers, and a number of species with names that end in "buck"—run with amazing elegance. One day our group witnesses a mother blesbok training her baby, leading him in a zigzag pattern across a meadow, with the youngster keeping up in pace and cornering. "They can reach pretty close to full speed," Juan says, "an hour after they're born."

Birds abound as well, from hawks to herons. The secretarybird delights us especially with his 747-landing style. Gliding toward the ground with his long wingspan extended, he comes in fast, touches down once, then scampers at a gradually slowing rate until he loses momentum and stops. The human-size ostriches are one of the gawkiest creatures on the reserve, perhaps helping to make them a dining favorite in the lions' den.

Tree Tops serves us ostrich once, too, as our Thanksgiving bird actually, though none of the staff knows about the American holiday. Each evening, the kitchen prepares two main dishes, one game and the other not. On this night, both disappoint, the only time that happens, with the ostrich undercooked and the lamb chops overcooked, resulting in tough meat in each case. It doesn't matter because the salads, vegetable side dishes, and desserts make a full meal in themselves, especially with the array of tasty condiments, including divine sweet-and-sour pickled figs, spicy chutneys, and fresh coconut. The brunches consistently please, providing choices of eggs in different styles, bacon, ham, and other meats such as venison sausage skewers with a chile sauce, sautéed mushrooms, baked tomatoes, fried potatoes, cheese, fruit, juices, jams, and breads.

Xhosa performers entertain us one night after dinner, demonstrating tribal dances (probably modified for show purposes), giving us a practice lesson in their drum rhythms, and trying to teach us to pronounce some of the click-clack sounds of their language. They stage the program by the blazing log fire pit, where the guests gather with wine before and after the evening buffet. All of us take photos of them, and then of the lodge cooks, a robust trio of local tribeswomen attired in flowing robes colored gold, mango, and purple, with head wraps to match and smiles as bright as the fabric.

The entertainment continues on our departure day from Lalibela on kulula .com, the discount airline with mostly online booking that we take between Port Elizabeth and Cape Town. The company flies vividly painted planes with lime-green leather seats and dresses their attendants in shirts the same hue as the chair cushions, which the crew wears over casual shorts and jeans. The Green Team, as they call themselves, points out the joy of reading the airline magazine, kulula .comic, and presents a safety demo as funny as it is thorough, grabbing the attention of every passenger. When the plane lands in Cape Town, one of the attendants gives us arrival instructions. "There are three no-nos inside the terminal: lighting up anything to smoke, cussing at the baggage handlers, and smirking smugly at people who arrived on South Africa Airways," the stodgier establishment competitor. In a rib on South Africa's reputation for crime, the speaker says, "If you are returning home from a grueling business trip and you parked at the airport, we sincerely hope your car is still where you left it."

> >

Crime is such a common problem in South Africa—the murder rate, for example, is twelve times higher per capita than in the United States—that residents joke about it to relieve the tension in the air. Along with poverty and high unemployment, it's largely a legacy of the harshly racist Apartheid policy that flourished in the last half of the twentieth century. Generations of blacks and "coloreds" (mixed-blood descendants of blacks, Europeans, and Asians) grew up in hovels in segregated townships with scant access to education, jobs, and basic liberties. The repression and total denial of opportunity bred bitter resentment, still widespread but ameliorating with time under a new government dedicated to racial equality and peaceful coexistence. In Cape Town, much of the hardship and violence is concentrated in the Cape Flats, a vast shantytown that visitors glimpse coming from and going to the airport.

Despite this and other areas of blight, Cape Town ranks near the top of any list of the most beautiful cities in the world. The mammoth profile of Table Mountain, often draped in a tablecloth of clouds, looms over the town center between the booming harbor and the striking beaches fronting the frigid Atlantic coast. Many tourists, including us, take the Explorer bus system around to the most attractive and interesting spots, hopping off to see various sights and then reboarding another bus later.

Our bus climbs the steep slope of Table Mountain slowly, providing grand vistas of the city and the hillside vegetation, including magnificent wild proteas, the exotic flower we've always associated with Hawaii. "At home," Cheryl says, "I pay $7 to $9 per stem for proteas, making this a million-dollar view." A midpoint cable car station offers access to the flat summit, but we bypass the chance for a nature hike in favor of strolling the shore along Camp's Bay Beach. Wide and deeply sandy, the beach brims with tanners and volleyball players, who have an arena with seating for their sport. Across the street, parked in front of small upscale shops and restaurants, a fast-food delivery car advertises "wheely good chicken" on the tires and on the sides, "perfect breasts, thighs, and legs for the beach."

Another stop on the tour casts a shadow over the pulchritude and playfulness. District Six, a large neighborhood on the fringes of downtown, stands almost completely in ruins. Once a poor but vibrant working-class area, home to thousands of Africans and coloreds, it slid into decline by the 1950s when the government and absentee landlords stopped investing much of anything in maintenance. The following decade, the Apartheid regime started a forced removal of the residents to the Cape Flats ghetto, declaring the neighborhood would be bulldozed and reserved for whites only in the future. The authorities displaced 65,000 to 70,000 people and demolished their homes, churches, and businesses, but the brutality of the relocation and destruction stirred up so much local and international furor that they never rebuilt District Six for whites. It remains a monumental scar in the center of Cape Town.

The District Six Museum documents the story with photos, physical artifacts, oral histories, musical recordings from the past, and more. Most poignant of all, it encourages former residents to serve as guides for visitors, recalling their memories of joy and suffering in the neighborhood. Joining a group of other travelers who arrived about the same time as us, we listen in wonder to an elderly gentleman as he relates tales of his home and family, and hear for the first time a recurring refrain: "We're not here to lay blame for mistakes of the past. We bear witness for the sake of humanity, not for the purpose of reprisal. All South Africans must move forward together into the future."

The Explorer bus trip drops us ultimately at the downtown tourism office, a good place to ask for directions to our choice for dinner, a restaurant known for good South African fare. Bill picks up a free city map and takes it up to the information desk to ask, "Are we in walking distance of Biesmiellah, the restaurant in the Bo-Kapp neighborhood?"

The woman looks back and forth at our white faces, the same shade as hers, and says, "Yes, theoretically at least. I don't know the exact location on the map, but I can show you the vicinity and street. Be aware you should not walk in Bo-Kapp, or downtown either, after dark, and you should not venture very far into Bo-Kapp even during the day. Also, you can't count on taxi transportation, especially coming back from the area. Cape Town has one of the lowest number of cabs per capita of any city in the world, something we're trying to correct. If you still want to go, do it early, planning to eat and leave by sunset."

Our walk to the restaurant takes us through the heart of the downtown shopping quarter, where we browse in African craft galleries, admiring in particular fanciful objects made out of scavenged materials such as telephone wire. The route continues into the thick of the vendor stalls on Greenmarket Square and across a busy boulevard onto Upper Wale Street, the location of Biesmiellah. The address at number 2 leads us to hope that the place might be near the intersection, but it's obvious within a block that it must be at the other end of the virtually deserted lane, which curves out of sight ahead before any sign of our destination. "I suspect it's safe to keep going, but we don't really know about that or how far the place is," Bill says.

Not usually one to emphasize caution, Cheryl balks as well. "The situation makes me nervous. I don't think it's worth the risk."

With the sun beginning to approach the horizon, we walk back to our hotel, the Protea Victoria Junction, a pleasantly standard business establishment with pretensions to being a local movie-industry mecca. Several restaurants nearby seem worth a look, but none of them entices us to a table, leaving us eventually to eat in the hotel dining room. Both of us get fresh fish, and Bill orders a bottle of good South African wine to share. When the waitress asks us about dessert, each of us responds, "Nothing, thank you." She returns several minutes later with cake plates bearing a handwritten note in chocolate saying "nothing," making us smile all the way up to our room.

After a late breakfast the next morning, we walk a short mile to the harbor, the departure point for four-hour tours to Robben Island, site of the notorious Apartheid prison where Nelson Mandela, among many others, lived for years. "Let's book the last boat in the afternoon," Cheryl says, "to watch the sunset over the water on our return. In the meantime we can wander through the waterfront mall development and have a combination lunch-dinner right before we take off." Bill agrees, buys the tickets, and we go in search of African crafts again, eventually buying a copper-wire-and-bead bracelet for Cheryl and some handmade Christmas-tree ornaments for ourselves and family members.

For our major meal of the day, we opt for the only harbor-side restaurant specializing in South African food, the Ikhaya. The waitress brings us a menu full of fascinating choices, and takes our order for a beer and a ginger beer, the latter a malty, yeasty version with strong ginger flavor. For appetizers, Cheryl settles on braised snoek, a favorite fish of the region, and Bill goes for spinach balls with a spicy *chakalaka* sauce. The kitchen flakes the snoek, simmers it with tomatoes and onions, and serves the dish over *steambread,* used as a bland foil. Cheryl needs to add almost a full shaker of salt to bring out the flavor. The spinach balls, baked with cornmeal rather than fried, arrive dried out, and the chakalaka—as much a warm salad as a sauce, combining beans, corn, tomatoes, and chiles—fails to enhance them.

Our main courses—*bobotie* and *piri piri* chicken livers—redeem the starters but don't appear for almost an hour due to an electrical blackout. The piri piri seasoning—the name is a pan-African term for chiles, the dominant ingredient—works great on the livers, and the curried lamb and vegetables shine in the bobotie, a widely popular local dish from the Malay Muslim tradition that resembles a shepherd's pie. Unfortunately, the waitress delivers the food only ten minutes before the scheduled boat departure, requiring us to scarf down tastes hastily, throw money on the table, and bolt out the door.

The Robben Island Museum depresses and exhilarates in the same moment, illustrating both institutional barbarism and the courage of prisoners who endured the malice and eventually triumphed. When the boat lands, the staff ushers the passengers onto waiting school buses for a circuit of the island. On our bus, a charismatic young black man greets us with an impassioned speech about freedom, emphasizing that the past is past and that South Africans of all colors must now work together. The driver and tour guide show us various areas, including one of the three limestone quarries used for forced hard labor and the building where prisoners were allowed to see family without any physical contact for thirty minutes every six months.

The bus stops later at the cell blocks that housed prisoners, and a former inmate takes us inside. He starts by telling us how he got sentenced here. "I was an activist in the African National Congress, like Nelson Mandela, but I was stationed outside the country doing intelligence work to help undermine the Apartheid government. I came back home with some associates on a sabotage job, and we were arrested. They held and tortured us for six months without bringing charges until one of the group cracked under the pressure and testified against the rest of us. I was sent to Robben Island for twenty-five years, and served six and a half years before the Apartheid regime collapsed."

"What happened to the guy who betrayed you?" one of the visitors asks.

"He got off more lightly, but I don't blame him for anything. Torture wears a man down. We must look ahead, not back."

The guide leads us through the cell blocks, explaining that even here the authorities segregated people racially, keeping blacks, coloreds, and Indians in separate sections; white political prisoners stayed in mainland jails. He and Mandela occupied the same building, with him in cell number 30 and the future president in number 4. Everyone got the same furnishings, still in place: a bench, a rudimentary cabinet, a thin blanket, and a miserably slight, small mattress on a basic bed frame.

On the boat going back to the harbor, when the sun is dropping toward the horizon, Cheryl says, "I'm too drained emotionally now to care about the sunset."

Bill agrees. "But I'm awed as well by what we're seeing. This is a country in birth throes. It's creating a new identity for itself right in front of our eyes, starting from scratch in many ways. Utterly amazing."

> >

The sign above the tasting-room door at the Kanonkop winery reads: "Pinotage is the juice extracted from women's tongues and lion's hearts. After having a sufficient quantity one can talk forever and fight the devil."

The first professor of viticulture at the nearby University of Stellenbosch, Abraham Izak Perold, created the Pinotage grape in the 1920s by crossbreeding two French varieties, the noble Pinot Noir and Cinsaut, a far humbler grape that thrives in the growing conditions of the South African Winelands. Kanonkop helped pioneer Pinotage wines and brought them to the world stage in 1991 when the estate's version won a prestigious international award. South African winemakers produce a range of good wines, but many of the most distinctive feature Pinotage by itself or in a red "Cape" blend with other grapes.

Kanonkop is our first stop in the Winelands, a lovely region of majestic mountains, pastoral valleys, and elegantly gabled Cape Dutch homesteads just an hour by rental car from Cape Town. In late spring, wildflowers frolic in the fields, and gardens abound with roses and dramatic agapanthuses with their violet, fireworks-shaped blossoms held high. Like most of the wineries, Kanonkop occupies serene, manicured farmland outside of the town of Stellenbosch and the village of Franschhoek, two of the main burgs in the area. The charming lady tending the tasting room pours us samples of a hearty 2001 Cabernet Sauvignon, a classy Bordeaux-style 2002 Paul Sauer blend, and a full-bodied 2003 Pinotage, loaded with luscious berry flavor, that lives up to the promise of the sign over the door.

At the Warwick Estate, just down the road, the 2004 Old Bush Vines Pinotage impresses us a little less, but we love the 2003 Three Cape Ladies, a blend of Cabernet Sauvignon, Merlot, and Pinotage, and the brightly crisp 2005 Sauvignon Blanc. Although the winery ranks among the most famous in the country, only one other couple joins us during our half-hour visit on the shaded terrace of the tasting room, which overlooks a pond guarded by a flock of guinea hens pecking away at the ground. "This is idyllic," Cheryl says. "Napa has more tourists and traffic at midnight than the Winelands at noon."

Bill glances at his watch. "Speaking of the time, we better get on to lunch," booked in Franschhoek at La Petite Ferme, where we're also staying for the next four nights. Our drive takes us down the single main street of the village, lined with small shops and restaurants that cater mainly to visitors but also serve the needs of the five thousand residents. European settlement here dates to the 1690s, about forty years after the Dutch established a supply base at Cape Town to provide fresh food—including wine to combat scurvy—for ships going around the Cape of Good Hope to trade in Asia. The Dutch called the valley "Oliphantshoek," because large herds of elephants roamed the area, before French Huguenots, fleeing the Protestant persecutions of Louis XIV, recognized the fertility of the soil and obtained land grants for farms. Within a few decades Franschhoek took its present name, meaning the "French corner."

Despite its diminutive size, promoters call the village "the culinary capital of South Africa," a bit of an understatement actually. By the end of our visit, Bill proposes a new boast: "The culinary capital of the world for affordable excellence," which is certainly true on a per capita basis at least.

The restaurant and five guest suites at La Petite Ferme (the little farm) overlook the town and valley from a fabulous perch on a mountain pass. A friendly, relaxed receptionist welcomes us and shows us to our Champagne Suite, a handsome cottage with a small swimming pool on the front patio that's in picking distance of a hillside of Sauvignon Blanc grapes. After dropping our bags, we stroll over to the dining terraces for lunch, the only meal served other than the breakfast provided to guests of the inn. As on most days, the restaurant is full, with many of the patrons lounging before their meal under stately pines on the grassy lawn, sipping wine while looking back and forth from the menu to the grand view.

Chef Olivia Mitchell and sous-chef Carina Bouwer give them plenty to think about in choosing dishes. The "femme-force," as owners Mark and Josephine Dendy Young call the duo, artfully meld African, Malay, and international influences into their ambitious and sophisticated cooking. Appetizers range from Asian fish cakes to warthog bresaola, but both of us are in the mood for vegetables on this sunny spring day. Cheryl orders green asparagus served over roasted parsnips with a green-olive tapenade and a cream reduction flavored with watercress and Sauvignon Blanc, and Bill opts for a toasted baguette rubbed with walnut-smoked paprika pesto and topped with sautéed porcini and shiitake mushrooms, goat cheese, and roasted cherry tomatoes. A sterling start.

The main-course selections include other vegetable preparations, as well as ostrich, calamari, and beef, but Bill is intent on the kitchen's most famous dish, a whole, house-smoked Franschhoek rainbow trout, deboned and served warm with a spaghetti galette and asparagus draped in fennel and an aioli with *naartjie* (African tangerine). "This is even better than the freshly caught trout I smoke at home," he admits.

Cheryl decides initially on a pan-fried duck breast marinated in hoisin, orange, ginger, and oak-wood chips with an accompanying plum tart tatin until the waitress describes, in loving detail, the special of the day, a local karoo lamb slow-roasted twelve hours before the fall-apart meat is wrapped in thin eggplant slices and served with mint yogurt over spaetzle. "I'm sure the duck would have been good, too," Cheryl says, "but this is sublime."

All the wines on offer come from the cellar below the restaurant, made by Mark from the grapes on the farm. Our choice is a Blanc Fumé, featuring a blend of Sauvignon Blanc from two vintages. A perfect match for the trout, it also adds a complementary crispy tang to the lamb. Our single dessert, shared between us, shines as well. The plate combines a trio of lemon wonders: Olivia's personal take on an icy limoncello liqueur, the house's lemon ice cream, and a warm lemon tart in a pine-nut shell, essentially a lemony crème brûlée in a crust with a topping of broiled sugar and caramelized pine nuts. The total tab for everything comes to about U.S.$75.00

During lunch, Mark acts as host, waiter, and probably dishwasher when needed. He stops by to introduce himself, knowing we're guests at the inn, and offers us a tour of the wine operation in the afternoon.

"Sign us up," Bill says.

At the appointed hour, he leads off with some background on La Petite Ferme. "My grandmother opened the restaurant originally, then turned over the kitchen to my mom, who helped to train Olivia. About thirty percent of the staff goes back to my grandmother's time, and another thirty percent came during my mother's tenure. My parents still live here, and my father stays active in the farming, but Josephine and I took over the helm in 1994. A major fire destroyed everything two years later, but we rebuilt and added the guest cottages."

He guides us down stone steps into the cellar and wine production room. "I made my first wine when I was eleven. It was simply part of life on the farm. I never studied enology formally, just learned from experience."

"How many different wines do you make?" Cheryl asks.

"Thirteen, but some of them on an irregular basis. The ones based on Sauvignon Blanc grapes are the most popular, and I focus a lot on them. Unlike many of the area winemakers, though, I seldom make Pinotage, like only twice in the last ten years." He gives tastes from the barrels of several developing wines, all finely crafted.

Before our arrival in South Africa, Bill had solicited the advice of the staff on dinner restaurants and asked them to make reservations on our behalf. The manager booked us tonight into a private dining room, Klein Oliphants Hoek, run by Ingrid and Camil Haas in their home. They serve only people staying in their eight guest rooms and outsiders recommended by one of five other local inns, including La Petite Ferme. Camil, from the Netherlands, does the cooking, and Ingrid, born in South Africa into a Dutch family, functions as the hostess.

She escorts us to a back terrace, where the dozen or so diners gather before the meal for glasses of a local sparkling wine (a combo of Pinotage, Pinot Noir, and Chardonnay) and a taste teaser, an oyster on the half shell with a Chinese black bean vinaigrette. The deck overlooks a huge flower, vegetable, and herb garden, where lavender and roses bloom brightly in the foreground of a magnificent sunset over the craggy mountain peaks in the distance. As the light dims, Ingrid invites everyone into the parlor restaurant, a comfortably elegant space with polished wood floors, a wood-beamed ceiling, and well selected contemporary art.

Our table provides a view through an open door of Camil and his bustling small staff at work in the kitchen, equipped with an old wood-burning stove that was one of the main attractions for the couple when they purchased the grand house, built as a missionary's residence in 1888. They installed a modern exhaust system above the stove, but altered nothing else, using its oven, grill, and burners of different heat levels for all the cooking. The choreography of the constant movement delights us, as Camil and his assistants juggle gumwood logs, pots, pans, and even a wok that goes over the hottest burner.

The set dinner consists of five courses, with options in a couple of cases, including two starter choices, one for each of us. The sashimi comes with wasabi mayonnaise and a scattering of ginger, and the salad of baby greens features crispy duck confit shreds, roasted pine nuts, and a fig wonton. Neither sounds novel for a contemporary menu, but the caliber of the ingredients and the care taken with them bring the dishes to their full potential.

Next up is the pasta of the day, a remarkable gnocchi, better flavored and lighter than any we've enjoyed in Italy or elsewhere. It's accompanied by roasted yellow tomatoes and a few Lilliputian mushrooms. The main course offers a selection between two fresh local fish, a panga in the snapper family with a Szechuan peppercorn sauce and a butterfish with curried basmati rice, melting baby leeks, and a sweet chile sauce. As usual in these situations, we get one each and share tastes. They contrast with each other smartly, with the butterfish living up to its name in richness and the panga hinting of citrus.

The cheese course continues the counterpoint theme, providing tastes of three different styles, an aged crottin chèvre melted over a baby brioche, a hearty blue, and a semisoft Tomme with applesauce. Ingrid suggests a break before our marzipan tart dessert, encouraging everyone to take a brief stroll through the garden, where tiny frogs are making a big racket. On our return to the table, Chef Camil excuses himself for the evening, explaining he has neighborhood security duty tonight. With a wine pairing for each course, including a private bottling in one case, the cost of the dinner for two is about U.S.$125. In New York or Paris, for similar food quality and intimate atmosphere with limited seating, the bill would soar above $500.

The next morning—after a tasty breakfast at La Petite Ferme of farm-fresh eggs, smoked trout, ripe fruit, and warm-from-the-oven breads and pastries—we take off in our rental car to visit wineries around Stellenbosch. The first stop is Thelema Mountain Vineyards, where the matriarch of the estate, the witty Edna "Ed" McLean, welcomes us and pours tastes. She and her husband became partners in the business with the winemaker, Gyles Webb, after he married their daughter Barbara, an accomplished triathlete who now handles the marketing end of the trade. Mrs. McLean is particularly proud of Webb's two Sauvignon Blancs, which she offers us along with samples of Riesling, Merlot, a vigorous Cabernet, and a beautifully balanced Muscat. Cheryl buys a bottle of the signature Sutherland Sauvignon Blanc for afternoon sipping.

Rustenberg Wines takes some effort to find and requires signing in at a gated residential area, but the historic farm, dating back to 1682, makes everything worthwhile. Lush pastures of rye and clover greet you at the entrance, providing sustenance to a herd of pampered Jersey heifers who the Rustenberg publicist calls "long-lashed ladies of impeccable pedigree." The cows graze across from and around the tasting room, the masterfully renovated former stables. Two servers barely beyond adolescence, Cindy Attwell and Florie Rossouw, attend us, pouring partial glasses of several whites before suggesting we try a newly bottled Cabernet Sauvignon. When Cindy asks us what we think of it, Bill searches his memory for appropriate wine terms, glances at the two of them again, and says, "Young and punky." They laugh appreciatively, taking the comment as a compliment for themselves, the wine, or both.

From the Rustenberg farm, our route to the Kleine Zalze winery takes us through the core of Stellenbosch, a sprawling town with a population of more than one hundred thousand people. In this case our interest is the estate's restaurant, Terroir, instead of the tasting room. From our table on the outdoor dining terrace, the sunny weather, ochre buildings, lavender in full bloom, and tall cypresses prompt an impression of Provence meets Tuscany. The small blackboard lunch menu ranges more broadly around the world, providing us for starters with cured tuna in ginger-shallot oil and prawn risotto, and for main courses, wood-roasted pork belly with applesauce and springbok venison medallions with cassis sauce and a parsnip-potato puree. The appetizers and the breads—a hearty peasant loaf and black-olive-and-tomato focaccia—make us think we're heading for another extraordinary meal, but the entrées disappoint us a little. On many occasions the lunch would leave us rapturous, particularly considering the value, but not after yesterday's feasts.

Still, we're amply satiated and decide to head back to our room for an afternoon of pool time and reading in the shade of our large covered terrace. The suite, like a small villa in size, cocoons us in the best of country style. The sitting area, with a sofa and chairs, faces a gas fireplace, attractive but less useful today than the ceiling fan and air-conditioning. The comfortable king-size bed and spacious bathroom both look out large windows toward the magnificent view, and everything sits under a wood ceiling that reminds us of Santa Fe, with sturdy beams (vigas in New Mexico) supporting split pieces of wood running perpendicularly (latillas). As the sun sets in a stunning fashion again, Cheryl says, "I really hate to leave here tonight, even for dinner."

Bill agrees but is resigned to the fact. "Our reservation is at Le Quartier Français Tasting Room, the most touted of the restaurants in Franschhoek. We can't miss it."

In the end, our longings work out. Le Quartier Français has accidentally booked us for the next evening, when our plans call for us to eat at Reubens, another well-regarded establishment but a lower priority. The hostess calls Reubens to try to switch dates because she is full, but it happens to be closed tonight for a private party. So we react like kids with a snow day away from school, bouncing across the street to the Pick 'n' Pay to get some local cheese, pâté, olives, and crackers to enjoy on our terrace with a bottle of the Three Cape Ladies wine purchased at the Warwick Estate. Watching the moon rise over the lights of the village below, we're as content as the Rustenberg Jerseys, wishing only that one of us had studied the stars in the Southern Hemisphere constellations before our trip. Neither of us can spot anything that resembles a Southern Cross.

Cheryl awakes to a wardrobe crisis the next morning, realizing one of her two pairs of cropped pants has shredded from all our walking and then discovering that a pair of panties has vanished somewhere between China and Africa. She recalls friends who lost all their underwear once in China when an unexpected windstorm blew them off a laundry's rooftop drying terrace. "Could that have happened at the Olivers? I'd hate to imagine a motor-scooter driver on the street trying to dodge flying red panties."

After breakfast, the receptionist at the inn promises to cancel our dinner reservation at Reubens, leaving us free for Le Quartier Français Tasting Room. Since it's a Sunday, wineries shut down, and we've scheduled a sightseeing drive on the dramatic Cape Peninsula south of Cape Town. The road into the area takes us over a mountainous spine, which descends on the other side to a different climate zone, misty and a little chilly. Simon's Town comes up shortly, offering a chance for a bathroom break and a stroll along the main street, lined with aging Victorian architecture. Noting the British Hotel and the Salty Sea Dog fish-and-chips shop, Cheryl says, "The place feels like a down-at-the-heels English seaside resort."

She's avidly focused on our next stop, Boulders Beach, home to a colony of African penguins popularly called "jackass penguins" because of their noisy braying. The tuxedoed birds moved to this site, now a part of Table Mountain National Park, only twenty years ago, to the chagrin of their affluent human neighbors, who have to put up with hordes of visitors trampling past their houses. "They wouldn't tolerate this in Malibu," Bill says.

Some four dozen of the penguins waddle, flop, and swim around today, awkward on the land but masterful in the water, where their two-tone coloring makes them practically invisible to birds above and sea predators below. Despite the protection, their numbers are dwindling, at least in part due to oil spills. In memory of the visit, Cheryl picks up some handcrafted wire-and-bead penguin key chains and goofy penguin socks for friends and family.

On the opposite coast of the peninsula, Chapman's Peak Drive provides thrills of a different sort on its wicked switchbacks, used in hundreds of car commercials and filmed chase scenes. The narrow highway, an engineering feat during its construction between 1915 and 1922, nestles between sheer walls of rock and a perilous drop-off high above the thundering sea. Since South Africans drive on the left side of the road and we're heading north with Bill at the wheel, Cheryl says in mock terror, "I'm hanging off this freakin' precipice." She clutches the dashboard and leans to the right as though she is trying to make a turn on skis, perhaps helping us to descend safely to the town of Hout Bay.

It's past noon at this point, time for a simple lunch that won't spoil our big dinner ahead. Bill spies a prospective eatery right off, a spot called Ice Dream that advertises "Real Italian Ice Cream." "If we get two or more scoops of different flavors," he advises, "it becomes a well-balanced meal." Unfortunately, there's no parking available anywhere within a mile. "Just like in Italy," he bitches.

Farther along, Cheryl notices a roadside fish-and-chips stand named Fresh. "Fried food is a fine substitute for ice cream," she says, "and it includes a healthy white vegetable." The proprietor cooks the hake and potato wedges fresh to order and both taste yummy.

Chef Margo Janse and her fine kitchen staff go leagues deeper in complexity and flavor at Le Quartier Français. The tasting-menu dinner ranks among our finest meals ever at any price, but costs only U.S.$150 for both of us, including a superb 2003 Akkerdal Wild Boar blend of Malbec, Mourvèdre, and Merlot. Among the all-star lineup of dishes, our favorite is the wild mushroom spaetzle, a forestful of mushroom varieties sautéed in butter with the tiny knobby dumplings, a poached egg, toasted almond slices for texture, and truffle foam. Two other courses reach similar heights, a terrine of salt-cured foie gras layered with tender shredded ham hock and quail and served with port-glazed figs, and a smoked zebra carpaccio (which tastes a bit like venison to us, though some compare it to horsemeat) with a warm composed salad of crispy sweetbreads, ox tongue, fresh lychees, individual leaves of tiny tatsoi, and a vinaigrette made of vegetable marrow and pureed butternut squash. Only a scattering of restaurants in the whole of the United States have the talent to match this trio of delights, and even fewer sport the gumption to put such adventuresome fare on a commercial menu.

Other dishes are merely outstanding. The sugar-cured impala venison loin comes with truffled honey jus and a foie-gras-enriched risotto colored a glorious shade of magenta by beets and a 1983 Shiraz. A small round of chilled rabbit porcetta has a splash of tarragon cream, a few pickled vegetables, and a bacon-and-apple vinaigrette. A foam of tangy nasturtiums and pineapple dresses the roasted warthog, which Janse plates with a side of turnip puree and an amazing confit of purple cabbage cooked down slowly to a tangle of melting vegetables and crispy tidbits. If we must quibble about something, the balsamic reduction seems slightly sweet in the pickled anchovy–prawn salad that accompanies a pan-roasted kingklip, a fillet of local white fish that flakes in big shreds like crabmeat.

Our final courses are salad and cheese combinations, an ideal way to wrap up this kind of meal. Cheryl's choice features a crumble of Gorgonzola, toasted pine nuts, sunflower shoots, finely cut bacon bits, and a streak of peach puree on the side. Bill opts for a walnut-crumbed, truffled goat Brie with three perfect endive spears. More restaurants should offer such savory treats as alternatives to sweets, which can overwhelm the sense of taste after a series of exquisite dishes.

Our last day in the Winelands brings more good food, visits to a couple of Franschhoek wineries, an amble through the local Huguenot Museum, and another spectacular sunset, this one a lingering display in which we can pick out nuances of light and shadow in the staggered tiers of mountains across the valley, where the front range remains a deep green, the most distant peaks bleed red and purple, and the intermediate crests shift through shades of white.

After sunset, it's a short hop for us across the road to dinner at Haute Cabrière, carved into a hillside in a handsome underground barrel-vaulted shape. Proprietors Matthew and Nicky Gordon run the restaurant—he in the kitchen and she in the front of the house—in collaboration with their winemaker, Achim von Arnim, who helps Matthew hone dishes well suited to his wines. The menu proudly announces, "There are no starters or main courses—just a series of taste sensations." It continues to state that everything comes in both small and large portions to allow diners to try as many different items as they wish. "Bravo for them," Cheryl says.

Each of us gets the same three small plates to maintain consistency in the food-and-wine matches. The waiter first serves us guinea-fowl boudin flecked with corn and accompanied by wilted savoy cabbage with smoky lardons and roasted carrots, turnips, and beets. The wine steward suggests a glass of a Chardonnay–Pinot Noir sparkler to go with the dish, and despite our doubts, its yeasty effervescence adds radiance to everything else.

For the next two courses of duck and lamb the sommelier recommends the Haute Cabrière Pinot Noir, so we get a bottle. The duck comes in three forms: as confit stuffed in a beignet; as rillettes with ginger; and as smoked breast with frisée and tomato-and-chile jam. The roasted rack of karoo lamb, crusted with green garlic, flaunts more fat than we're used to at home, both on the surface and in internal marbling, to delicious effect. "Bravo again," Bill says. It sits beside spinach so fresh it squeaks in our teeth and al dente black mushroom cannelloni filled with an inky duxelle, a mince of earthy mushrooms cooked down in butter. The Pinot Noir complements the food superbly, as does a light estate brandy with our shared dessert of little doughnuts brimming with tiny wild blueberries, served with a scoop of a properly tangy Granny Smith apple sorbet.

On our way out, Cheryl raises her head to the heavens to ask, "How on earth can there be so much great food in this tiny village, a place I never heard of before we started planning this trip?"

No one above responds and Bill doesn't hazard a guess until we board our flight in Cape Town to leave the country. "There's a jolting level of energy in South Africa, a passionate sense of renewal and wide-open possibilities. It seems to lift all aspects of life, even the creative aspirations in the cooking."

THE NITTY-GRITTY

LALIBELA GAME RESERVE
www.lalibela.co.za
Eastern Cape between
Port Elizabeth and Grahamstown
27-41-581-8170   fax   27-41-581-2332

PROTEA VICTORIA JUNCTION
www.proteahotels.com
Somerset and Ebenezer Roads,
Cape Town
27-21-418-1234   fax   27-21-418-5678

ROBBEN ISLAND MUSEUM
www.robben-island.org.za
Cape Town
27-21-413-4200

KANONKOP WINE ESTATE
www.kanonkop.co.za
R44 between Stellenbosch and Paarl
27-21-884-4656

WARWICK ESTATE
www.warwickwine.com
R44 near Stellenbosch
27-21-884-3145

LA PETITE FERME
www.lapetiteferme.co.za
Franschhoek Pass Road,
Franschhoek
27-21-876-3016   fax   27-21-876-3624
Delightful in all respects.

🔁 KLEIN OLIPHANTS HOEK
www.kleinoliphantshoek.co.za
14 Akademie Street,
Franschhoek
27-21-876-2566   fax same

🔁 THELEMA MOUNTAIN
VINEYARDS
http://thelema.co.za
Stellenbosch
27-21-885-1924

🔁 RUSTENBERG WINES
www.rustenberg.co.za
Stellenbosch
27-21-809-1200

🔁 TERROIR
www.kleinezalze.co.za
Strand Road (R44), Stellenbosch
27-21-880-8167   fax 27-21-880-0862

🔁 LE QUARTIER FRANÇAIS
TASTING ROOM
www.lqf.co.za
16 Hugenot Road, Franschhoek
27-21-876-2151   fax 27-21-876-3105
Fabulous food.

🔁 HAUTE CABRIÈRE
www.hautecabriere.com
Franschhoek Pass Road, Franschhoek
27-21-876-3688   fax 27-21-876-3691

Cape Malay Bobotie

SERVES 8

Filling

1	tablespoon vegetable oil
1	tablespoon butter, preferably unsalted
2	medium onions, finely chopped
1	or 2 garlic cloves, minced
2	pounds ground lamb
1	tablespoon curry powder
1	teaspoon ground turmeric
1	teaspoon salt
¼	teaspoon freshly ground pepper
½	cup fresh breadcrumbs
1	large egg, lightly beaten
1	tart apple, such as Granny Smith, peeled and chopped fine
½	cup raisins
½	cup chopped dried apricots
⅓	cup slivered almonds

Grated zest and juice of 1 small lemon

Topping

3	large eggs
1	cup milk
½	cup half-and-half or additional milk
¾	teaspoon salt

Store-bought mint chutney or other chutney

Preheat the oven to 325°F. Butter a large shallow baking dish, like one you would use for lasagna.

In a large heavy skillet, warm the oil and butter over medium heat and add the onions. Sauté until the onions are soft and translucent, stir in the garlic, and cook about 1 more minute. Spoon into a large mixing bowl.

Return the skillet to the heat and add the lamb, breaking it up evenly while it cooks. As soon as it loses the raw look, pour off any fat and stir in the curry powder, turmeric, salt, and pepper. Cook for about 5 minutes longer. Spoon into the mixing bowl and add the rest of the filling ingredients. Stir together well, then spoon into the baking dish. Cover and bake for 1¼ hours.

Meanwhile, whisk together the topping ingredients.

Take the bobotie from the oven and uncover it. Raise the oven temperature to 400°F. Pour the topping evenly over the baked meat mixture and return it, uncovered, to the oven. Bake for 13 to 15 additional minutes, until the topping is set and golden brown. Cut into squares and serve with chutney on the side.

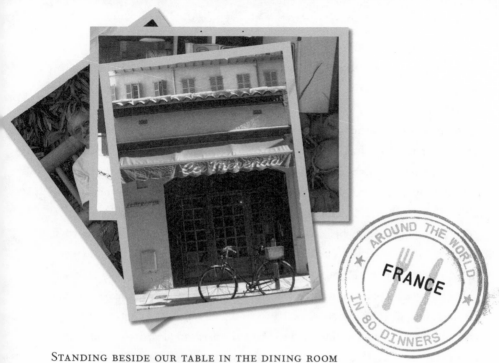

STANDING BESIDE OUR TABLE IN THE DINING ROOM
at La Riboto de Taven, Christine Thème tells us, "When I was a small child, I
used to think of this space that we're in now as the sheep's bedroom, where they
went to sleep at night. Jean-Pierre and I were born right next door in our parents' house, when the restaurant was the barn on our family farm. From as far
back as we can trace deeds, to 1610, the land has been in our family." That's basically why we love La Riboto, because it's truly home in all respects to the hostess,
her husband, Philippe, and her brother the chef. When they welcome you to their
small plot in Provence, they welcome you wholeheartedly into their lives.

When one of us mentions to other people that we go as often as possible to
Les Baux-de-Provence to enjoy a wonderful hotel with fabulous food, most of
them who know the town assume we're talking about Oustau de Baumanière,
a famous restaurant that boasts some classy rooms for overnight stays. About
twenty years ago, we dined there during the haute cuisine phase of our French
travel, but it no longer appeals much to us. In those days we took the Michelin
Red Guide seriously about making any detours necessary to get to places awarded
three stars, covering almost half of them eventually. Many of the heralded restaurants awed us, particularly the two led by Alain Chapel and Joël Robuchon in
their prime, but we grew weary of the pomp, the frilly excesses of the multiple
courses, and what seemed an increasing frequency of preparations structured for

the sake of showiness rather than flavor. After an awful evening in 2001 at one of the most lauded of today's establishments, now called La Maison de Marc Veyrat, we retired pretty much from the hautest of haute cuisine.

Michelin recommends La Riboto de Taven, even paints it red to indicate special character, but the inn voluntarily gave up its culinary star a number of years ago, just before we discovered it in odd circumstances. One of Bill's most skilled and daunting local poker opponents, Bernard Trenet, comes from France, where most of his family still lives. During a game of no-limit Texas hold 'em—Bill's recreation of choice long before it became popular, going back to the days when saying you bet on cards was akin to bragging about debauchery—Bernard mentioned he would be in France the following summer, at a time that overlapped with a visit we were planning. He told Bill that his cousin Claire had married a talented chef, Jean-Pierre Novi of La Riboto, and suggested that we meet up with him at their auberge. Bill checked up on the place and learned that it used to have a Michelin star, but no longer did. He figured it was going downhill, though he couldn't say that to Bernard, so we just went. Maybe the lesser expectations boosted our initial reaction, but La Riboto stunned us in all ways, with its rooms, food, beauty, and genuine human warmth.

Second and third visits soon confirmed our first impressions, and made us curious about the family behind the extraordinary inn. Philippe Thème credits much of the appeal to Christine and Jean-Pierre's parents: "Decades ago, when automobile tourism began to boom, they made a bold move in turning their farm into a restaurant. Maybe the founder of Oustau de Baumanière inspired them a little, because he tried to buy their property for his new restaurant as soon as he arrived in town. As farmers, the Novis knew and loved food and eventually earned a Michelin star for their kitchen.

"Christine and I came here to help them," Philippe says, "when they wanted to cut back on their heavy time commitment. The two of us had already worked together for a number of years as hotel managers, first in the Camargue region, where we met and got hooked up."

Christine overhears the last comment and joins the conversation. "He was so handsome, as you can see, and quite the smooth operator."

"Anyway," Philippe resumes, smiling, "running a restaurant required similar hospitality skills."

"Until you fired the chef," Christine interjects. "We got bored with his heavy cooking," she explains, "and decided he had to go. It's hard to sack someone in France, particularly a professional. What an ordeal. For a whole year, Philippe had to take over the kitchen himself, which made us nervous about losing our Michelin star. It worked out fine in the end, after Jean-Pierre became our new chef in 1990."

"Introducing his elegantly crafted contemporary dishes," Cheryl says.

"Yes, he and Claire were living then in England, where he had already been awarded a Michelin star for his cooking. Both of them were keen to come back, and we're sure glad they did."

With the two children at home again now, the Novis and Thèmes decided to add a couple of hotel rooms on a midlevel plateau of the soaring limestone cliffs above the restaurant. They carved these "troglodytic suites" into the rock face of the bluff, giving them a magnificent cavelike feel, and romantically named them Vincent and Mireille, the Romeo and Juliet of Provençal poetry. As you enter Mireille, our chosen roost, you're struck immediately by the limestone out-cropping that surges above and around the large canopied bed. Fossil indentations and gradations of color, from ochre to gold to rose, enrich the creamy stone that continues along the walls into the bathroom, where it juts massively over the large soaking tub and helps to enclose a corner shower. A high, pitched ceiling arches over a sitting area with velvet-covered chairs, and mullioned windows look out to a patio ideal for lounging in warm weather. From the terrace, guests have an incomparable view of the walled medieval city of Les Baux as well as the inn's wonderfully groomed grounds, featuring olive, cyprus, pine, and plane trees interspersed with shrubs, hedges, grasses, and flowers.

"The addition of those suites," Jean-Pierre tells us one day, "made a big dif-ference here, but the really decisive changes came in 2000. We closed for much of that year to build a new residence for my parents on the property and to con-vert their former house into four additional guest rooms."

"Christine showed us the rooms once," Bill says, remembering them as com-fortable, spacious quarters in the style of a Provençal mas (farmhouse).

"More important," Jean-Pierre continues, "we reorganized the business completely so that Christine, Philippe, and I could do everything ourselves without other employees except a maid and a gardener. Previously, with the kind of broad à la carte menu you need for a Michelin star, we had to maintain a full kitchen staff year-round despite big fluctuations in reservation levels between high and low seasons. That didn't make financial sense for us, and created labor headaches, too. So we rebuilt my kitchen for the needs of a single chef, changed to a table d'hôte menu with limited choices, and gave up our star without any fanfare."

"That's really the key to La Riboto's personality, isn't it?" Cheryl says. "The family takes full responsibility for every little detail. It's like a good mom-and-pop operation with two talented pops. What a team you make!" Though Jean-Pierre just grins without comment, Bill knows she's right. Christine and Philippe take care of guests personally in the front of the house with utmost professionalism and charm, and Jean-Pierre cooks for them personally with the consummate skills of a great French chef.

Life on the road—even in the grandest of hotels or at anyone else's home—just doesn't get much better.

> >

So we're returning to La Riboto again, simply because it doesn't seem right to go around the world without visiting our favorite inn in the world. Apart from that, a stop in France doesn't make much sense on our itinerary. It pulls us away from the warmth of the Southern Hemisphere, where all of our other destinations dwell, and takes us to the cusp of winter in a region north of some parts of Canada. New experiences lure us on our journey, a chance to see places we've never been, a longing to broaden our cultural and culinary horizons. France is familiar turf for us, a country we know reasonably well. It must appear we're abandoning fresh paths to indulge a passion and sacrificing adventure to have a fling. Yep, low temptation thresholds.

Our flight from Cape Town arrives in Nice shortly before midnight and we depart again the next morning in a rental car bound for Les Baux-de-Provence. Since we're coming back to the Mediterranean city in a few days, we don't pause for anything now other than sleep and a satisfying French breakfast of strong coffee, fresh juices, crusty baguettes, fluffy croissants, and hard-boiled eggs so fresh that the mother hen might still recognize them.

As we pull out of Nice onto the autoroute heading west, our first planned stop is the town of Les Arcs, to have lunch with Kristin Espinasse, her husband, Jean-Marc, and their two children. Cheryl became e-mail pen pals with Kristin several years ago when we stumbled across her delightful Web site, French-Word-A-Day. Originally from Arizona, she came to France during college and stayed to marry Jean-Marc, who exports wine to the United States, including his family's Domaine du Banneret Châteauneuf-du-Pape. In her Web site and now in a new book, *Words in a French Life,* Kristin chronicles her wrestling match with the French language, smartly using stories about everyday experiences in Provence to amplify her points.

While all of us snack on briny home-cured cracked green olives, Jean-Marc pours the adults a round of a good sparkling wine, less yeasty than most versions and full of Pinot Noir character. He's cooking *sanglier* (wild boar) for lunch, provided courtesy of his cousin. He got the recipe, he explains, in Phoenix from Vincent Guerithault, the French chef-owner of Vincent's on Camelback, who ironically began his cooking career in Les Baux at Oustau de Baumanière. Jean-Marc serves the tasty meat with a robust red-wine sauce studded with garlic, and brings out a bottle of his family's Châteauneuf-du-Pape as a perfect accompaniment. With the food, wine, and a spirited conversation about writing, publishing, and working at home with a spouse (which they do, too), we lose track of the time and get back on the road late. Since we're joining other friends for dinner at La Riboto, we race off into the sunset at European speed, averaging close to one hundred miles per hour.

Sunshine Erickson and her husband, Alain Garcès, drive in from the opposite direction, from their home in Montpellier. Sunshine used to work for our former publisher in Boston and has been a friend for at least a decade. Alain, a research scientist, did graduate work at MIT, met Sunshine in the city, and returned to France with a wife as well as a degree. She's now studying wine marketing at a Montpellier university and doing an internship with an online retailer and wholesaler of old vintages. They arrive a little before dinner, as we suggested, to see Mireille and sip an aperitif, a light Côtes de Provence wine we pick up in Les Arcs at the appellation's Maison de Vins. Sunshine brings us a wedge of carrot cake with cream-cheese frosting, left over from their American-style Thanksgiving dinner. Cheryl gobbles it a bite at a time for the next two days, savoring it like a rare delicacy.

Christine and Philippe greet us jovially in the dining room, gracefully switching between French and English in their welcome. Because it's late November, their slowest period, we're the only guests tonight, as we will be the following two nights. For an opening nibble, they bring out crispy cheese puffs, tapenade, and their version of home-cured cracked green olives, obviously a popular premeal snack during this olive-harvest season. Bill asks Philippe if he could present one of his patented olive-oil tastings to Sunshine and Alain, as he's done for us in the past. Philippe produces three small carafes of local oil and some pieces of bread, inviting us to sample and savor. They range from mild and buttery, resembling most of the good oils available in the United States, to one that we recognize as Castelas, intense and peppery with hints of almond and artichoke. When Philippe seeks our opinions about the differences, he tells us he likes them all for varying uses. "The one Christine and I drink for breakfast, though, is the Castelas."

During the tasting, we survey the evening's table d'hôte menu, featuring an appetizer selection of skate salad and a tian of Provençal vegetables, followed by a main course of either roasted lamb loin or fresh rascasse (a Mediterranean fish used in bouillabaisse). The four of us give Philippe our choices, making sure that collectively we get at least one of all the possibilities, and ask his advice on a wine that will go well with the range of flavors. He suggests a full but soft red such as the 2002 La Pialade Reservé de La Riboto de Taven, a Côtes du Rhône bottled exclusively for the inn for forty years.

Everything sparkles, including his recommended wine. The tian distills the essence of Provence in a single dish, offering tomatoes, eggplant, and zucchini perfectly roasted in their own juices and seasoned with a few grains of flaky salt and a splash of sage-infused olive oil. The boomerang-shaped skate wing comes with greens and a tartarlike sauce grebiche enriched with olive oil and dense with cornichons and capers. Jean-Pierre serves the lamb rosy with jus smelling sweetly of thyme and roasted garlic, and tops the rascasse with a sauce of garlic and late-harvest olive oil. On the side of both, he places a ragu of seasonal vegetables with tender baby Brussels sprouts, fennel, roasted potato, green beans, and Romanesco broccoflowers.

When we finish, Philippe clears the table, preparing the way for Christine's turn at center stage. She always handles the cheese course, presenting a cart full of tasty alternatives. She knows each intimately because she's responsible for the affinage, the art of aging cheese to realize its optimum flavor. Our quartet focuses on the goat and sheep options tonight, appreciating in particular the heady Roquefort and the pert Banon that oozes out of its chestnut-leaf wrapper. For dessert, we wrap up with an ethereal chestnut soufflé with a hint of brandy before parting company with Sunshine and Alain and wishing them a safe drive home.

In the morning, we return to the restaurant for breakfast, which consists at La Riboto of pots of coffee, tea, or hot chocolate, a basket with chunks of baguette, whole-grain rolls, and croissants, a tray of jam and preserves, a bowl of fresh fruit, and, if you wish, yogurt. The Thèmes prefer to seat people at night facing the fireplace, and in the morning, looking out over the dining-room terrace. The swimming pool, we notice, supports a faint glaze of ice today. Christine asks about our plans for later, and Cheryl says we're going to wander around medieval Les Baux and maybe drive over to nearby Saint-Rémy de Provence. Christine sensibly suggests waiting on Saint-Rémy until Wednesday, a market day, and tells us about a Christmas fair in Arles that we might want to see. She offers us free tickets that she won't be able to use this year and we accept gratefully.

An ancient Roman city, with the ruins to prove it, Arles is a quick twenty kilometers away. Grabbing a parking place within walking distance of the convention center, we join the throngs at the bustling fair, which sprawls through several halls packed with booths selling crafts, textiles, furniture, books, artisanal food products, and more. The popular snack bar near the entrance makes an American counterpart seem as counterfeit as a crayon Picasso. Instead of corn dogs, cheese nachos, and funnel cakes, shoppers stop by for small plates of duck foie gras with mesclun, crawfish salad with marinated tomatoes, hanger steak with morels, leg of lamb from the Alpilles roasted with garlic, and carpaccio of beef with capers and local olive oil.

From the café, aisles of baubles, bangles, and brocade radiate in all directions. Cheryl picks up a few small Christmas gifts, but we pause mainly at food stands, sampling apples at a booth with dozens of different varieties, admiring handmade chocolates, liqueurs, honeys, and confitures. That's all before we discover an entire hall at the rear of the complex devoted to culinary products, including huge rounds of *pain d'épices,* a gingerbread larger than our heads; candied fruits such as whole minipineapples; nougat sold by the thick slice in flavors like coffee, coconut, bergamot, and praline; a wealth of tapenades and oils made from olives grown within kilometers of Arles; truffle cream and Arborio rice infused with truffle slices.

The stimulation whets our appetites for lunch, leading us back to a booth providing sample bites of incredible ham and selling sandwiches of the same. Artisan charcutier Jacky Gruson of Le Carré de Picq makes his own ham from Rosa d'Etienne pigs that he raises himself on a diet of corn, barley, and peas. He cuts us paper-thin slices of the meat and places them on whole buttered baguettes, a treat as simple as a grin but good enough to be considered for a last meal.

On our way out of the convention center, we pick up a bottle of Bandol, one of our favorite wines, from a boutique producer, Domaine de Cagueloup in Saint-Cyr-sur-Mer. The vintner, Richard Prébost, tells us next week is the annual Fête du Vin du Bandol and encourages us to come. Bill tells him we'll be in Brazil by then, but will keep it in mind for the future. The winemaker smiles and starts dancing a solo samba, giving us a merry send-off from the Christmas fair.

In contrast to the scene in Arles, the historic center of Les Baux is quiet today, the main reason we decide to see it again. Most of the year, busloads of tourists swarm the place as if they've been invited to a sneak preview of Heaven. The towering hilltop location alone lures many of them. The Provençal poet Frédéric Mistral compares it to an eagle's nest, soaring high above the rest of the distinctive local white limestone formations. The fabled history also draws in the crowds. Celts built the first defensive fortress on the site in the second century B.C., but the powerful lords of Les Baux, beginning in the eleventh century A.D., turned it into the "impregnable" stronghold of the Middle Ages, which didn't fall until Louis XIII laid a royal siege.

Even though we have the old streets and sights mostly to ourselves on this blustery day, we find little to detain us for long. Right before we leave, Cheryl peers over the city wall next to the castle ruins to search for Mireille in the valley below. She spots her and blows a kiss, saying we're on our way home, from where the historic city looks even more majestic, particularly on moonlit evenings.

Before dinner, Christine and Philippe tell us about the origin of the name of their inn. "Riboto," they explain, refers to a communal feasting table in the old Provençal dialect. In Mistral's epic poem about Mireille and Vincent, Taven is the good witch who helps to unite the lowly basket maker's son and the aristocrat's daughter. Charles Gounod turned the story into an opera that Christine and Philippe once saw in Avignon. They swear the set looked exactly like their property.

For an appetizer, Bill selects the lamb-sweetbread salad, with crisply tender sweetbreads that Jean-Pierre allows to cool slightly before adding greens and a saffron dressing. Cheryl opts for the langoustine ravioli, luscious little pouches of seafood swimming in a broth of squid ink and olive oil. Both of us follow up with a roasted veal sirloin with sautéed cèpes and parsley, which comes with baby root vegetables. As with many of Jean-Pierre's dishes, the jus elevates fine ingredients into a spectacular success. Philippe matches the veal flawlessly with his wine recommendation, a locally produced 1999 Château Dalméran blending Syrah, Cabernet Sauvignon, and Cinsaut grapes.

Each of us holds back on the cheese course, sticking with just a wedge of Saint-Marcellin, because we know additional cream is on the way with dessert. Alongside an apple tart, a spiral of roasted apples on buttery pastry, Jean-Pierre scoops a globe of vanilla ice cream churned just minutes before. On top of that, he dribbles a sundae crown of golden, light olive oil, which works beautifully. Only in Provence.

The next morning we drive down the road a couple of miles to drop in on olive-oil producers Jean-Benoît and Catherine Hugues, who make Castelas. The couple jumped into the business about a decade ago when they bought a house and six hectares of trees from a family that had cultivated olives on the land since the seventeenth century. The original owners, who had no heirs, would only sell to people who promised to take excellent care of the trees. The Hugueses must hug each one every night judging by the oil they extract.

The trees don't deserve all the credit, however. The Hugueses press their oil on the same day that they harvest the olives, usually within six hours, and they use a production system designed by Jean-Benoît to obtain optimum flavor. A professional engineer with a specialization in automated processing, he showed us his custom-built machines with great pride on a previous trip. Jean-Benoît employs water in his scheme only in the initial step of bringing olives to the right temperature for pressing. A blower dries and destems the fruit and eliminates leaves. Another apparatus pushes the olives through a grate just slightly smaller than them, so that they crack but aren't crushed, as happens with stone grinding.

The next machine tumbles them into a paste in an airtight tube and a centrifuge drains out the oil, which stays in stainless-steel vats until bottling. The label on the final product proclaims its Appellation d'Origine Contrôlée (A.O.C.) status, just like French wines enjoy, under the region called the Vallée des Baux de Provence.

Just around the corner, Mas de la Dame makes some of the best local A.O.C. wines. The old farmhouse looks the way it must have for decades, if not centuries, featuring limestone block architecture with a faded red tile roof. In the tasting room, bottles of current vintages sit on the counter, including our two favorites from past experience, the Coin Caché and Le Vallon des Amants. After sipping a little of each, Bill buys a bottle of Le Vallon, the longer-lasting of the pair. Cheryl starts looking closely at the lovely holiday baskets on display and Bill goes en garde. In France, Cheryl sometimes buys and hauls home some of the most unwieldy items in the country—the worst excess being a fragile, three-foot-high walnut-drying rack that she carried back as checked luggage after begging yards of bubble wrap from shops in Saint-Tropez, of all places. This time she exercises restraint.

After escaping unburdened, we drive south a dozen or so kilometers to Saint-Martin-de-Crau for lunch at Auberge La Pastourello, another of our treasured spots in the area. You enter the restaurant through the bar, which Monsieur attends, and pass a miniature living room furnished with a sofa and a TV that's always on and tuned to a game show around the noon hour. The proprietors and their family station themselves here before and after meals. The adjacent dining room, which Madame oversees, is exuberantly decorated with a collection of antiques and objets (not all d'art) that define the essence of eclectic. Wherever you look on the walls and shelves, you see musical instruments, operatic masks, ceramic ware, copper pans, carpenter's tools, *santon* figurines, paintings, and kitchen implements such as coffee grinders. An enormous cooking hearth blazes today at one end of the room, directly across from a grandfather clock and a piano.

In warmer months, when we've come before at lunch, La Pastourello sets out an expansive buffet of Provençal fare. In this slower period, the restaurant offers a recited menu of daily specials for a three-course prix fixe meal with house wine. Cheryl starts with a "pizza" on a puff-pastry base with cheese melted over tomato and ham, and Bill leads with a custardlike mussel terrine accompanied by an anchovy-laced salad. For a main course, both of us order dorade (sea bream) in pistou, the Provençal equivalent of an Italian pesto. Delicious fillets float on creamed chard, and pistou swathes the fish. Cheryl chooses the *île flottante* (floating island) dessert, while Bill has a *tarte au citron* that's as close to a lemon meringue pie as we've ever seen in France. At ten minutes until 2:00, the restaurant clears completely as all the other patrons head back to work.

In the afternoon, we read lazily, learning later that Christine, Philippe, and Jean-Pierre are toiling hard at the same time, helping with the olive harvest. It doesn't diminish their spirits at dinner. Unusual for us, we decide to get the same dishes this evening, foie gras for an appetizer, followed by roasted *macreuse*, a cut of beef unfamiliar to us. The sautéed foie gras rests on a thin potato cake, crispy and garlicky, and drips dabs of red currant sauce. A glass of Muscat from the Languedoc mates perfectly.

The macreuse, Philippe tells us, comes from the top front of the shoulder, guaranteeing full beefy flavor, and is cut in a way that increases tenderness. Jean-Pierre presents it in medium-rare scallops with a caramelized shallot–red wine jus, and nestles it with a mélange of fall vegetables—fennel, baby turnips, green beans, roasted potatoes, and marble-sized Brussels sprouts almost as sweet as fruit. As Philippe clears the table, we somehow get into a discussion of American barbecue sauces. The ones he has tried all overwhelm and mask the food, he says, a flaw we've seen also in some French sauces. Jean-Pierre's meat sauces do the opposite, complementing and melding flavors because they are reductions of the original juices minimally but skillfully enhanced with garlic, wine, and other seasonings.

When Christine arrives with the cheese cart, we're still drinking the red wine we had with the beef, a local 2000 Château Romanin that combines Grenache, Syrah, Mourvèdre, and Cabernet Sauvignon. To match the wine, she picks for us two aged sheep cheeses and an Alsatian Muenster. Dessert is sautéed pears with a pine-nut praline and intensely fragrant lavender ice cream, dribbled again with olive oil.

Bill takes a glass of Armagnac back to our room, and we relive our dinners of the last three evenings, concluding that the food is as satisfying to us today as most of what we've had at three-star restaurants in France in previous years. Although the style of the meals is less elaborate, the attention to detail, the overall quality, and the pacing reflect the same seriousness about dining well. The conversation leads to a momentous decision that both of us take an oath to uphold: as soon as Bill wins the World Series of Poker, which he says will be any year now, we'll retire permanently to La Riboto.

> >

The next day, we return to Nice, stopping first at the open-air market in Saint-Rémy, the town where Vincent van Gogh committed himself to an asylum after cutting off his left ear. The artist painted many landscapes here, often depicting the local trees that still form a canopy above lots of village streets. Today, gnarly but elegant plane trees, cut back in winter, cast shade and shadows over the downtown market area.

You can buy most anything of personal use from one vendor or another: stocking caps and coats suitable for the weather, ladies' lingerie less heedful of the cold, shoes and boots, books, CDs, Laguiole knives, diminutive grapevines, even roses and tulips. Among the numerous food booths, we find one selling only kiwis, another specializing in oysters and mussels, and a third just roasting chestnuts. Other stands boast loads of leeks, turnips, and other root vegetables, chickpeas dried and fresh, walnuts, hazelnuts, eggs, hearty breads, honeys, and sausages flavored with herbs, fennel, and pepper. As usual at a Provençal market, a man stirs a huge paella pan full of rice and seafood, an Asian stand offers spring rolls, samosas, and other fried treats, and spits loaded with chickens and meats spin at a rotisserie truck, where the proprietor watches distractedly as he bites off chunks of a baguette to wash down with red wine.

In Nice, we drop off our rental car and check in at La Pérouse, a seaside hotel in the old center of town where we've stayed several times before. When Bill made the reservation, he requested one of two specific rooms that enjoy the same great view, and the accommodating reception staff—generally cheery young men and women fluent in many languages—oblige. Our preferred rooms are small, but feel almost spacious because of the expanse of glass on two sides. A big shuttered window opens fully toward the city, and French doors gaze out to the Mediterranean and lead to a standing-room-only balcony that overlooks the whole of the bay, the beach, and the hotel pool. The higher of the two rooms, where we land today, abuts the top of La Colline du Château and offers exactly the same perspective on the town and the water, a view that virtually every tourist pays to see for a couple of minutes. While they come and go, we sit and stare at the vista for hours at a time.

The hill (colline) and the remains of its château beside us figured prominently in Nice history. In the fourth century B.C., Greeks routed Ligurians living in the vicinity and established the trading post of Nikaia (the basis of the city's current name), placing the town on the plateau as a natural vantage point for protecting the port. The residents had built a cathedral on the site by the eleventh century, and next to it, the ruling counts of Provence put their castle, eventually razed in later battles of succession.

Control of the strategic city changed a number of times before France finally established lasting sovereignty in 1860. Through the frequent political turmoil, the people of Nice remained remarkably independent of their rulers, as if they owned the fiefdom themselves. They still annually celebrate the courage of Catherine Ségurane, whom they credit with saving Nice from the Turkish fleet in 1543 by mooning the invaders. Maybe she misunderstood Machiavelli, who must have said somewhere that when the odds are against you, attack from the rear.

Shortly after we arrive, we find ourselves on a street named in honor of the heroine. It descends from La Colline du Château into Old Nice, where the population gradually expanded around Ségurane's era. It's always fun to walk the maze of narrow pedestrian lanes in this neighborhood and that's what we do on our first afternoon, after making an initial stop at La Merenda to secure a dinner reservation, which is always necessary despite the restaurant's refusal to install a phone for that purpose. In the heart of the old town now, we wander aimlessly, admiring the historic architecture, browsing a few stores, and absorbing the food aromas.

Almost equally split between local and visitor appeal, the mix of shops fascinates us. At one we buy a toddler's backpack for our granddaughter Chloe, engraved with the French spelling of her name with an accent over the last letter. Just a block or so away, we gape at a boned whole, head-on suckling pig resting in a case in front of a *boucherie*. It's known as *porquetta*, a trademark dish of the area stuffed with ham, artichokes, mushrooms, and other vegetables, and then roasted until the skin is crackling crisp.

Other Niçoise food specialties abound as well, most of them seldom found elsewhere. Cheryl gets a *pissaladière* snack to go at the same storefront eatery that Calvin Trillin once raved about in a *Gourmet* article for its local *pan bagnat*. Resembling a pizza, *pissaladière* is flatbread covered with onions cooked down slowly to their essence and then topped with a smattering of black olives and anchovies. *Pan bagnat* consists of a split loaf of round bread rubbed with a garlic clove and then filled as a sandwich with tuna canned in olive oil, lettuce, tomatoes, hard-boiled egg slices, and maybe radishes, scallions, celery, artichoke hearts, or anchovies. Made simply with chickpea flour and olive oil, *socca* looks like a giant, thin pancake, and the equally unfussy *tourta de bléa* features chard and pine nuts in a savory pie. The original mesclun, in contrast to salads that go by that name in the United States, brings together greens gathered mainly in the hills of Nice, particularly dandelion stalks, purslane, arugula, small bitter lettuces, and chervil.

By dinnertime, we're eager to eat. La Merenda raised eyebrows in the French food world when it opened years ago because chef-owner Dominique Le Stanc quit a prestigious haute cuisine position heading the kitchen at Chantecler, in Nice's grand Négresco hotel, to start cooking the kind of food he personally likes to eat. He has dubbed it "family cooking," but that doesn't translate well in American terms, since few families in the United States sit down to such regular menu dishes as tripes à la niçoise, andouillette (tripe sausage), and stockfish (pungent salt cod soaked for days and cooked with onions, tomatoes, and white wine for a couple of hours). The restaurant also stirred a little indignation at its inauguration by doing two seatings for dinner, at 7:00 and 9:00. Normally in France, when you book a table, it's yours all night. At La Merenda, they pace the service to get you out within two hours. Dastardly.

Promptly at 7:00, the early shift arrives, including us and all the other two dozen patrons who can fit knee-to-knee and elbow-to-elbow in the tiny space. Tonight, as we know is usual from past visits, the blackboard carte offers six appetizers, a similar number of main courses, an optional cheese course (the server just asks whether you want a goat, sheep, or cow variety), some desserts, and water or house wine to drink. The waiter carries the portable menu from one table to the next, expecting guests to choose and order quickly. Bill starts with a *tarte de Menton*—basically a *pissaladière* without the anchovies—so deservedly popular that the night's complete supply disappears by 7:15. Cheryl's house-made spinach tagliatelle with pistou also shines, a model of everything pasta can and should be: al dente, flavorful itself, and dressed with a perfect amount of basil-rich pistou.

For our main courses, Cheryl goes for the *daube* with *panisse* (chickpea fries) on the side. Our favorite style of beef stew, shaming all Anglo-Saxon versions, daube must be cooked for hours in an ocean of red wine, as Dominique Le Stanc does artfully. Bill's sausage with lentils features a fresh pork *saucisson,* fragrant with fennel and garlic, served a touch soupy in a shallow bowl with plump green lentils simmered with chard. Finishing with cheese—goat for Cheryl and sheep for Bill—we stagger out happily about 9:00.

The next morning we resume our vigil on the balcony, watching a half-dozen swimmers brave the frigid water. Although we've never been here at Christmas or Carnival, even colder periods, some residents reportedly celebrate those occasions by skinny-dipping in the bay. These polar bears today wear regular suits, which they deftly slip off their legs when leaving as they pull on warmer clothes over their heads. The beach promenade is far more active at this early hour, lively with joggers, bikers, Rollerblade enthusiasts, and plenty of walkers, many of them tethered to a dog. Our strolls around the city frequently lead us to the busy promenade, but we seldom go below to the uncomfortable beach, formed by rocks instead of sand.

Six mornings a week, including this one, a big pedestrian boulevard in Old Nice, cours Saleya, hosts an open-air market, with produce and prepared foods at one end and flowers at the other. Ambling over, we find it noticeably slower at this time of the year than in sunnier months, with fewer vendors and visitors both. At least the invincible Thérésa shows up, looking as striking as ever even bundled up for the weather. Chez Thérésa has been a mainstay of the market, and a Nice icon, since the 1920s. She's not that old herself, being the third Thérésa to run the business, but she upholds the legacy with regal pride, selling *socca, pissaladière, pan bagnat,* and *tourta de bléa* like they're her crown jewels. Her name isn't really Thérésa—it's Susy—and she's not from Nice—lived much of her life in Israel actually—but no one complains about food fraud.

A local man, whom we take to be her husband, does the cooking a couple of blocks away. Our last time in town, we were watching him work through the window of his small storefront kitchen when he waved at us to join him inside. He showed us his wood-burning oven, more than seventy-five years old, and demonstrated how he makes the socca. A biker pulling a cart transports the food to the market and Thérésa keeps some of it warm on the top of a big barrel that sits over a charcoal fire. She stations herself most of the time right behind the barrel, smiling and showing off her socca with the coy conceit of a new mom.

For lunch, we wind up right across the street from her booth at another Chez, named after Freddy in this case. Both of us yearn for local seafood and the restaurant provides gargantuan plates of it. Cheryl gets oysters on the half shell and *moules frites* (steamed mussels with French fries). Among a variety of paellas, the house specialty, Bill picks the one with the most goodies, including shellfish, fish, rabbit, chicken, and chorizo. The waiter plops it on the table in an iron skillet so loaded with the promised provisions—as well as a thick stew of tomatoes, onions, and garlic—that Bill can hardly locate the rice. It's far from a Valencian version, but this is Nice, not Spain, and everything here is distinctly Niçoise.

Isabelle and Michel Vernaud always guarantee that at Lou Pistou, our dinner restaurant this evening. Next-door neighbors with La Merenda—at the same physical address in fact—it shares much in common with its competitor, from the size of the space to a similar menu of well-executed local classics. The two differ primarily in personality, and on that measure we prefer Lou Pistou, a quintessential mom-and-pop bistro. Michel takes care of the cooking by himself in the small, fully open kitchen, always looking calm and collected in an apron-draped T-shirt while he manages a dozen tasks simultaneously. Isabelle, whose hair is so red she seems to be on fire, handles the front of the house alone with boundless energy. They love what they do and it makes you love them and their food.

Cheryl starts with an arugula salad, which Isabelle tosses at the table with hefty chunks of Parmesan and balsamic vinaigrette. Bill has grilled red bell peppers, topped with chopped garlic. When Isabelle brings the plate to the table, she hands him a can of olive oil to pour over the appetizer to taste. We both follow up with daube and pasta, but in two different preparations, with Bill's beef served over tagliatelle and Cheryl's stuffed in ravioli. For dessert, we opt for a lemon tart and a honey-rich nougat glacé, full of pistachios and candied fruit. It's all superlative, on the same level of quality and delight as our dinner at La Merenda. Incredibly, the bill is exactly the same in both places, €76 for three courses each and a bottle of wine.

In the morning, after a long gander at our view, we linger over breakfast, since it's going to be our last meal in town. Our hotel sets out a cold buffet daily worthy of indulgence. The baguettes, croissants, and pain au chocolat excel, as do the selections of French cheeses and charcuterie. Bill dives into the bowl of hard-boiled eggs, while Cheryl favors the quiche and yogurt, both of us leaving ample room to wrap up with fresh fruit salad. After another walk through Old Nice and a shower, it's time to head to the airport.

Our taxi driver turns out to be a talkative young woman. She asks about our stay and Bill says we've had a wonderful visit, enjoying the food in particular. Cheryl tells her about our meals, and the driver tells us about her mother's cooking, bringing us to mutual agreement about the culinary bounty. Then when she pauses at a red light, she turns and looks at us seriously to say, in a typically feisty Nice way, "It's not like this in northern France, you know. Parisians understand nothing about olive oil. Their food is so heavy, they might as well be eating the rocks on our beach." An apt parting thought, true or not.

THE NITTY-GRITTY

La Riboto de Taven
www.riboto-de-taven.fr
Les Baux de Provence
33-4-90-54-34-23
fax 33-4-90-54-38-88
Worth a detour from a different continent.

Castelas Huile d'Olive
www.castelas.com
Les Baux de Provence
Available in the United States from www.zingermans.com and other online retailers.

French-Word-A-Day
www.french-word-a-day.com

AUBERGE LA PASTOURELLO
Saint-Martin-de-Crau
33-4-90-47-40-44
fax 33-4-90-47-06-43
lunch and dinner

HÔTEL LA PÉROUSE
www.hotel-la-perouse.com
11 quai Rauba-Capeu, Nice
33-4-93-62-34-63
fax 33-4-93-62-59-41
*Great location and grand views from
some of the rooms.*

LA MERENDA
4 rue Raoul Bosio, Nice
*lunch and dinner (reservations usually
necessary, but no phone or fax)*

CHEZ FREDDY
cours Saleya, Nice
*lunch and dinner
(reservations not necessary)*

LOU PISTOU
4 rue Raoul Bosio, Nice
33-4-93-62-21-82
lunch and dinner

Beef Daube

Serve with broad flat egg noodles, other pasta, polenta, or simple boiled potatoes.

SERVES 8

Marinade

2 tablespoons olive oil

1 large onion, chopped

2 carrots, peeled and sliced into rounds

1 whole head of garlic, cut in half horizontally

1 bottle full-bodied tannic red wine, such as a Bandol

Large bouquet garni (about 6 large sprigs of parsley, 4 large sprigs of thyme, 1 bay leaf or sprig of rosemary or winter savory)

1 strip orange peel, about 3 inches long and ½ inch wide

2 cloves

2 teaspoons salt

4 pounds boneless beef chuck roast, or other similar beef for stewing or braising, cut into pieces 2 to 3 inches square

¼ cup duck fat or olive oil

½ pound chopped pancetta, *ventreche,* or blanched bacon

2 large onions, cut into small chunks

2 to 4 garlic cloves, minced

4 medium carrots, peeled and sliced into rounds

¼ cup Armagnac or brandy

½ pound celery root, peeled and chopped, or 2 celery hearts, chopped, optional

1 small pig's foot, optional

1 ounce bittersweet chocolate

Salt and freshly ground pepper to taste

Zest of 1 medium orange

Handful of chopped parsley

Thyme sprigs, optional

Make the marinade, first warming the oil in a large saucepan over medium heat. Add the onion, carrots, and garlic, and sauté about 5 minutes, until the onion is translucent. Pour in the wine, add the remaining marinade ingredients, and bring to a boil. Reduce the heat to low and simmer covered for about 30 minutes. Uncover and cool to room temperature.

Place the beef in a Dutch oven or similar large pot. Pour the marinade over it, cover, and refrigerate overnight or up to 24 hours. With a slotted spoon, remove the beef from the marinade and reserve. Strain the marinade, reserving only the liquid. Rinse and dry the pot. Add the duck fat or olive oil and pancetta, and sauté over medium heat until it colors lightly, 5 to 7 minutes. Using a slotted spoon, remove and discard the pancetta.

Stir the onions into the pan drippings and continue cooking over medium heat several minutes, until limp. Add the garlic and carrots and continue cooking until the vegetables just begin to brown, 5 to 7 minutes. Raise the heat to high, add the meat, about one-half at a time, stirring until the first batch is evenly browned before adding the rest. Pour in the Armagnac. Add about 1 cup of the marinade and scrape up from the bottom to dislodge all the tasty brown bits, or fond. Add the rest of the marinade, and the optional celery root and pig's foot. Bring to a very slow simmer over medium heat, then reduce the heat to low, cover, and cook until the meat is very tender, 2 to 3 hours. Remove the pig's foot, if used, pull any meat from it, shred the meat, and add the shreds back to the pot, discarding the rest. Add the chocolate, salt and pepper, orange zest, and parsley, and simmer for about 15 additional minutes. (If the liquid seems watery at this point, simmer uncovered for these remaining minutes.) Serve hot, garnished with thyme if you wish.

BRAZIL

OUR LONG BUT COMFORTABLE BRITISH AIRWAYS
flight, via London and São Paulo, arrives in Rio de Janeiro at midmorning on a
Saturday, always an auspicious day in the city. "Think of it like Thanksgiving," Bill
tells Jan and Mary, two friends joining us in Brazil. "Only it happens every week."

"And instead of a big, bland bird at the center of the table," Cheryl adds,
"you get the most sumptuous pork and beans on the planet."

"Of course, you can eat *feijoada* anytime—it's the national dish, after all—
but Saturday lunch is the traditional feasting hour," Bill says. "Few cooks or
restaurants serve the whole *completa* version at night because it's too much food
for then. They reserve it instead for a leisurely midday weekend meal, when everyone can take a nap afterward, preferably on the beach."

Mary Jablonsky agrees to the idea with resignation. A close friend of Cheryl's
for decades, she's always game for any adventure—like her traveling companion,
Jan Kohler—but Mary is also apprehensive about some of our eating enthusiasms. "Just don't expect me to try any ugly pig parts. You guys have never had to
inspect slaughterhouses, like I did in my early years at Kraft. I've seen plenty of
hog chow that will never cross my lips."

"If you end up with a trotter on your plate," Bill says, smiling, "pass it along
to me. You may not know it, but I've got a bit of a foot fetish."

Mary and Jan flew into Rio from Chicago and Boston, respectively, the day before, and have just welcomed us to the Ipanema Plaza Hotel, our mutual residence for the next three nights. "So where do you want to go to satisfy your little obsession?" Mary asks.

"I've narrowed the choices to two," Bill replies. "The nearby, posh Caesar Park Hotel has a feijoada buffet on Saturday, though the setting doesn't seem right. This is a slave dish, after all, not an upper-crust meal. But the best alternative, an old institution called Confeitaria Colombo, is downtown, a fair distance by cab."

"Let's go there," Jan says. "It will give us a chance to see more of the city."

The trip certainly does. Our inexperienced but eager-to-please taxi driver, unaccustomed to requests to go to the rather dowdy Centro, can't find the restaurant. He's heard the name, and knows the general location, but takes us around in circles for more than an hour before finally dropping us off. By the time we're seated, around 2:00 in the afternoon, most of the other patrons are moving on to dessert, and when we leave three hours later, no other diners remain.

Confeitaria Colombo opened in 1894, just as the historic downtown entered its golden age. For the first half of the twentieth century, until the national government began moving in 1960 to the new capital of Brasilia, this square mile of metropolis glittered more brightly than any spot in Latin America. It housed not only both branches of Congress and a multitude of ministries, but also Brazil's most prominent theaters, newspapers, banks, hotels, restaurants, and dance halls.

Few places represented the vibrant magnificence better than the Colombo. Portuguese immigrants founded the establishment as a pastry and sweets salon (hence, *confeitaria*) and added a fashionable ladies' tearoom in 1922 that evolved into a restaurant. It still looks today like it did then, brimming with belle époque splendor. A massive stained-glass ceiling splashes tinted sunlight across display cases filled with cakes and candies, tables topped with Italian marble, ornate French fixtures, Portuguese tile floors, and, best of all, eight monumental Belgian mirrors that each weigh as much as a car. In its heyday, the Colombo hosted the political, business, and intellectual elites of the city, including such regulars as poet Olavo Bilac. This Saturday, the restaurant, like the rest of the Centro these days, has to settle for ordinary folks like us.

Following custom, we start our *feijoada* banquet with a *caipirinha,* our first of dozens over the days ahead. A potent blend of Brazilian *cachaça* (strong sugarcane brandy) and coarse sugar muddled with the juice of a lime cut into small chunks, the drink supposedly cuts the fatty richness of *feijoada*. Whatever: it tastes great. While we sip the cocktails, Cheryl and Mary regale Jan and Bill with stories of their first trips together in Europe, when they both spent a year abroad at Salzburg College. Mary laughs about some of the guys Cheryl attracted, particularly a vagabond sailor in Majorca, saying, "Even Bill the reprobate was a better catch than him."

Cheryl retorts, "At least I wasn't loony enough to jump into Venice's Grand Canal."

"Those jerks who made the dare promised me a bottle of Jack Daniel's for that and never even gave me a drop."

The tales stop temporarily with the appearance of two formally attired waiters, a grizzled veteran of fifty-two years with a sly sense of humor and a more proper young man who speaks some English. They motion with a broad sweep of their arms at the buffet setup, ready apparently to give us a joint tour of the goodies. Pointing one at a time to a variety of big iron pots on a large central table, the younger gent recites, "Black beans, pork ribs, smoked pork loin, peppered pork sausage, *carne de sol*," which is salted, sun-dried beef. His colleague starts adding emphasis now to the enumeration by indicating different parts of his body. "Beef tongue, pork ears, pork feet, and pork tails."

A second long table nearby offers a profusion of possible accompaniments, accents, and side dishes: rice, vinegar laced with hot malagueta chiles, sautéed collard greens, orange segments, *farofa* (toasted manioc meal), sautéed plantains, and banana fritters. Another smaller table presents a dozen desserts, mostly custards and meringues. Starting with a foundation of beans, guests fill their plates—repeatedly in our case—with any combination of foods they desire.

Mary and Jan, feeling their way gingerly into the new cuisine, stick with familiar meats and a healthy assortment of vegetables, grains, and fruits. The two of us, having eaten sanitized American versions of *feijoada* before, are eager to try the real deal, and we dive in more fully. Cheryl samples a little of everything except the earthiest meats, while Bill skimps on the sides and desserts to leave ample room for all the pork and beef parts. The cooking isn't stellar, but the bounty is, leaving all of us happily satiated.

When the waiters bring the check, the older one, grinning infectiously, hands each of us a souvenir caipirinha glass with the name and logo of the restaurant. It's a goofy memento, the kind of kitschy curio we stopped collecting years ago, but we keep the tumblers and haul them all the way home. They will be a reminder for life of an indulgent Thanksgiving afternoon in Rio de Janeiro.

> >

As the urban energy ebbed in the historic Centro, it flowed straight toward the shore, especially the beaches of Copacabana, Ipanema, Leblon, and, more recently, the relatively distant Barra de Tijuca. Though it may seem odd today, most of the world, including Rio, didn't discover beaches as potential playgrounds until the twentieth century. Before then, they attracted little interest except as handy anchorages for fishing boats, or for the adventurous, serene spots for a stroll or a swim. In Rio and elsewhere, few people could even reach a grand beach before modern transportation provided access on rails, roads, and airways.

Using tunnels cut through the mountains south of downtown, trams arrived in 1892 at Copacabana, the closest of the major beaches, prompting the construction of some isolated summer residences. More substantial development didn't begin for another thirty years, until a wealthy visionary opened the opulent Copacabana Palace as a retreat in Rio for international royalty and the merely rich of the world. Within the following thirty years, the population of the neighborhood increased tenfold and started spilling farther south toward Ipanema, only a small bohemian enclave at the time.

Tom Jobim and Vinicius de Moraes enjoyed that offbeat spirit in Ipanema but accidentally helped to change it forever. Drinking beer together one day in a scruffy bar by the beach, they watched a lovely young girl walk by, swaying her hips gracefully. Jobim composed a lilting bossa nova score to extol her graceful cadence and Vinicius contributed lyrics for the tribute. When João and Astrud Gilberto teamed up with Stan Getz the next year, in 1963, to record "The Girl from Ipanema," suddenly every man on earth—most of all, twenty-one-year-old Bill—wanted to rush to the area and fall into step right behind her.

Bill spots her on Sunday, dozens of times, and again just as often on Monday when we return to the sand for a second visit. She's everywhere along the seaside, generally arm in arm with the Boy from Ipanema. Wherever we look in the crowds on the long, broad shore, we see them sashaying and playing, usually in such a carefree, guileless manner that it grabs our attention over and over. The attire is different each time—though always so skimpy that it never taxes the imagination—and most reassuringly for old, overclothed white folks like the two of us, the ages, shapes, and skin colors encompass the full range of human possibilities. The Girl and Boy are forever young but also maturing well, hefty and light, lanky and squat, black, brown, bronze, pink, and every hue in between.

Cheryl marvels at the jaunty, easygoing mood. "This is such a local scene, not at all like a stilted tourist beach or a pretentious resort beach." No hotels or other buildings intrude on the atmosphere. The closest structures—mainly tasteful mid-rise, multifamily residences interspersed with an occasional hotel or restaurant—sit well back from the sand across a broad boulevard, certainly visible but not at all imposing. As far as we can determine, not a single T-shirt or other ticky-tacky shop exists within blocks.

Even the ubiquitous beach vendors respect the laid-back mood, pushing their jewelry, sunglasses, press-on tattoos, pareos, and other goods only when someone shows interest. The four of us pass on everything except the charcoal-grilled cheese, sold by guys who lug around a hibachi loaded with glowing coals and a small ice chest holding thick slices of a Halloumi-like cheese on a stick. They sear the outside of the cheese over the fire and serve it warm, with an herb coating or a hot sauce if you wish. "Now this is what people are meant to eat," Mary tells Bill.

After our first outing on the beach, a short tree-lined block from the hotel, we take a taxi to the top of the town. The view from Corcovado Hill, towering 2,300 feet above the coast, astounds us and everyone around us—except maybe the ones trying to take in everything through the lens of a video recorder—and confirms our impression that Rio enjoys the most spectacular natural setting of any city we've ever visited. Though other mountains block part of the perspective to the south, you can see all of the striking Guanabara Bay, the Centro, Sugar Loaf Mountain, the principal beaches, dozens of residential areas, including some of the *favela* slums, and of course, rising another one hundred feet above you, Brazil's most famous postcard image, the art deco statue of Christ spreading his arms wide to embrace the faithful. Even the ride up and down thrills our crew, winding around the humpback contour that gives the peak its name through the world's largest urban forest, the Tijuca National Park, an immense jungle that makes New York's Central Park seem like a suburban backyard.

When we return from the heights, we ask our cabdriver to drop us at the main market square in our Ipanema neighborhood, Praça General Osório. During most of the week it functions as a full-blown food market—offering everything from luscious tropical fruit to whole chickens, complete with their blood in a bag—then on Sundays becomes the scene of the Feira Hippie (yes, Hippie Fair). Our quartet finds a trove of oddball treasures in the stalls, but not a single identifiable hippie. Mary and Jan pick up some belts, jewelry, and Christmas gifts, while we browse seriously with less success through several tables of handmade crafts.

In the end, the two of us lay out money only at a lunch and sweets booth operated by Baianas (ladies from the state of Bahia, our next stop in Brazil), who enjoy fame across the country for their great street food. To check whether they're offering the real thing or a big-city imitation, at first we just share one of the signature black-eyed pea fritters called *acarajé*. After frying the cake in *dendê*, a red palm oil, the cooks split it and give us a choice of toppings. Cheryl chooses for us the fiery red chile paste *vatapá* (a puree of shrimp, bread, nuts, and coconut milk) and *caruru* (stewed-down okra and shrimp sometimes compared to gumbo). Glory be, it's heavenly. Cheryl rushes off to get Mary and Jan, drags them back, and all of us dig in with gusto, ordering more *acarajés*, coconut patties, flan, and an unusual banana pudding with layers of cake and meringue.

Too bad the Baianas are not in the kitchens at the two churrascaria restaurants we try, both of which could use a little help with the food preparation. A Brazilian institution exported in recent years to other parts of the world, including the United States, a churrascaria specializes in meats served *rodízio*-style at the table by a parade of waiters carrying cuts of beef, pork, lamb, chicken, and sausage on large metal cooking spits. For a starter course, diners graze an extensive buffet, usually including a variety of salads, sushi, and fish dishes, supplemented by starchy sides—such as empanadas and *pão de queijo* (tasty mozzarella-like cheese balls)—brought directly to the table. After guests are stuffed with meat and signal that by turning a card in front of them to the *"não, obrigado"* side, they return to another section of the buffet for a choice of desserts. The format emphasizes quantity over quality, of course, but it's too local to overlook.

Our initial experience goes pleasantly at Churrascaria Carretão, a short walk from our hotel and chosen in part because of that. Rio has a reputation as a dangerous city for tourists, a place where thieves often prefer confrontational robbery to purse-snatching or pickpocketing. None of us ever sees anything suspicious or feels the least threatened, but we stay cautious when we're out on foot. The Carretão surprises us at first with its merry ambiance, reminiscent of what we've seen earlier in the day on Ipanema Beach. The reason quickly becomes apparent: most of the customers came directly from the sand, hardly bothering in many cases to slip a modest cover-up over their thong bikinis and Speedos.

During dinner, right after one scurrying waiter almost spears a barely clad behind with his spit, Mary asks us about our last stop in France, where the three of us have traveled together before. "Actually," Bill says, "there are surprising similarities between Nice and Rio. Take Carnival, for example. Nice invented it in the Middle Ages and Rio re-created it for modern times, just for the sake of lusty amusement in both cases. The cities even look a little alike, sitting on big bays below lofty hills, and the residents of each clearly have a local style of their own, a kind of trademark joie de vivre."

"Do you know that the first European settlers of Rio were French?" Cheryl asks. "French pirates came first, followed by an official colony called 'Antarctic France.' In a good book I'm reading about Rio right now, Brazilian writer Ruy Castro says most of the pioneers went gaga over the local Indian women, who apparently were a male fantasy, always naked and horny. Their commander, a strict Catholic, got fed up with frequent orgies and declared he would start hanging raunchy settlers. That caused so many men to desert and move inland, the colony collapsed."

Looking around the room at the nearly naked patrons, Jan says, "Maybe the honcho misunderstood Rio's destiny. By the way, has anyone noticed where guys keep stuff like wallets and house keys in a Speedo?"

Several *caipirinhas* and the ongoing floor show make up for the shortcomings in the food, leaving us in a jovial mood as the evening ends. So we head to another churrascaria the next night, this one a taxi ride away in Leblon, but it disappoints us compared with the Carretão, distinguishing itself primarily by a stuffier atmosphere, more condescending service, and a check three times greater. The sole redeeming grace of the evening is the trip back to our hotel, which takes us by a lagoon festooned with a giant Christmas tree—twenty-seven stories high—floating on a barely visible barge. Approximately three million lights blaze through revolving patterns of display, casting dazzling color across the water and the sky.

On our last morning in town, just hours before our departure for Salvador, Bahia, Mary pushes the rest of us to go to the Carmen Miranda Museum, despite reports that it's tiny and has frustrated many fans. Humoring her initially, we end up thanking her profusely. The bunkerlike building is minuscule, severely limiting the display space, but the costumes, photos, and film clips turn us from curious, detached observers into awed admirers. The dynamic little lady—five feet tall on tiptoe—truly presented the best of Brazil to the world during her music and movie career from the 1930s to the 1950s, when she reigned as one of the queens of Hollywood.

Our perspective totally flip-flops on the most fanciful aspects of her stage and screen persona. Her whimsical headdresses, we learn, drew their inspiration from the distinctive turbans worn by the Baianas and, for practical purposes, compensated for her height, allowing her to star in movies alongside the much taller leading men of the day. Her elaborate outfits, bountiful bangles, and sensual hand movements also mimicked Baiana style, and her sense of rhythm in songs and dances reflected the booming music scene in Rio at the time. What once seemed caricature to us now seems brilliantly real, even when she dons tropical dress on celluloid and sings a "Home on the Range" tune about "where the cows and the cantaloupes play."

The women are incredulous that the Museum lacks a gift shop, but Mary discovers right before we're ready to leave that the small administrative office sells a few souvenirs. Our group buys out much of the stock, including jewelry boxes, purses, magnets, and shirts, demurring only on the Barbie-style dolls in Carmen costumes. Cheryl even considers getting one of them as a girlfriend for

Flat Stanley but settles for taking a photo of him flirting with the whole troupe.

Jan and Bill depart, trying to pressure Mary and Cheryl to hurry up. With the impatient ones gone, the office manager asks the dallying pair, "Would you care to try on a replica of a Carmen headdress?" It's like asking our editor if she wants this manuscript on time.

"This is really heavy!" Mary exclaims. "How could she possibly carry and balance it on her head through one of those bouncy dance numbers?"

"Just stand still and smile like a pinup girl," Cheryl says, taking her photo multiple times. Switching roles, Cheryl poses next, trying to be both coy and sultry in a Carmen way.

"You got it, girl," Mary says. "Now take a big bow for the camera without losing your crown."

"Oh no!" the manager intervenes. "Don't try that. You'll dump out the bananas."

> >

Among all of our destinations on this trip, only Bali has been on our priority list for longer than Salvador. Rio becomes a fine bonus on the way here, significantly exceeding our expectations, but we're eager now to see the place that gave birth to Brazil and continues to define its soul.

A thousand miles north of Rio, approaching the spot where South America juts east into the Atlantic and seems to point directly at Africa, Salvador served as the capital of colonial Brazil for the first two hundred years of the nation's history. For even longer, its port controlled most foreign trade, exporting great quantities of sugar, the white gold of the northeast, and the real gold and diamonds extracted from southeastern mines. Some of that wealth stayed behind, financing magnificent homes, grand baroque churches, and steady growth. At the time of the American Revolution, Salvador surpassed any city in the future United States in population and splendor. Within the Portuguese empire, only Lisbon eclipsed it in prestige.

Slavery made it all possible. By the middle of the sixteenth century, sugarcane cultivation dominated the economy in the Bahia and Pernambuco regions around Salvador. In the eyes of the landowners, the arduous, relentless work in the fields required chattel labor from Africa. Brazil became the first area of the New World to exploit African slaves, and the country maintained the practice longer than any other, up to 1888. Of the eleven million people sold into slavery in the Americas, almost 40 percent came to Brazil, more than to anywhere else.

That kind of heritage definitely leaves a legacy. A proud European poise remains in Salvador, ingrained in the mores in many ways, but the city is fundamentally African, more so than any other place on this side of the Atlantic. It's not just the ancestry of the population—90 percent wholly or partially African—but more critically, the traditions the residents maintain. In religion, music, movement, food, and more, Salvador exudes an indigenous Creole spirit unlike any other on earth.

The vitality of the city almost overwhelms us on our first night. Our flight arrives late due to a delay in Rio, pushing us into the thick of evening rush-hour traffic, which creeps in this city of two and a half million people. The taxi takes us past industrial zones, high-rise office buildings, shopping complexes, and sprawling residential areas before finally reaching Barra, the seaside neighborhood where we're staying. When our driver gets to the Monte Pascoal Praia Hotel, we dump our bags in our adjoining rooms and take a quick look from our balconies out to the local beach, still buzzing with life under bright streetlamps.

Without wasting any more time, we're off to Pelourinho, the historic center of town a few miles away. Our original plan called for us to be in the old city well before sunset, to get our bearings in daylight. This is Tuesday, the prime day of the week for local bands to perform on outdoor stages all around Pelourinho, and it's also the first Tuesday of the month, a major payday and party day in Salvador. Our advance reading suggests the area is going to get crowded and boisterous, but what we find still bowls us over.

Our cab drops us at Praça da Sé, a plaza one block from the main square, Terreiro de Jesus. Right in front of us, as we shut the car doors, a large children's chorus is singing Christmas carols in Portuguese. Most of the kids stand on an elevated stage, but some range farther afield, including in the windows of an adjoining colonial building. Massive speakers—they like the volume high in Salvador—boom the music to an appreciative, packed audience occupying every square inch of available space. The carols enchant us, especially "Silent Night," though it seems curious to us at first that "silent" translates as *feliz* (happy or merry). Later in the week, we realize that the English word would have a negative connotation here; in a city so full of music, a silent night would seem dreary.

Just beyond the choir, in the midst of a swarm of people, Santa sits in a pretty, tinsel-covered, one-room house, taking requests from a long line of admiring youngsters. A dozen teenage elfettes, cloaked in red satin and faux ermine, assist Santa, as do a red-shirted security guard, three hunky shepherds with crooks, and several young women in Christmas tree and star outfits. Mary comments, "This is like going through Disney's 'It's a Small World' in a speedboat."

After the cheerful overture with the children, we plunge into bigger adult crowds on Terreiro de Jesus. At food and drink stands lining three sides of the square and spilling into the streets, Baianas preside regally, attired in traditional white, with billowing skirts, puffy-sleeved lacy blouses, and blossomy turbans. A bandstand occupies the fourth flank, facing the cathedral. A few people watch the group playing now, but most cluster with friends, talking, laughing, gesturing.

On the dark fringes of the plaza, two young men dance acrobatically, not so much with each other as at each other. Bill recognizes the thrusting, fading, fluid movements as capoeira, a martial art that slaves brought from Africa and refined in Brazil, particularly in Bahia. Slave owners distrusted the skill, as you might expect, and eventually got capoeira banned, but it continued to flourish underground. Though it has spread around the globe now, Salvador remains the center for the teaching and practice of the ritualized craft. Performers pop up regularly around the city, always attracting a circle of fans.

The horde of revelers and the maelstrom of activity quickly disorient us. Without a map, and no streetlights to guide us beyond the busy square, we have no sense of where we are in relation to anything else in Pelourinho. Music reverberates dimly in the distance, but not clearly enough to follow the sound. Dodging and weaving our way through the throngs, the four of us wander aimlessly for a while before deciding to retreat inside for drinks and dinner at Axego, a second-story restaurant right off the plaza.

According to a story Bill came across on a good Salvador Web site (www.bahia-online.net), Manoel dos Santos Pereira founded Axego accidentally. He liked to cook on weekends for friends at his rustic summer home, which had a large terrace great for alfresco dining. One day a French guest at the nearby

Club Med saw this happening, assumed the place was a lively restaurant, sat down, and ordered the dish of the day. Manoel served him happily, but when Monsieur asked for the check, the host tried to explain the situation, saying the meal was a gift. Probably not comprehending the Portuguese, the Frenchman came back the next weekend with a group of buddies determined to pay this time. Manoel took their money and went into business.

The menu—only in Portuguese, as is common in the city—offers Bahian specialties mainly, along with a smattering of other popular Brazilian dishes. In need of a calming elixir, we order a round of *caipirinhas* and some *pão de queijo* for nibbling. Then each of us gets an appetizer course of *casquinha di siri,* deviled sea crab served in a ceramic, shell-shaped dish with *molho de pimenta,* a hot sauce made in this case with bits of fresh red chile, onion, and tomato in a vinegar base. For an entrée, two large plates of pan-fried whole local sea bass amply satisfy our gang.

Since we arrived, a band has been playing somewhere below the restaurant's back windows, but about the time the fish comes, a new group takes the stage and kicks up the beat substantially. The music now rocks the restaurant, sending us and the other guests into motion, tapping toes, beating fingers, shaking heads. Although we don't know it yet, it's the first of our several encounters with the amazing Olodum, which electrifies the Salvador Carnival parade each year with two hundred drummers, a number of singers, and thousands of dancers.

After leaving Axego, we head back to the bandstand on the main square, where an exceptionally energetic group is now performing to an enthralled audience. Three young female singers and dancers lead the ensemble, belting out lyrics while shimmying and pumping their pelvises, hips, arms, shoulders, and heads with such fervent abandon that you wonder how their bodies stay intact. Jan quietly says, "I've never seen anything more erotic in my life." Bill stands agape, speechless. Our more restrained trio of ladies drags him to a nearby taxi and deposits him in the front passenger seat, alone with his reveries.

Our driver promptly jerks us all back to reality. He does the 0 to 60 routine in less time than it takes to grab a breath—without bothering to turn on the headlights, which he uses only occasionally later on the darkest streets we encounter. Red lights slow our suicidal momentum two or three times, though the driver ignores at least a dozen other stop signals, sometimes braking briefly for a glance in other directions but usually just zooming through intersections without heed. He gets us back to the hotel in one-third of the normal time, in direct but inverse correlation with the surge in our heart rates.

> >

Over the next few days we settle in and sort out the pieces of our first-night experience. Gradually, we get to know every cobblestone street and many of the hidden courtyards of Pelourinho, learn that everyone disregards some red lights when they feel it's safe to do so, and immerse ourselves in local food and music, both intricately tied to religion in this city. Eventually it dawns on us that Salvador is far and away the most exuberant city any of us has ever visited and that's why it felt a bit overwhelming initially. Life gets seriously heady here.

Jumping in like most tourists, we start with the two primary attractions for visitors, the sights of historic Salvador and the lively beaches. Everyone goes early in a stay to Pelourinho, the core of the colonial city during its glory days and now a UNESCO-designated World Heritage site. Dignified though rather stern colonial structures surround the Terreiro de Jesus, including the seventeenth-century cathedral, a couple of smaller baroque churches, and a former school of medicine that now houses the Afro-Brazilian Museum.

Opposite the cathedral, a wide street leads to the Igreja de São Francisco (Church of St. Francis, the patron saint of the city). In the week we're here, the avenue in front of the church slowly takes on a festive Christmas air, complete with an oversized Nativity scene and a giant effigy of a well-tanned Santa with cornrows in his white hair. The church itself, built in high baroque style between 1708 and 1723, echoes the grandness of scale in a more solemn way. The sugar barons of the wealthy city covered the intricately carved interior with more than one hundred kilograms of gold, enough to cast a sheen outside at night when the doors stand open.

Pelourinho brims with boutiques these days, like all tourist areas. Since this is our last stop on the trip, and we don't have to haul our bags anywhere except home, we're ready to load up on Christmas and other gifts. The fetching Mariana at Planet Bahia obliges us eagerly, getting us to try on almost everything in the shop over the course of several visits. She lived briefly in Los Angeles with her aunt and speaks English well, a rarity in Salvador. When she mentions once that she spends her days off at the beach, Bill asks which of the dozen possibilities she prefers. Mariana says, "Usually Flamengo, all my friends agree it's the best," which sounds like a solid recommendation to us. She finally sells us a bunch of colorful hair doodads for our daughter and granddaughters as well as a bright beaded necklace and earrings for Cheryl. Elsewhere in Pelourinho, we also pick up local music CDs, an Olodum T-shirt, jars of malagueta chiles, and some gemstone jewelry, mostly for presents.

A large crafts bazaar in the nearby Comércio district, the Mercado Modelo, offers little of interest to us, but farther along the shore to the north, the Feira de São Joaquim proves livelier and more remarkable. Almost a miniature city, it encompasses an earthy food market, stalls with kitchenware and baskets, shops selling a range of local merchandise, and snuggled behind it all, some shanty-town living quarters that make us wince. Our cabdriver, Wellington—who speaks no English but starts calling Cheryl "Hillary" after learning Bill's name—insists on escorting us for security purposes. He takes us past stands packed with produce, including greens, okra, manioc and other knobby tubers, malagueta and Scotch bonnet chiles, sugarcane, and cashew fruits, which look like voluptuous calico bell peppers with a curved, green-brown nut on top. Butchers cut meat for customers, vendors hawk dried and fresh shrimp by the bushel, and a live frog the size of a guinea pig croaks at shoppers from a cage. A man brushes by us on the way to his car with a bellowing goat, feet tied together, in a sack slung over his shoulder.

Continuing north on the same taxi trip, we visit the Nosso Senhor do Bonfim church, a beloved eighteenth-century sanctuary associated with miracles. Outside, vendors sell us *fitas,* good-luck ribbons in a variety of colors that we tie around our wrists in the traditional fashion. Making our way inside through crowds of the faithful, we go to a back room where people seeking cures and giving thanks for them leave testaments in the form of photos and replicas of afflicted body parts.

From the divine to the worldly, after a few days of sightseeing and shopping we're ready for some beach time. Barra beach, actually, has been omnipresent since our arrival, greeting us enthusiastically every time we step out on our hotel balconies. Tanners and swimmers congregate down the shore from us, while sporting types gather directly below our perches. Surfers, often in droves, ride the waves, and joggers dodge pedestrians on the sidewalk and cars on the street. From early morning until night, football teams compete constantly in the game Americans call soccer, always keeping the ball in play even when it bounds far into the sea. On occasion, it's just a few guys and gals, using goalposts made of sticks, but now and then, full squads show up with regulation equipment, uniforms, and referees.

On our first weekend morning, trombones wake us at 7:15, when a festive parade passes along the beachfront. A jazz band leads the procession, followed by a truck loaded with beer, coconuts, and people blasting fireworks over the water. Bringing up the rear, a woman wearing a fancy headdress and sash guides scores of celebrants in identical white T-shirts toward a sandy destination somewhere ahead. Figuring the ruckus roused even the late-rising Mary, Cheryl calls their room to say, "Let's hit the beach."

On Mariana's suggestion, we head to Flamengo, as far from Barra as public transportation goes. The bus trip along the coast takes an hour and a half, in part because street parades (different from the one that woke us) delay us twice. Other passengers, all quite friendly, regard us as oddities, particularly the two young girls engrossed with Mary; when they pantomime a question about whether she has children, Mary tries to say she has a cat but conveys instead that she *is* a cat, eliciting delighted laughter. An elderly gentleman in front of us, who once worked for Xerox and spent time at the company's Connecticut headquarters, coaches his shy four-year-old grandson, Jaime, to tell Cheryl, "Hi. I love you." When she responds in kind in English, the foreign language startles him, and he bursts into tears.

The palm-lined Flamengo and other nearby beaches look a little meager compared with Ipanema, but they feel more natural, largely secluded from urban and resort development. Most beachgoers settle in at tables with chairs and umbrellas provided free by dozens of *barracas*, food and drink stands. Following the routine, we pick a place close to the bus stop. Over the next several hours, a stream of waiters brings us limeades and cheese "crepes" on a stick, the specialty of our barraca. Scads of vendors stop by, selling everything hawked in Rio plus oysters on the half shell, fresh fish, blow-up Santas, coconut-shell planters with live flowers, cigarettes by the pack or individually (with a free light), and ashtrays decorated with crab shells. Jaime and his grandfather also stroll past us on a walk and the child waves at us cheerfully like we're longtime neighbors.

The next day, Sunday, is the busiest of the week for the beaches. Multiple generations of families show up together, including grandparents in some cases with swimsuits as ample as ours. Wanting to try a different beach, we decide on Patamares, mainly to have lunch on the shore at Caranguejo da Dadá after our time in the sun. Today, in addition to other services, our barraca sets out inflatable plastic kiddie pools for toddlers, and a really enterprising vendor cooks fish and sausages on a commercial-size charcoal grill mounted to a three-wheel cart that he pushes through the sand.

The food at Caranguejo da Dadá is terrific, especially the *bobó de camarão*, made with jumbo shrimp, dried and grated fresh cassava, green peppers, onions, tomatoes, and coconut milk. The kitchen sautés the ingredients first in dendê and then stews them together until the flavors meld and the mixture thickens. It may not be the most appropriate dish for a hot summer day on the beach, but it's as well crafted as anything else we see or purchase in Salvador.

> >

Getting comfortable now with the surface charms of the city, we're ready to delve deeper into its character and fervent energy. The key, many experts suggest, lies in religion, not so much in the Catholicism practiced in the venerable churches that we and other tourists visit, but in the Afro-Brazilian blend of beliefs called Candomblé. The creed prospers in many areas of the nation, and shares a heritage with other African-based religions in the New World, but Candomblé comes originally from Bahia and exerts its broadest overall influence in Salvador.

Our first glimpse of this side of the city comes on taxi trips that take us past a small lake near the center of town. A dozen colorful sculptures, each about twenty feet tall and grouped in a circle, rise from the water. Mistaking them initially from a distance as Christmas trees, like the one we saw in Rio, we finally realize they are *orixás*, the deified forces of nature worshipped in Candomblé. Slaves brought a devotion to them from their homelands, but the Church in Brazil firmly banned the ancient African religion. Rather than acquiescing, the slaves discovered they could secretly maintain their faith in the orixás by disguising them as Catholic saints and syncretizing those identities. Omolú, who possesses feared and respected power over disease, for example, became associated with Saint Lazarus. By praying to a saint for spiritual intercession, slaves could also appeal directly to their orixás for protection and help.

As the sculptures in the lake proclaim clearly, Candomblé is no longer an underground religion. Many of its adherents remain Catholic as well, but even more important in its impact on local culture and cuisine, a lot of nominal Catholics in Salvador also openly revere the orixás. Since the orixás love and respond with appreciation to song, music, dance, and offerings of food—rites employed in their worship for centuries—their enthusiasms spill over to the human population.

To gain any appreciable understanding of Candomblé, it seems important to us to experience a worship service. Dinner shows advertised in Pelourinho include a Candomblé presentation, but that won't do. After asking around about opportunities to attend an authentic ceremony, the tourist office informs us there's only one open to the public during our week in town. The four of us sign up eagerly, agreeing to a stipulation that we dress conservatively and don't wear black, a color that offends many of the orixás. This requires Cheryl to go shopping for something other than the few black slacks she's carrying. She looks at some beautiful white dresses typical of the area but reluctantly returns them to the rack as too extravagant to wear at home. In the end, she opts for a more versatile pair of soccer pants that can be rolled into capris.

A minibus picks us up at our hotel in the early evening, then stops at other places for ten additional guests from a variety of countries before delivering all of us to a white house in a humble residential neighborhood, where our guide, Carlos, joins us. Shortly before 9:00, we follow people from the neighborhood in filing down a narrow walkway on the side of the house to a covered outdoor terrace. This is the only section of the *terreiro*, or sacred space, where visitors are allowed. Earlier in the day in private areas of the terreiro, according to insiders, initiates of the order have sacrificed animals in a ritual butchering to prepare the favorite dishes of the orixá being honored tonight. They set the hallowed fare on an altar erected on the open-air terrace, and after we and other outsiders leave at the end of the public service, they will feast literally on the food of the gods.

Our vanload of guests troops onto the terrace and takes seats around the sides. Above us, a simple handmade chandelier, bare lightbulbs, and strips of white fabric hang from the corrugated-tin ceiling. The spiritual leader, or *ialorixá*, of this house of worship enters wearing white lace, with a flowing skirt and a puffy-sleeved blouse. A turban covers her head and beads dangle from her neck and wrists. A septuagenarian, we guess, she circles the space swinging an incense burner, the same kind Catholic priests use, and presents all of us in the room with a little manioc flour in our cupped hands, blowing more of it to the corners of the terrace.

Three other mature women assist the main priestess in conducting the rites that follow. A half-dozen younger female initiates also take an active but more subservient role, and three men in the same age range play drums and other simple percussion instruments. Tonight, they want to summon the spirit of Oxóssi, the *orixá* of the forest and the hunt. The musicians set a beat that's known to appeal to the god, and the ladies dance in a circle in a distinctive shuffling, swaying style, to further entice him.

Men from the congregation gradually join the circle, and one by one, a number of them begin to shake and tremble, sometimes stumbling and falling in a trancelike state. Oxóssi has possessed them, joining the ceremony in their bodies. The elder women lead these men away, escorting them to another room behind a closed door. Later, after a couple of hours of drumming and dancing, the possessed men reappear in the attire of the *orixá*, wearing simple woodlandlike costumes and smoking big cigars. Now a link for the night between humankind and the gods, they mingle with the crowd, offering and receiving blessings.

Seeing the ceremony makes the connection between Candomblé and Salvador's street music viscerally real to us. Two kinds of bands dominate the music scene, *afoxés* and *blocos Afros*. Both orient their year around the city's Carnival, which is less formal and more robust in many ways than the same celebration in Rio. To prepare for the annual event, they rehearse publicly before live audiences, usually once a week and often in Pelourinho.

Afoxés basically perform a nonreligious rendition of Candomblé music, with a similar percussive rhythm and lyrics in a ritualized vein. The first *afoxé* joined Carnival in 1895, and a decade later, another of the groups broke the color barrier in the annual festivities, simply marching into the then segregated white parade. Today's largest and best known *afoxé* is Filhos de Ghandy (Sons of Gandhi), formed in 1949 to honor the recently assassinated Indian leader and his spirit of peaceful resistance to oppression.

On a Sunday night, when the group rehearses, we happen to wander by their headquarters in Pelourinho. Hearing music, we hesitate outside, unsure whether it's an open performance until a young man at the door motions us in. He leads us down a flight of stairs, crammed with people coming and going, and through a crowded bar out to a covered terrace where the band is playing. It looks much like the ceremonial space at the Candomblé service, down to the strips of fabric hanging from the ceiling, and the percussive beat and shuffle style of the dancing are nearly identical. When Carnival rolls around again, the Filhos will come out five thousand strong in Indian robes to celebrate this cadence and movement on the streets of the city.

Blocos Afros go several steps further in secularization. They maintain African roots as fully as the *afoxés* but adapt the ancient percussive rhythms to contemporary music. Dozens of them flourish in Salvador and some, especially Olodum (featured on Paul Simon's *The Rhythm of the Saints* album), have achieved considerable commercial success and international recognition. One night in Pelourinho, we catch an Olodum performance at a fund-raising concert for a local food bank, paying an admission of a sack of sugar each. Twenty or so drummers, under the lead of a professional conductor, rock the concrete stage with such intensity you think it's going to crack the floor. A young boy in front of us tries to keep up with the beat on an imaginary drum, banging it furiously with two empty water bottles. A Brazilian sports star, who we never identify, saunters in after us, signing autographs and shaking hands. He stands a head taller than anyone else, proudly displaying an extraordinary hairdo in synch with the vibrant music, a masterpiece of beads and woven rags in Day-Glo lime and fuchsia.

Strolling through Pelourinho on another evening near the end of our stay, we fall into step behind one of the newer *blocos Afros,* an all-woman ensemble called Dida that's led by a former music director of Olodum. They move slowly down the street, playing as they go, toward a performance stage, stopping often and collecting an entourage of dancers and other enthusiastic followers. It's a spontaneous party, bubbling with excitement. By now, we're beginning to expect this kind of thing. It's just another routine night in the hometown of Candomblé.

> >

Our long-standing interest in Salvador derives, as you might guess, from the food, specifically the city's great reputation for Creole cooking. In all bastions of Creole cuisine, the culinary tradition is closely tied to other aspects of the local culture, but we had no inkling of how in this case until now.

In the United States, people often take a narrow, parochial view of Creole food, associating it exclusively with New Orleans. This perspective even mutates into a fixation sometimes when a curious person tries to sort out clear and absolute differences between Creole and Cajun cooking in Louisiana. The two, in truth, are city and country cousins, related by virtue of belonging to the same extended family of New World Creole cuisines. Other branches of the family flourish in the French West Indies, parts of the Spanish Caribbean, and in Bahia. More distant cousins live around Veracruz, Mexico, and in the past, across various areas of the American South from Biloxi to Charleston. They generally share great-grandparents, one African and one southern European, an affection for New World ingredients employed in robust preparations, a coastal location that provides easy access to the bounty of the sea, and a temperate climate that encourages a taste for the spicy.

Oddly, few of the relatives know each other, and they tend to regard their cooking as unique. One night in Phoenix, during a culinary conference, we had dinner with a superb New Orleans chef at an authentic Mexican restaurant. He asked us about one of the menu items, *huachinango a la veracruzana* (snapper Veracruz), and we said it's similar to the New Orleans favorite named courtbouillon. Laughing, he said, "That's impossible. New Orleans cooks created courtbouillon strictly out of local inspiration and it remains unlike any other fish dish in the world." He ordered the huachinango, recognized the affinities, and apologized for his presumption. Neither of us worked up the courage to tell him that French Caribbean islanders also claim exclusive rights to another variation of the same dish, which they even call courtbouillon themselves.

To us, this broad Creole food tradition is the signature cuisine of the Americas, and one of the most fascinating culinary syntheses on earth. Except for Bahia, we've visited all of the centers of Creole cooking in the past and have gone to many of them multiple times in recent decades. Salvador became gradually but steadily the biggest case of unfinished business on our food agenda. It is our main reason for visiting Brazil, to plop into place the final piece of a jigsaw puzzle that we've been carrying around for years; anything else we enjoy here is gravy.

The local cooking, it becomes clear early, resembles other Creole cuisines in many respects. Some of the common combinations of ingredients look almost identical to those elsewhere, particularly the rice with beans or peas and the shrimp with okra. The casquinha di siri here brings to mind the crab *farci* on Guadeloupe and Martinique. The most popular kind of molho de pimenta, mixing fiery chiles with vinegar, recalls Caribbean hot sauces, and occasionally you even see a molho in the familiar New Orleans Creole style, with tomatoes, bell peppers, and onions.

Not surprisingly, though, Bahian cuisine remains more purely African than other varieties of Creole cooking. That's due in part to the prominent role played by dendê, an African ingredient virtually unknown in other Creole capitals; the palm oil adds an inimitable musky accent to loads of local dishes. You also have to credit the Candomblé influence again. The *orixás* brought many of their favorite dishes almost intact from Africa. They demanded a faithful execution of the original or at least tastes as similar as possible with available ingredients. Even today in terreiros, initiates hew to old recipes and preparation methods in the kitchen in an attempt to maintain continuity with former African versions of the fare. They perpetuate an allegiance to African foods and flavors within the Candomblé community, which for practical purposes means all of Salvador.

A direct Candomblé connection probably even exists to some of the best restaurant chefs of the city, mostly women of a traditional bent. Like Guadeloupe with its *cuisine de mères,* Salvador boasts its own *comida de mãe,* cooking defined and refined by mothers with boundless energy and saintly authority. Our most memorable meals come from their kitchens.

Alaíde da Conceição, respectfully known as the "Queen of the Beans," prepares the first of these local feasts late one afternoon before she closes her tiny restaurant at sunset. Dona Alaíde began cooking with her mother almost a half century ago at a stand in the Comércio district, and remains at the stove at Alaíde do Feijão, located on a narrow side street in Pelourinho. When we arrive, two large groups have commandeered most of the tables and chairs, stringing them together for one office Christmas party occupying most of the inside space and another on the street, blocking all but the most determined traffic. The din reaches decibels unimagined in American restaurants, but it's fun to watch the celebrations—our only option anyway, since conversation would be impossible.

Dona Alaíde specializes in feijoada and a locally popular *rabada* (oxtail stew). Our group gets a couple of plates of both, preceded by a cup of a simple but sub-lime bean soup. Unlike the *feijoada completa* we had in Rio, this one arrives with the major components already in the bowl. To the brown beans, rice, and various meats in the mixture, you can add condiments at hand on the table, including a relish of chopped tomatoes and onions in a saucer and dendê-sautéed farofa in a shaker jar. The *rabada* differs from the *feijoada* mainly in the flavor of the meat because it's served with the same beans and rice. Both dishes thrill us. They couldn't be more elemental, and rustically Bahian, but Dona Alaíde cooks them to such perfection that they taste transcendent.

A few blocks away, Dona Juana displays a similar command of local foods. She hails from the countryside herself and makes that evident in many ways. She christened her restaurant Uauá in honor of the small village where she grew up, and decorated the pretty second-story space in a rural theme, with faux adobe walls, laced with sticks and straw, that display farm tools, pottery, old photos, and folk art. The menu offers country meats as well, ranging from roast goat to pig and sheep innards.

The four of us stick with specialties from the sea. Mary and Jan share a heap-ing plate of fried fish and shrimp on skewers, filled out more than amply on the side with steamed vegetables, rice flecked with corn, and a yucca mash that we like more than they do. Our choice is a *moqueca de peixe,* a hearty fish stew that we ladle over rice and sprinkle to taste with farina. It brims with chunks of firm white fish, possibly cod or haddock, simmered with dendê and a mixture of chopped onion, bell pepper, and tomato in coconut milk. Big windows directly behind us open over a small Pelourinho plaza, bringing in the sounds of the streets to complement the aromas and tastes of the table.

Going from excellent to extraordinary, we have our best meal at Sorriso da

Dadá. The name comes from the chef-owner's dazzling smile, depicted in a number of portraits on the walls. Aldacir dos Santos, who goes by Dadá, moved to Salvador from the Bahia interior at the age of fourteen to work as a domestic servant. She liked to cook, so she opened a restaurant in her backyard, Tempero da Dadá, where diners dodged the drying laundry and scratching chickens. Gaining fame for her food—and some attention, too, for the underwear she hung on the line—Dadá branched out, expanding to several locations, including the beach restaurant we enjoyed at lunch on Sunday and this intimate, white-tablecloth operation in Pelourinho.

The menu encompasses a broad spectrum of Bahian favorites. You can start with acarajés, fried or steamed in banana leaves, fish fritters made with fresh or salt cod, and chowders of shellfish or octopus. All of us choose crab in the form of casquinha de siri, which the kitchen prepares with a little coconut milk and leaves soupy enough to absorb a dusting of farofa. After a few squeezes of lime and small dollops of molho de pimenta, it becomes one of the best dishes of our entire trip.

Entrée options vary from carne de sol and beef tenderloin with cheese sauce to a variety of *moquecas* (crab, shrimp, fish, lobster, and crawfish) and *ensopadas* (the same kind of stew without the palm oil). Mary and Jan select shrimp with vatapá paste, a luscious mating of tastes and textures. The two of us go for *moqueca de siri mole,* soft-shell crab in an exceptionally rich and complex coconut-milk-and-dendê broth redolent of cilantro. It boasts, like the rest of the dinner, a sophisticated balance and blending of flavors that proclaims pure and exalted Creole magic.

You don't find that on every street corner unfortunately. The buffet break-fasts at our hotel are downright shameful, based largely on commercially pack-aged, poor-quality breads, pastries, and cereals. In a country that rightfully prides itself on *sucos* (fresh fruit juices), the versions here reek of a can and taste diluted as well. Nowhere else is nearly that bad. More often, typical of restau-rants around the world, some dishes shine and others lack luster. That's the case, for example, at the most elegant and upscale establishment in town, the interna-tionally oriented Trapiche Adelaide. The kitchen excels with carne de sol in gnoc-chi and a seafood vatapá, but the shrimp with mustard and pineapple is too sweet and the molten chocolate cake lacks oomph.

Still, Salvador elates us with the best of its Creole food and its intense exuberance for life. The verve may wane occasionally, but it pops up again around the next bend, delighting us over and over gastronomically, musically, intellectually, and sensually. Arriving with high hopes, we leave in even higher spirits.

THE NITTY-GRITTY

⊡ IPANEMA PLAZA HOTEL
www.ipanemaplazahotel.com
Rua Farme de Amoedo 34,
Ipanema, Rio de Janeiro
55-21-3687-2000   fax 55-21-3687-2001
Moderately priced business hotel run by a good European chain, Golden Tulip. Spacious deluxe rooms, but few balconies and good sea views are limited to the rooftop pool terrace.

⊡ CONFEITARIA COLOMBO
www.confeitariacolombo.com.br
Rua Gonçalves Dias 32,
Centro, Rio de Janeiro
55-21-2232-2300
lunch only
Maybe not worth the trip downtown except on Saturday.

⊡ CHURRASCARIA CARRETÃO
www.carretaochurrascaria.com.br
Rua Visconde de Piraja 112,
Ipanema, Rio de Janeiro
55-21-2267-3965
lunch and dinner

⊡ CARMEN MIRANDA MUSEUM
Av. Rui Barbosa, Flamengo, Rio de Janeiro
55-21-2299-5586

⊡ MONTE PASCOAL PRAIA HOTEL
www.montepascoal.com.br
Av. Oceânica 591,
Barra, Salvador
55-71-2103-4000
fax 55-71-2103-4005
Basic, moderate-size rooms, but the full-sea-view quarters offer what they promise from their balconies. Small hotel with a good location and mediocre service.

⊡ FERIA DE SÃO JOAQUIM
Salvador
On the waterfront just north of the ferryboat terminal.

⊡ AXEGO
Rua João de Deus 1,
Pelourinho, Salvador
55-71-3242-7481
lunch and dinner

⊡ Caranguejo da Dadá
Patamares Beach, Salvador
55-71-3363-5151
lunch and dinner (no reservations)

⊡ Alaíde do Feijão
Rua 12 Outubro 2, Salvador
55-71-3321-3634
lunch and early dinner
Pure Salvador.

⊡ Restaurant Uauá
Gregório de Matos
36 Pelourinho, Salvador
55-71-3321-3089
lunch and dinner
(no reservations)

⊡ Sorriso da Dadá
Rua Frei Vincente 5,
Pelourinho, Salvador
55-71-3321-9642
lunch and dinner
Wonderful cooking.

Casquinha de Siri
Bahian Deviled Crab

SERVES 6

Molho de Pimenta

- 4   to 6 pickled malagueta chiles, or other fresh or bottled tiny hot red chiles, or more to taste
- 1   teaspoon salt
- ⅓   cup chopped onion
- 1   garlic clove, minced
- ⅓   cup cane vinegar, rice vinegar, or fresh lime juice, or a combination

Deviled Crab

- ¼   cup dendê (palm oil) or vegetable oil in which 4 to 6 annatto seeds have been briefly sautéed until the oil has turned golden (seeds then discarded)
- 1   cup dried coarse bread crumbs
- 1   small onion, minced
- ¼   cup minced green bell pepper
- 2   garlic cloves, minced
- 1   red-ripe plum tomato, squeezed of its seeds and watery liquid, chopped fine
- ¾   teaspoon salt, or more to taste
- ¼   cup coconut milk
- 1   tablespoon Molho de Pimenta, or more to taste (above)
- 1   pound lump crabmeat
- ¼   cup grated aged grana cheese or other aged hard cheese like Parmesan

Preheat the oven to 400°F. Oil or butter six ramekins or scallop shells and place them on a baking sheet.

For the molho or sauce, mash together in a mortar or with the back of a fork, the chiles and salt until roughly pureed. Scrape out into a food processor or blender and add the other ingredients. Puree the mixture. Pour into a small serving bowl and let sit while you prepare the crab.

Warm 2 tablespoons of the oil in a small skillet over medium heat and stir in ½ cup of the bread crumbs. Heat until the bread crumbs just begin to crisp and color lightly, about 2 minutes. Spoon out into a small bowl and reserve for a topping.

Warm the remaining oil in a medium skillet over medium heat. Stir in the onion, bell pepper, and garlic. Sauté until the onion is soft and translucent and add the tomato, salt, coconut milk, the remaining ½ cup of bread crumbs, and the 1 tablespoon of molho. Heat until the milk bubbles, then gently stir in the crabmeat. The mixture should be moist but not soupy. If needed, cook just briefly to eliminate excess liquid.

Spoon into the prepared ramekins. Mix the toasted bread crumbs with the cheese and top each ramekin with a portion of the mixture. Bake for 10 to 12 minutes, until medium brown and crisp. Serve immediately, accompanied by the remaining spicy molho.

LET'S
DO IT AGAIN

"SO WHAT WAS YOUR FAVORITE PLACE?" EVERYONE, FROM OUR CLOSEST FRIENDS to the checkout lady at the grocery store, asks the same natural but impossible question.

After a few stumbling, muddled efforts at an answer, Bill starts saying, "That's like asking me to name my favorite body part. I'm rather attached to all of them, from my eyeballs to my toes. All the countries are different, like eyes and feet, but each is special in some way."

Most people, alarmed by the prospect of hearing about every stop, move on to other pleasantries at this point, but some of the intrepid just change tack. "It must have been tough being gone that long. I'm sure you missed home."

"Didn't even think about it," Bill consistently and truthfully replies.

Both more tactful and verbose, Cheryl elaborates when she's present. "We certainly missed you and the rest of the gang, and coming back feels great, but we were having too much fun to fret about anything."

"Yeah, that," Bill says.

Don't get us wrong. No one we know is fonder of their hometown and their actual, physical home as we are individually and jointly, and each of us regards our families and friends as the most special parts of our lives. But the trip unfolded in fast-forward, like most joyful and vital experiences. Three months seemed like three days, hardly long enough to begin longing for somewhere else.

Maybe a few extra calamities would have made us homesick. Bill lost his ATM card in Bali, as you may remember, and in the Hong Kong airport temporarily misplaced his jacket with our passports, credit cards, and cash, but pickpockets, purse-snatchers, and other thieves left us alone. Beyond our bout with bronchitis in New Caledonia, which dragged us down for a week, and a messy nosebleed Cheryl suffered in South Africa, neither of us got ill. Though the monsoons tormented us in Thailand, and a mistral blew through Provence, bad weather didn't disrupt many days on the whole and the balmy temperatures never brought out bothersome bugs. Our cache of antibiotics, first-aid supplies, insect repellents, and other precautionary paraphernalia sat mostly unused at the bottom of our bags.

A marauding monkey kidnapped the original Flat Stanley early in the trip, but his stand-in soul mate suffered no mishaps on the rest of the journey and now enjoys the care of his creator, our granddaughter Bronwyn, who keeps him with his official photo album and bag of miniature souvenirs. When Cheryl started telling the seven-year-old about the abduction, Bronwyn focused immediately not on Stanley's fate but on the courageous struggle her grandmother waged on his behalf against the jungle beast. In relating the tale to her first-grade classmates, Bronwyn depicted Cheryl as Wonder Woman, a superhero who never flinched in the face of evil.

"You got lucky on that one," Bill says.

Except sometimes for quirky Qantas, the ONEworld and other airlines treated us well, providing comfortable seating and commendable service on most flights, even the long-haul journeys we always dreaded. They never canceled one of our segments, arrived significantly late, caused us to miss a connection, or lost a single bag, depriving us unfortunately of outstanding story opportunities. The odds of such luck on three dozen consecutive flights in the United States must be akin to the chances of Tiger Woods giving up golf for shuffleboard.

Little irritations stayed that way instead of growing into real problems. Our cell phone/PDA, Mobi, couldn't find a network in a few remote spots, but it, the camera, and tape recorder functioned well on the whole and they made it back intact. When we spilled food and drinks on ourselves, predictable enough to wager on, our Tide to Go stain remover sticks and laundry detergent did their jobs admirably. Our clothes, however clean, became obnoxiously familiar by the end, like guests who overstay a welcome, but we simply dumped all the offending garments on our last stop in Brazil. Cheryl in particular gleefully left behind a hefty pile of discards, though she surprised herself in the end by keeping the tatty old cashmere cardigan she wore on planes and a Chico's T-shirt that survived the strains of travel remarkably well.

Arriving home two weeks before Christmas, a frosty time in the New Mexico mountains, we're looking forward to holiday visits with family and friends, but our first priority is a green-chile cheeseburger, grilled outside despite the cold. Other home-prepared comfort foods follow quickly, including beefy Texas chili, richly creamy mac and cheese, bagels and smoked salmon with cream cheese for Cheryl, and for Bill, a peanut butter and mayonnaise sandwich on a fresh flour tortilla.

After settling in for a spell, we start cooking favorite dishes from the trip to relive our memories. Those that work best in an American home kitchen are presented here in recipe form. Unsurprisingly, many of the dishes we tried didn't travel as well, often because of variations in the ingredients available. The success of some preparations, particularly ones featuring seafood, depends on a level of freshness seldom found in the United States. Even a good whole fish purchased "fresh daily," about the best you can get anywhere in this country, differs in taste and other characteristics from a fish still alive in the cook's hands.

Freshness obviously matters as well with produce, but that's less of an issue these days for a careful American consumer because of the increasing number of farmers' markets, roadside farm stands, and groceries and restaurants committed to buying from local suppliers. Diversity of varieties can be a bigger problem. Asian cooks don't just put fresh eggplant in a dish, they pick a specific variety of eggplant to impart a desired and distinctive flavor and texture. A mother-and-daughter team of New Mexico farmers, Eremita and Margaret Campos, once grew many of the dozens of eggplant varieties common in Asia— even the pea-shaped type that adds zesty bitterness to some Thai specialties— but they couldn't sell them. Our cooks and their guests, both in homes and restaurants, aren't ready for such complexity.

Before leaving on the trip, we thought the United States in recent decades was catching up to international culinary capitals in its understanding and appreciation of food. Our experiences abroad undermined some of that parochial confidence. In Australia and South Africa we saw contemporary chefs taking a bold leadership role in transforming the tastes of their nations. They presented exciting, unconventional dishes, exploring the frontiers of fresh local ingredients and elevating the expectations of patrons instead of pandering to them.

American chefs are just as creative and skilled, but the bottom-line consciousness of their restaurants and the resistance of their customers to daring flavors exerts a powerful restraint on their ability to lead in a similar way. Some buck the odds and take risks to appeal to serious eaters, but many of our top talents are content to cook for people who have too little real enthusiasm for eating to bother with doing any cooking of their own. For main course dishes in particular, these chefs offer one of everything—a steak, a chicken ("free-range," of course), a fish, a pork dish (probably tenderloin), etc.—in tasty but standard preparations that won't challenge many palates and can easily be matched or even surpassed by good home cooks. In Australia and South Africa, we found lots of real restaurant food, fare that went beyond the limitations of a home kitchen and made eating out a wonderful adventure.

Our meals in France and China illustrated another kind of strength generally lacking in our country, the devoted respect for a classic tradition. In Hong Kong, Provence, and Nice, and at our incredible TV-show banquet in Chaozhou, the best dishes reflected treasured regional tastes that resonated with a sophisticated, contemporary understanding of the core concepts. With a solid grounding in their roots, the chefs refined the old to make it brightly new. In the United States, perhaps only New Orleans possesses a range of fine restaurants with a similar commitment to honoring and honing a venerated local heritage. In most of the land, Americans are so nervous about food and obsessed with this month's health fad that little or nothing from grandmother's table appeals.

Even in the realm of fast food, where we supposedly lead the world for good or bad, we've got lots to learn from street-stand cooks in Singapore, Thailand, Brazil, and other nations, who make and serve their specialties as quickly and efficiently as any eatery in the United States but also offer astonishing levels of flavor and complexity. Despite the well-intentioned preachments of the Slow Food folks, speed is not culinary enemy number one. The big problem is the forgotten joy of eating sensuously and the human fulfillment of sharing that with others.

Neither of us had thought before in quite these terms about travel. We simply assumed that we travel, therefore we eat, and we should make the most of the eating opportunities. The three-month trip changed the correlation in our minds in a subtle but significant way. Now it seems to us that we eat, therefore we must travel to enjoy the pleasure as fully and passionately as possible.

That would be true wherever we live, in the United States, Australia, France, Singapore, or anywhere else. It's not because you can't get good food at home—you just have to be more selective in some places than others—but you can't get all of it in any one spot. Robert Frost once described poetry as "a way of taking life by the throat." So are some kinds of travel.

A few months after our return, friends come to dinner at our house and bring Cheryl a hostess gift of beautiful small cacti in a strikingly colored ceramic pot. She takes one look at the container and says, "I know this seems rude, but I've got to look at the brand name on the bottom of the pot." She does and smiles instantly. "I thought it looked familiar. This Norcal line comes from our friends' factory in Chaozhou, China, where we saw similar pieces."

Cheryl makes northern Thai khao soi for dinner, and while feasting on it, we tell our friends about other great food we had on the journey, refreshing our excitement about the whole experience. Bill wakes early the next morning, as usual, boots his computer, and logs onto the Internet to check our frequent-flier miles. He doesn't say anything about it to Cheryl until the evening, when we're looking together for a place to put our cherished new pot.

"You remember how we started thinking about our trip four years before we went?"

"Yeah, when we realized that we had enough reward miles to begin planning something special."

"Well, I figured out this morning that we're in a similar place now, mainly because of miles we earned from credit-card charges on the trip. And it's four years from our twenty-fifth anniversary. What do you think?"

"Let's do it again!"